PRETTY GIRL KILLER

Andrew Byrne is an award-winning former UK national newspaper journalist, now based in Sydney. Andrew has run the news desk on both *The Sydney Morning Herald* and *The Daily Telegraph* in Australia and *The Sunday Mirror* in London, and for the last few years has been working on current affairs shows such as *Sunday Night*. Much of his career has involved investigating and writing about some of the world's most horrific crimes, including those committed by the Yorkshire Ripper, Jeremy Bamber, Ian Brady, David Birnie and Bradley Murdoch.

This book depicts scenes of violence and sexual assault based on reported events.

THE PRETTY GIRL KILLER

andrew byrne

VIKING
an imprint of
PENGUIN BOOKS

VIKING

UK | USA | Canada | Ireland | Australia
India | New Zealand | South Africa | China

Penguin
Random House
Australia

Viking is part of the Penguin Random House group of companies
whose addresses can be found at global.penguinrandomhouse.com.

First published by Viking, 2019

Cover design by Alex Ross © Penguin Random House Australia Pty Ltd
Cover photography by Siegfried Layda/Getty Images
Back cover photography by Rapeephan Bucharattanakul/Shutterstock
Typeset in 12.5/18pt Adobe Garamond by Midland Typesetters, Australia
Printed and bound in Australia by Griffin Press, part of Ovato, an accredited ISO AS/NZS 14001
Environmental Management Systems printer.

A catalogue record for this
book is available from the
National Library of Australia

ISBN 978 0 14379 674 9

penguin.com.au

MIX
Paper from
responsible sources
FSC® C009448

INTRODUCTION

This is the chilling and definitive true story of one of the world's most extraordinary serial killers, infamous in both Australian and American criminal history.

Christopher Bernard Wilder, born in the leafy suburbs of Sydney, was the perfect model of an Australian playboy, who became the most wanted man in America and the perfect model of a psychopathic killer. How this surf-loving son of a decorated naval war hero grew up to become a sadistic monster, slaughtering as many as sixteen women, is as fascinating as it is frightening.

The ruthless and terrifying Wilder had been sexually harassing, molesting, abusing, kidnapping, torturing and murdering young women and girls for over two decades when he went on the run in one of the most notorious killing sprees in US history. On his frenetic final odyssey, Wilder would drive thousands of kilometres, crisscrossing the US, abducting and murdering a string of innocent victims. He had more than 500 FBI special agents and hundreds more local sheriffs and police officers pursuing him in the country's biggest ever manhunt.

Wilder's modus operandi was faultless, honed to perfection over the best part of two decades. He targeted only pretty girls, bewitching them with a few carefully rehearsed flattering words, brazenly walking up to them on crowded beaches, in busy shopping malls and at beauty pageants. Adorned with flash jewellery and expensive suits, he would pretend to be a professional photographer and lure them with promises of modelling careers. They were young, good-looking and vulnerable to a smiling stranger who promised to make them famous. Once captured, he tortured them for hours, sometimes days.

There were occasions when Wilder was accused, investigated, arrested, even charged and put before the courts, but he was never jailed and always walked away with the most lenient of sentences, free to abuse and kill more women. This incredible ability to – quite literally – get away with murder was due to a few crucial factors.

He was wealthy, which meant whenever he did end up before the courts he could call on the best and most expensive defence lawyers.

It is important to remember, too, that Wilder operated in an era in which sexism and misogyny were still deeply ingrained, particularly when he started out in the 1960s. Although a second wave of feminism started in the 1960s thanks to books like Betty Friedan's *The Feminine Mystique*, life for women in the late sixties and early seventies was still far from ideal. They were badly underpaid compared to men, still doing the lion's share of the housework and child rearing, still considered too sympathetic and fragile to be on court juries in most US states and remaining banned from several prestigious colleges such as Yale, Princeton and Harvard. Although the birth control pill was legalised in 1960, it could still only be prescribed to married women, pregnancy was still a sackable offence, only 6 per cent of doctors were women and one of the most popular TV variety shows was Hugh Hefner's *Playboy's Penthouse*. Many of the screen icons were a hangover from the fifties – highly sexualised but vulnerable and in need of protection, such as Marilyn Monroe. Stars like Jane Fonda and Brigitte Bardot may have been less vulnerable, but they still got their star rating from being overtly sexual and the plaything of the male hero.

It was a time, in both Australia and the US, when police and the courts turned a blind eye to domestic violence (not even a term until the mid-seventies) and often lacked earnestness when it came to the investigation of sex crimes against women. There was too often a culture of blaming the victim, and too many of these vulnerable women chose not to speak out or seek justice. Looking back with the benefit of hindsight, there is plenty of fault to find in the various law enforcement investigations of Wilder, everything from the wrong identification of victims to missing evidence, to petty internal one-upmanship politics to downright incompetence. It was also an age before real technological advance or proper centralised databases, which meant everything moved at a snail's pace and in frustrating silos.

Mostly, however, it was Wilder's phenomenal charm, and his extraordinary ability to manipulate not only his victims but everyone around him, that allowed him to develop into such a horrendous serial killer. He managed to fool his family, colleagues, girlfriends and his wife; and outsmart cops and deceive psychiatrists, therapists and judges.

What most serial killers have in common, when you scratch away long enough at their personalities, is an inability to completely conceal their true nature. The murderous intent is always there, lurking in the background, if you look hard enough. Wilder was different. He was clever at hiding not only his crimes but, more importantly, also his core self. Wilder was – to his girlfriends, mates, colleagues and acquaintances – a handsome businessman and sports car racer. A bit of a womaniser, but harmless enough. A guy who loved dancing and drinking expensive cocktails. His chilling charm, impeccable sophistication and unfaltering manners duped all those around him.

Over the course of twenty years, Christopher Wilder committed hundreds of appalling crimes, from Australia to mainland USA as well as Hawaii. He matured into the most depraved and merciless killer it is possible to imagine, but his bloodlust and carefully concealed malice against women, especially those that were both young and pretty, started on a desolate and windswept beach on Sydney's southern fringes.

I

WANDA BEACH

MONDAY 11 JANUARY 1965
WANDA BEACH
SYDNEY, AUSTRALIA

It was eleven days after New Year and shaping up to be a sticky Australian summer. Teenagers all over the country were still hoarse and in the throes of Beatlemania after the British band's tour just a few months earlier. The Vietnam War was a looming cloud with compulsory military service for twenty-year-olds recently introduced, but most families were optimistic about the future, unemployment was less than 2 per cent, front doors were left unlocked and in many cases wide open, and children played safely in the street unsupervised. It was a time of flower power and the beginnings of feminism.

Fifteen-year-old Marianne Schmidt and her best friend from next door, Christine Sharrock, were busily pulling together a picnic to take to the beach. The two girls were like peas in a pod, the same age and height, both slim and attractive with curly dark hair. Although they went to different high schools, they were inseparable, always in and out of each other's Sydney homes on Brush Road, West Ryde. Typical teenagers, they loved fashion, gossiping about boys, listening to music, and learning the steps to the latest dance craze. If it wasn't the Stomp, it was the Mashed Potato, the Hitchhiker or the Jerk. Marianne's favourite was the Climb; she was a huge Elvis Presley fan and the two girls had recently seen his latest movie *Viva Las Vegas*. Three days earlier Marianne had written in her diary, 'Happy Birthday, Elvis. I think I love Elvis. Not for his money but himself. Heard Elvis's songs all day.'

The girls' bond was strengthened by their shared grief – both had lost their fathers. Christine had been living with her nan and grandad, Jim and Jeanette Taig, since her father died and her mother, Beryl, remarried. Marianne's father, Helmut, had also died, from Hodgkin's lymphoma, two years earlier. Money was tight in the Schmidt household, and the family only managed to scrape by thanks to the Smith Family charity and the kindness of neighbours. Marianne's mother, Elizabeth, who had arrived in Australia with Helmut and the children in an influx of immigrants from Germany in September 1958, had recently had to go into hospital for hepatitis, and Marianne had been left in charge of cleaning and cooking for herself and her younger siblings, Norbert, five, Wolfgang, seven, Trixie, nine, and Peter, ten. On a recent visit to her mother in Sydney's King George V Hospital, Marianne had asked her if she and Christine could take her brothers and sisters to the beach at Cronulla. Her mum had easily agreed, since the girls were sensible, it was a simple enough journey and she knew how much they all loved the beach.

Marianne had got up early that morning, put on her one-piece black swimming costume with a multi-coloured sleeveless blouse over the top, and started making Marmite, cucumber and tomato sandwiches. She packed them into her blue-and-white striped beach bag along with some oranges and apricots, a thermos of cold water, and a radio so they could listen to music. Her eldest brothers, Bert and Hans, decided to stay home, paint the kitchen and mow the front lawn as a surprise for their mother when she came home from the hospital. Marianne was relieved. She wanted to explore Wanda Beach again, which was 2.5 kilometres further up from the popular beach near Cronulla Station where they always hung out. She knew if Hans tagged along, he might stop her exploring the isolated and beautiful stretch of sand, a known haunt for nude bathers and courting couples, which had been the filming location for the 1940 Australian war movie *Forty Thousand Horsemen* and held a fascination for Marianne. Next door, Christine Sharrock, wearing white shorts and a green-and-white patterned sleeveless top, was making a flask of green cordial. Her nan, Jeanette, had given her a one-pound note to buy lunch. Jeanette thought her granddaughter was wearing a lot of jewellery – a heart-shaped locket, gold bracelet, gold signet ring with the initials 'BT' and pierced gold earrings – for a trip to the beach but didn't bother commenting. She believed Christine, whose good looks had already attracted several admirers, was a level-headed girl. A couple of weeks earlier, visiting her aunt's house at Christmas, Christine had asked her uncle during a game of backyard shuttlecock, 'If a boy attacks me, how do I defend myself?' Her uncle had replied, 'Kick him between the legs. That'll make him turn away.'

'It would be fun if we could walk across the sandhills again,' Christine now said to her nan, packing her beach towel.

'Don't go today, love,' Jeanette replied, 'you've got four little ones with you, it's too far.'

'But we'd only be away from them for half an hour,' said Christine, eager for approval.

'No, you stay with the children,' her nan told her firmly. Ten minutes later, the teenagers and their four young charges left Brush Road, the colourful lorikeets tumbling and jostling each other high up in the trees, galahs screeching, the magpies swooping. They didn't bother waiting for a bus and even though it was already hot, the humidity making their clothes stick to their bodies, they walked three kilometres to West Ryde station. By the time they arrived at Cronulla it was just before 11 a.m. and the sky was overcast, the briny smell of the sea strong on the gusts of wind. They trooped across the street and down a lane that led through Cronulla Park to the main surfing beach, but the signs were up warning the beach was too dangerous for swimming, because of the strong southerly winds causing high seas. Undaunted, Marianne and Christine led the way like pied pipers to the southern end of the beach, holding the kids' clammy hands in their own, and then sat everyone down on the rock wall and had a picnic with the sandwiches and cordial they'd brought. After a while, seven-year-old Wolfgang, who could never sit still for long, pestered his big sister to go in the water, and Marianne took him for a splash in the shallows. Christine, who had disappeared for a while to buy some lunch with the money her nan had given her, joined them, even though she wasn't in swimmers.

Later, Trixie and Wolfgang saw a 'surfie' teenage boy, with fair hair, hunting for crabs. Wolfgang noticed he had a knife in a holster, similar to one his brother Bert had at home, and a short spear about a metre long, which he was using to prise crabs out of the cracks in the rocks. The younger kids noticed Marianne and Christine chatting to the boy, and soon after Marianne suggested they all go for a walk to the sandhills at Wanda Beach. It was still windy and overcast, and there weren't many people around, so the gang left their bags hidden at the rock wall and set off along the cement promenade to North Cronulla Beach. It was there they cut across down onto the sand past Elouera Beach and carried on past the Wanda Surf Club. Shortly before 1 p.m. they trudged off the beach, which was being pounded by large waves, and sought shelter in the dunes from the gusting wind that had been whipping up the sand and stinging their legs. Marianne, who liked to entertain the young ones by singing her favourite Elvis songs while dancing like her idol, sang '(You're the) Devil in Disguise' as she placed all the beach towels over their heads so they could lie underneath and play. She handed Trixie the radio for them to listen to and said she and Christine were going for a walk and would collect their bags and come back for them. They walked over the sandhill back towards the sea, but then started heading north, away from where they'd left their belongings. Ten-year-old Peter shouted out they were going the wrong way, but they just turned around, laughing, and carried on. After a short while Peter told Wolfgang to go and see where they were, and his younger brother, who didn't need an excuse to go scampering about, ran over the dunes and saw Marianne and Christine in the distance walking along the beach. Later he would be able to tell detectives that the surfie youth he'd seen crab hunting earlier was walking between them with his hands on their shoulders. He remembered the boy's greasy, fairish long hair, which had been combed back and was blowing about in the wind, and that he was barefoot and had a blue towel slung over his shoulder.

Running to catch them up, Wolfgang got within 10 metres when he heard the youth, whose back was turned to him, ask one of the girls what her name was. Neither Marianne nor Christine replied, and Wolfgang could tell they weren't laughing or joking as they walked along. He later said the boy appeared angry by the way he spoke and walked. Wolfgang fell over and by the time he picked himself up, the girls and the youth had disappeared into the dunes at the top of the beach, so he ran back to the others and made sandcastles and listened to the radio. After a while, Wolfgang got restless and went searching for his sister again. He was walking up the beach, near the water's edge, when he saw the same youth walking towards him. Wolfgang noticed he was still wearing the holster, but it was empty and there was no sign of the knife or the spear gun he'd been carrying earlier.

'Where are the girls?' he asked him as he drew close, but the teenager walked straight past him and completely ignored the question. Wolfgang told detectives later that the boy had been shaking.

Back in the dunes, Peter was becoming increasingly worried about little Norbert, who was only five and hungry. As soon as Wolfgang returned he led the four of them back to the rock wall at Cronulla Beach, found their bags and fed them the remains of their packed lunch. The four Schmidt children looked around for Marianne and Christine for as long as possible before running to catch the 6 p.m. train home. They got back to Brush Road at 8 p.m., and when they knocked at Christine's door and explained what had happened, Mrs Taig put on her coat and went straight to Ryde police station to report the girls missing.

———

Many terrible crimes capture headlines, but the sexual assault and murder of Marianne Schmidt and Christine Sharrock on that windswept beach in Sydney, in 1965, also stripped away the innocence of the 'Lucky Country', as Australia was known. Marianne was the first to be butchered, with fifteen separate stab wounds from a serrated-edged fishing or hunting knife. Christine tried to escape, but her killer was bigger and stronger than her, and she never stood a chance. He caught up with her, bashed her in the back of her head, fracturing her skull, then stabbed her repeatedly. She was dragged, leaving pools of blood in her wake, 34 metres back to the body of her best friend. He ripped off her bloodied white shorts and sanitary pad and tried to rape her, but the brave, dying teenager fought him off, battling to her very last breath. Enraged, he smashed her violently in the face and head and then stuffed her white shorts into her vagina. In a final act of degradation, he tried to rape Marianne as she lay dying, cutting out the crotch of her black one-piece swimming costume and yanking it up around her breasts, masturbating and ejaculating over her brutalised body.

Twenty-four hours later Peter Smith, walking in the dunes after lunch with his three nephews, saw feet sticking out of the sand and thought, at first, he'd found a discarded shop mannequin. It wasn't until he'd dug away some sand and scraped aside the long black hair that he realised it was a human face and found the lifeless eyes of a young girl staring blankly back at him. When police removed the rest of the sand, Marianne was found to be lying on her right side with her left leg bent at the knee at right angles to her body. Christine was facedown, her right arm bent at the elbow and her forearm close to her face as if she had been trying to protect herself. The two girls were in line with each other, Christine's head against Marianne's left foot. Doctors confirmed they had died within half an hour of each other. The same weapon, a knife with a blade of 6.5 centimetres, was used to kill both girls. It was never found.

The crime scene was more than a kilometre from the nearest road, Captain Cook Drive, and several hundred metres from the closest track. Police said it was an area used by lovers and often frequented by perverts. It was cordoned off and an initial search was undertaken, identifying recently made car tracks leading from where the bodies were discovered, as well as bloodstains 30 metres up the beach that had been covered by shifting sand, though it couldn't be determined whether deliberately or by the weather. The bodies were taken to the Sutherland District Hospital, where Christine's grandfather took on the grim task of identifying the girls.

The next day, Marianne's devastated mother spoke to reporters from her hospital bed, 'I bear no malice toward the killer,' she said. 'My little girl has gone to a new life. The killer has still to face his existence in this world. He will be hunted and haunted by the memory.'

With his mother still in the hospital, the responsibility for looking after all his siblings fell to Bert, and at sixteen he struggled to keep the press at bay. While the Taigs ignored every reporter who knocked on the door, it was an open house at the Schmidts' and all the children attracted enormous attention, especially Wolfgang, who soon became the most photographed little boy in Australia. 'HE SAW THE SURFIE' screamed one front-page headline under a photograph of Wolfgang, looking nervous, standing on Wanda Beach talking with a detective. At a news conference, police told reporters the mystery teen was the main suspect and the focus of their investigation. Wolfgang was interviewed multiple times by different dark-suited detectives in their trilby hats. They gave him lollipops and sweets to suck on as they questioned him for more than three hours at Cronulla police station. When he was taken back to Wanda Beach along with Trixie and Peter – Norbert was considered too young – and asked to retrace their steps on the day Marianne was killed, a large posse of reporters, photographers and TV cameramen followed behind. Each of the three Schmidt children gripped the hand of an accompanying detective, hiding their faces as photographers edged closer to capture their every move and expression. It was the start of a media frenzy that would engulf their lives for years. Trixie, in a little checked dress with a blue cardigan and white socks and shoes, looked dazed as she sat in the back of an unmarked police car with her two brothers for the journey back home.

Detectives thought Wolfgang was a lively, intelligent boy, and he stuck to his story so strongly they were convinced the surfie youth was the key to finding the killer. Although Wolfgang's story about him never changed, details about his description did, so the depiction police finally settled on was quite vague: about sixteen years old, medium height and build, light-coloured long hair, facial hair, wearing zinc cream and long grey pants.

WEDNESDAY 20 JANUARY 1965
SYDNEY, AUSTRALIA

The funeral services for Marianne and Christine took place on the same day, nine days after the murders, and the city's afternoon newspapers carried heartbreaking photographs of both mothers on their front pages. The service for Marianne was held at the Metropolitan Funeral Home chapel in Burwood, and afterward a cortege of twenty-two cars wound its way to Rookwood Crematorium, where her father had also been cremated. A simple sheaf of white flowers lay on the white casket, a final tribute from Marianne's mother, and Elizabeth Schmidt had to lean heavily on the arm of her eldest son, Bert, as she left the service. She had dressed her daughter in her prettiest high-necked dress, but the knife slash marks had still been visible above the collar when she had visited the open casket to say goodbye. Meanwhile, at St Michael's Catholic Church in Meadowbank, 200 mourners gathered for Christine's service. At her gravesite in Liverpool Cemetery later, the family's parish priest

Father Davey asked them, in the name of Christian charity, to also pray for her killer. It is doubtful many did.

WEDNESDAY 20 APRIL 1966
CORONERS COURT
SYDNEY, AUSTRALIA

More than a year later, the inquest into Marianne's and Christine's deaths opened before the city coroner, JJ Loomes, in a packed courtroom. Every seat in the public gallery was taken and extra chairs had to be installed to cater for the reporters who spilled out from the press bench. Elizabeth and Bert Schmidt were given permission to sit at the bar table by the coroner, so they could follow proceedings closely. It was well before the days of DNA forensics and testing, but on the second day of the inquest, the lead police investigator told the court that police knew the blood group of the killer. The third day was taken up with evidence from Trixie and then Wolfgang, who was the star witness and clearly very nervous. He looked tired and there were dark patches under his eyes. Asked by the coroner if he felt okay, Wolfgang replied in a raspy voice that he had a cold and a sore throat. 'You can stand up if you would rather do that,' said Coroner Loomes, asking the little boy what his friends called him at school. 'Wolfie,' he replied, making everyone smile.

Asked about the teenager he saw on the beach three times that day, Wolfgang told the hushed courtroom about a 'big boy, carrying a knife in a belt pouch,' walking between the two girls when they had gone into the sandhills. His voice surprisingly firm for one so young, he said the boy had returned alone without the knife. He was questioned for three hours before the coroner delivered his findings, ruling that Marianne had died from a haemorrhage caused by her throat being cut and wounds to her chest, and that

Christine's death resulted from the knife wounds to her chest and a fractured skull, which had injured her brain.

While six knives were later found on Wanda Beach, none of them was the murder weapon. Two items were discovered which gave more credibility to Wolfgang's recollection: a homemade crab spear with a wooden handle made from a packing crate, found on Wanda Beach the day after the killings but not handed in to police until fourteen weeks later, and a blue towel that washed up nineteen days after the murders. The towel was described as an important lead and sent to the police scientific bureau for testing, but no traces of blood were found.

There were mysteries about the case that baffled police from the beginning. Had the surfie youth Wolfgang saw lured Marianne and Christine away from the little ones and off the beach into the sand dunes, and if so, how? Autopsy results, which upset Christine's grandmother, revealed Christine had a blood alcohol level of 0.015 – the equivalent of a middy glass of beer. Had the killer met her at the shops, given her something to drink and arranged to meet her and Marianne at Wanda Beach? Had the girls known their killer?

Criminal profiling was not a formal science in the 1960s, but the leading NSW forensic psychiatrist Dr John McGeorge described the unknown killer as a late teenager or in his twenties, with a split personality. 'His bloodlust would not be apparent to friends or strangers,' said the doctor. 'To those who know him well, he would appear to be a bit withdrawn, unsociable and not very friendly. He might appear as a quiet, reserved kind of fellow and a bit peculiar in his mannerisms. He is young, cunning and given to sudden violence.'

He had just described, in unerring detail, a teenage Christopher Wilder.

———

Former chief petty warrant officer third class Coley Chapman Wilder, a US war veteran who'd survived the Japanese attack on Pearl Harbor, was twenty-five years old and on shore leave in Sydney when he met June Ducker, the daughter of a tram conductor, nineteen years old and still living with her parents and younger sister in Potts Street, Ryde. They fell in love and married in April 1944 at June's local church. Less than a year later, on 13 March 1945, Christopher Bernard, the first of their four sons, was born. He was premature and not expected to survive. The delivery doctor rang Coley and told him he didn't think his baby was going to pull through, suggesting he might want to call a priest to give the newborn his last rites. Coley, a hard, cold, no-nonsense man, told the doctor to forget the baby's soul and get on with saving his life. Wilder had two more near-death experiences as a child. He almost drowned when he was fourteen months old and was in a coma for six days when he was just five.

For fourteen years the family moved wherever Coley Wilder was stationed, never staying in one place long enough to settle or make lasting friendships. After moving to the US, they lived in Illinois, California, New Mexico, Virginia and Nevada. At one stage they even moved to the Philippines, to the giant US naval base there. The marriage was rocky and at one stage Coley moved out, but midway through 1959, after a second posting in the Philippines, Coley retired, and June insisted on returning to Australia with the whole family to begin a new life. They set up home in a weatherboard cottage in Meta Street, East Ryde, not far from June's parents and only a few kilometres from Christine and Marianne, the Wanda Beach victims.

When they arrived back in Australia, Wilder was fourteen years old and was enrolled in the nearby Epping Boys High School. But the 'service brat' lifestyle and constant upheavals and school changes meant Wilder was well behind in his studies, and he got into trouble in and out of the classroom. He wasn't particularly close to his brothers, and he was a quiet, odd and broody teenager who soon became isolated, teased by the other boys for his funny accent. He didn't like the popular Aussie sports – rugby league, soccer and cricket – and found it impossible to make friends. Wilder had suffered regular disciplinary beatings at the hands of his father, a heavy drinker, all his life. By the time he was a teenager he hated his father's 'southern redneck mentality' – the Coley family originated from Alabama – and the pair had a fractious relationship.

The warning signs about his sexual perversions started in the US when he 'tried to do something to a girl'. He was only nine years old. When they were living in Las Vegas he began peeping at his mother when she got undressed, later telling therapists this was where his obsession with big breasts started. He used to masturbate while wearing his mother's clothes. Soon after arriving in Australia he molested a girl he had a crush on, zipping her inside her jacket so she couldn't move her arms, and then fondling her breasts. He would roam the neighbourhood, peeping in windows to satisfy his burgeoning sexual fantasies. He was caught peeping by neighbours one evening when he was fifteen, and his embarrassed parents took him out of school and started him on a carpentry apprenticeship, in the hope that keeping him busy would improve things.

In 1963, when he was seventeen, Wilder read an article in *Pix* magazine, an Australian scandal rag that had racy photos of bikini models on the front cover, about a successful photographer who started out going to the beach and photographing girls in their swimming costumes. It was also the year *The Collector* by John Fowles was published, the novel that would become Wilder's obsession. The main character, Frederick Clegg, a clerk with relatives in Australia, is afflicted by extreme sexual insecurity. Clegg kidnaps a young woman and tries to make her his friend and sex slave, using his camera as an instrument of extortion. Two years after the book, the movie based on it was released and Wilder's infatuation extended to the actress Samantha Eggar, who played Clegg's victim Miranda and won an Academy Award nomination for her role. Many of Wilder's victims would bear more than a passing resemblance to this strikingly beautiful brunette.

In 1963 Wilder was arrested as the ringleader of a gang sexual assault on a teenage girl at a beach. He'd been with another youth, when they cornered the sixteen-year-old and plied her with alcohol. After his arrest Wilder openly admitted what he'd done. A rape charge was dismissed, but he pleaded guilty to charges of taking away the girl by force and sexually assaulting her. He was sentenced to a year in juvenile detention, suspended on condition he 'enter into a recognisance to be of good behaviour for a period of twelve months in the sum of twenty pounds'. Prior to sentencing he spent a couple of weeks in custody, initially at a reformatory, where he underwent a psychological evaluation. The experience haunted him, he would later tell lawyers who represented him on both sides of the Pacific.

'He had a terrible fear of ever being locked up again,' said Clifford Brown, the Australian solicitor who defended him twenty years later. 'He was terrified. Something happened to him in there.'

Wilder returned to his apprenticeship after the court case and started working on construction sites all over Sydney, including in Cronulla. At weekends he would head to the beaches with his long board and camera to catch a few waves and get close to the pretty teenage girls in their bikinis. While he found it impossible to form any close male friendships, according to his brother Stephen, Wilder was very different around girls. Stephen would tell reporters later,

'Chris had it made. He was blonde, good looking, a good athlete. He used to surf and play baseball. Being an American in Australia in the early sixties was classy. He was from the land of Elvis Presley, he could put on the accent. If you were reasonably good looking, and he was, all he had to do was open his mouth. Chris was always able to go up and talk to girls; he could do that without any problem. He always had a line that would satisfy a girl.'

Meanwhile, his mother had been hiding her eldest son's escalating sexual problems and perversions from neighbours, friends and most of the family. One neighbour, Cathy Edwards, said the family couldn't have been more nondescript and normal. She remembered June telling her once, 'I have some family secrets I have never told anyone,' but in truth, the only thing memorable about the family was that they were so unremarkable.

When Wilder was nineteen, his mother became so desperate she asked a friend who worked in a mental hospital about the controversial electroconvulsive therapy, which in the 1960s doctors believed could treat a range of psychological 'disorders', from depression to homosexuality and sexual deviancy. Unlike with today's ECT therapy, patients weren't given anaesthetic or muscle relaxants, and the treatment was considered by many to be barbaric, as portrayed in the 1962 best-selling novel *One Flew Over the Cuckoo's Nest*.

June took Wilder to the sessions, which involved him being strapped down and connected to the device, then shown photographs of naked women. Some machines involved a strain gauge – a flexible, mercury-filled rubber ring with wires attached – being fitted over the penis once the pubic area had been shaved, with electric shocks administered automatically when the electrodes detected any change in size. After three treatments an enraged and humiliated Wilder refused to return. He told his therapist years later he tried to block out the terrifying experience and was angry at his mother for subjecting him to it.

Later it was revealed his father, a navy-trained electrical engineer, made a DIY version of the device which could be plugged into the mains electricity. It's not known if he ever used it on Wilder, but he was still subjecting his son to violent punishment. Wilder's brother Stephen recalled one occasion when Chris had accidentally run the battery flat on his father's car. The corporal punishment his father had dished out had been 'brutal', he remembered.

Just weeks after the Wanda Beach murders, Wilder's mother was arranging more psychiatric treatment – this time group therapy – for her aberrant son. It isn't clear why, but she must have had reason to think the ECT therapy had not worked. Did she believe her son was responsible for the murders? The circumstantial evidence was strong. Wilder was living in the same suburb as the Wanda victims, frequented the shop where Christine worked, knew the train station well, and, because it was the height of summer, the building sites he worked on would have been shut down for the holidays. It is also not hard to imagine that Marianne would have been taken in by a good-looking teenager with an American accent, who sounded just like her idol Elvis in his surfing movie, *Blue Hawaii*. The most damning evidence against Wilder, however, would not surface for another four years. When it came, it would be from the most unlikely of sources. His wife.

SUNDAY 15 JANUARY 1967
PALM BEACH
SYDNEY, AUSTRALIA

Two years after the Wanda Beach murders, Wilder, now nearly twenty-two years old, was spending every available daylight hour on hot weekends driving around Sydney's coastline in a little red Austin-Healey Sprite sports car, stalking sunbaking pretty girls.

He noticed Christine Paluch, twenty, and her sister Elizabeth, sixteen, straight away. They were on a family day out at Palm Beach on the northern beaches of Sydney and were listening to music down near the water while their dad, a wealthy Sydney banker, and their mum, Marie Louise, watched on from a patch of grassland nearby. Wilder sat staring at the two girls as they sunbathed and swam until 3 p.m. Quite a few times they walked right past him to join their parents, but it was only when the family were packing up to leave, and their mother called them in from the beach, that he introduced himself, hopping over to the girls, a noticeable bandage on his ankle. In a thick American accent, which they both thought was cute, he offered to take them to an even better beach the following day.

Marie Louise had noticed the man watching her daughters all day and saw him talking to them as they walked back from the beach. She didn't have a good feeling about him, and the next day when the red sports car turned up outside their home and he knocked on the door, it led to the first of many rows with her eldest daughter about Wilder. But Christine was old enough to get her way, and Wilder ended up taking both girls to Warriewood Beach for the day. The next few days he kept calling up, wanting to talk to the younger daughter, Elizabeth. The third time he called, Mr Paluch answered and told him in no uncertain terms that Elizabeth was far too young to go out with a man of his age. Wilder immediately switched his attention to Christine.

One Saturday morning he picked her up, as usual, for a trip to the beach, but after a few kilometres, with no explanation, he pulled off the road into bushland. He grabbed a camera from the back seat and turned to Christine: 'Come on, get out of the car.'

The day was prickly hot, the cicadas were deafening and a lone kookaburra was calling out from high in the trees as a nervous Christine watched Wilder spread out a picnic blanket on the dry, crackly undergrowth, full of paperbark tree flakes. She felt uneasy; he was always telling her she could be a model, but she was shy and self-conscious, and when he asked her to lie down on the blanket and pose for him, she started protesting.

Wilder ignored her protests but gave her one of his big smiles and started flattering her as he took photos. Christine tried to cooperate, smiling gamely and trying to loosen up, but soon the smiles and flattery stopped, and Wilder's mood abruptly changed. He threw the camera down and lunged at Christine's blouse, tugging at it so the buttons popped off. Christine attempted to pull away, but he grabbed her bra, tearing one of the straps. She was stunned, completely baffled about what was happening, pleading with him to stop, and sobbing.

Wilder didn't care. He looked at her coldly and told her flatly, 'Either take your clothes off, so I can photograph you naked, or I'll force you to have sex.'

The more distressed Christine got, the more excited Wilder became and, ignoring her tears, he roughly pushed her down onto the blanket. She was struggling beneath him, the smell of his sweat mixed with the scent of eucalyptus making her feel sick. She shouted, babbled at him desperately, 'If you do anything, I'll never go out with you again!' Just as abruptly as he'd started, he stopped.

Christine didn't tell her parents about the incident, but they were still horrified when six months after he'd gatecrashed into their lives, he persuaded Christine to leave home.

Wilder was high on the power and control he now had over Christine, and a day after she moved into a girls hostel, he paid a visit to her mother. Marie Louise was alone at the family home when Wilder crept up behind her in the hallway. Jolting back-wards, her heart thumping, she squawked out a half scream. 'What are you doing here, how did you get in?'

'The back door was open. I want to talk to you, Marie,' he said, plonking himself down on the carpet in the lounge room. He patted the space next to him, 'Sit down here.' She ignored him and pulled out a footstool, sitting down and staring at him, her body tense, ready to run. He laughed, as if he was indulging a small child, got up and sat down in a chair next to her and then leaned over and gently started removing the bobby pins from her hair. Marie Louise was petrified, her insides plummeted, she felt sick. A smack or a punch would have been less terrifying to handle. She jumped up and walked towards the hallway, trying to get away from him, but Wilder followed her.

'I want to know something about sex, what would a young boy like me know about sex?' he asked her, his eyes excited but not meeting hers, looking instead over her shoulder.

Marie Louise, nerves jangling, stepped backwards and took a deep breath. Her body wouldn't stop shaking. She deliberately raised her voice. 'Get out. Leave me alone. Why are you talking to me about things like that? You should ask your father.'

He ignored her. 'I watched you that first day on the beach, in your bikini. You looked good. I would like to take photographs of you in that bikini.'

Marie Louise looked at him, horrified. 'Don't be ridiculous, it is far too cold today for a bikini,' she told him, flustered, looking around her for an escape route.

He stood in silence for a moment, blocking her way, and then pointed to her bedroom. 'That's where I want you,' he said, launch-ing himself and clawing at her jumper.

'Get out or I'll kill you,' Marie Louise shouted at him, but he wouldn't let go. 'Get out or I'll call the police,' she screamed, even louder this time.

'You wouldn't dare,' he challenged, his eyes blazing.

'Wouldn't I?'

He stopped, let go of his grip on her arms, turned around and marched to the front door, slamming it shut behind him. Marie Louise, her insides churning, strained to hear the sound of his retreating footsteps as she steeled herself to lunge forward and slide across the security bolt that would lock him out. There was a split second of silence before Wilder's clenched fist smashed through the door's glass panel. Marie Louise's terrified scream drowned out the sound of Wilder's feet crunching the gravel in the driveway as he stomped angrily back to his car.

SATURDAY 17 FEBRUARY 1968
SYDNEY, AUSTRALIA

Thirteen months after first stalking her on the beach, Wilder converted to Roman Catholicism and, despite the objections of both sets of parents, married Christine, who had just turned twenty-one. The newlyweds set up home in a housing commission unit in Union Street, West Ryde. Within a few months the marital bed had become a terrifying place of pain and torture. Wilder revelled in hurting his new bride. The more she cried or complained, the more sadistic he became, bruising, slapping and shaking her, and insisting on anal sex night after night. If she was menstruating, he would become even more insistent, her pain stimulating him even further. He was demanding sex up to three times a night; if she refused, he became violently angry and after raping her would go straight into the bathroom and masturbate to the memory of how he had just dominated and abused her.

Three months into their marriage, Christine left him for the first time, after she found photographic equipment and a pile of negatives of naked women. Wilder soon persuaded her back with gifts and apologies, but the rows and abuse continued, and Christine started fearing for her life, especially when the brakes mysteriously failed on her car and within a few weeks the steering suddenly froze. Wilder often came home with scratches down his neck and back, and – even though he obsessively bit his nails to the quick – tried to claim he'd accidentally scratched himself. One weekend in November she opened the boot of her car and discovered a briefcase full of *Playboy* magazines and negatives of women in various stages of undress, taken on local beaches and in bushland. There were sheets of paper and envelopes filled with his handwriting, detailing the names and addresses, phone numbers, descriptions and measurements of dozens of women. He'd even noted alongside their names whether they were married or not. Many of the women were wearing Christine's bikini bottoms or her lingerie. He was taunting her. She walked out again, but somehow, within days, he had wooed her back. Then one late summer evening came the final straw.

FRIDAY 14 FEBRUARY 1969
UNION STREET, WEST RYDE
SYDNEY, AUSTRALIA

It was 10 p.m. on Valentine's Day. 'What a joke that was,' Christine thought, as she watched Wilder fiddling with her car in the parking area beneath their building. He had his shirt off and wrapped around his waist. Another couple, Laurie and Wendy, who lived in the same block, had joined them and were chatting and laughing, smoking and drinking bottles of VB. The smell of barbecuing snags wafted down from one of the balconies, mixing with the cigarettes and strong tang of engine oil.

'Hey, did you notice that cop car that's been parked up the road a bit? Been there for hours,' Laurie said.

Christine started to feel uneasy. She looked at Wilder bending over the open bonnet of her car, and even though he didn't react or say anything, she could sense him tense up. For the past two nights he had been up and down out of bed, pacing the apartment with the lights off, peering through the venetian blinds for hours. His nails were bitten down so badly they were bloody.

A while later, the two cops approached their group.

'What's going down?' Laurie called out.

'We're investigating the disappearance of women's clothing, lingerie mostly, from the communal clothes lines over there,' the younger detective said, pointing.

Remembering the photos she'd found, Christine's heart sank.

'Seen anything?' the older cop said, looking over at Wilder, who was still bent over the engine of the car.

Laurie and Wendy both shrugged their shoulders. The detectives looked at Christine, who was digging her thumbnail into the palm of her other hand in a bid to calm her nerves. She shook her head.

'What about you, sir?'

Wilder looked up briefly. 'I don't know what you're talking about.'

When the detectives had retreated back into the shadows, Wilder became agitated and short tempered, and he quickly packed up his tools, locked the car and headed back upstairs. Christine sighed at his retreating back, said goodnight to Wendy and Laurie and told them she hoped they could hang out again soon, before following him up to the unit. Less than an hour later, when there was a knock

on the door and she opened it to find the two detectives standing
there, she didn't say a word, she just stood aside and let them in.

––––––––

Police had been watching and investigating Wilder for almost two
weeks after a distressed teenage girl, accompanied by her mother,
had reported that a man was stalking and blackmailing her for sex.

Jane, an eighteen-year-old student nurse at Sydney's Royal
North Shore Hospital, had been walking along The Corso, a pedes-
trian-only street, to do some sunbathing on Manly Beach several
weeks earlier when Wilder had persuaded her to model for him.
He told her his name was Chris Warrell, and in return for helping
him he said he'd give her a lift home. It had been that easy. He took
her to the cliffs above nearby Fairy Bower Beach and pretended to
film her, with his Rubica movie camera, against an ocean backdrop.
Then he took her to some nearby changing rooms, handed her a
bikini and told her to swap it for the one she was wearing. She'd
tried it on but then came out bellyaching that it was too skimpy.

'It's too brief,' she said.

'Well just put the top on, I just want a few shots.'

He laughed to himself when she dutifully plodded off back in and
put on the top. After a bit more fake filming they got back into his car
and drove to Balgowlah Oval, which he said was on her way home.

'Hold up your towel and take off your costume,' he told her,
as she posed at the entrance to the shower room.

Jane, who'd been getting more and more uneasy, started pro-
testing. 'No, I won't.'

'If you do this, no-one else has to see the photos I've already
taken,' he said.

Horrified at the thought of what her parents would say, she took off her clothes and, shaking, held the towel out in front of her.

'It's a movie,' he said, as if coaching her, 'go over and take a shower.'

Humiliated, she nervously put the towel down and stepped under the water. It was a double shower and she had her back to him. He swiftly stepped into the other shower recess so he could see more of her. He was holding the camera up pretending to film. Jane started sobbing.

Before taking her home, he made her write down all her telephone numbers and then, for days afterwards, pestered her at work and home. She tried to ignore him, but he kept calling and claiming if she didn't meet him, he would have the film developed and would send copies to her parents and management at the hospital. She eventually relented.

He drove her to a beach and ordered her to approach every pretty girl they saw, question her about modelling, then report back to him what they'd said. The control and dominance he had over Jane was so exhilarating that the next afternoon he rang and demanded to see her again. He picked her up and told her to lie down on the front seat of his Falcon ute, so she couldn't see where he was taking her. The love song 'Eloise', by Barry Ryan, was playing on the radio as he drove her to the unit where he lived with his wife, Christine. Almost immediately on entering the flat, he started to abuse Jane and when she tried to fight him off, he picked up a film canister, waving it in front of her, taunting her. 'You wouldn't like anyone to see the photos, would you?' he jeered at her.

Jane started crying. Wilder ignored the tears and had sex with her.

Wilder remembered how the next time he'd tried calling Jane her mother had answered and angrily threatened him with the police.

Now here they were. He couldn't believe Christine had invited them straight in, right into their fucking living room. The older detective, with a look in his face, weary disgust. The younger one, cocky, too much attitude. The older detective pedantically took them through all of Jane's allegations. Well, there was one upside. He would always treasure the look on Christine's face when he openly admitted to the cops that he had indeed fucked Jane in their bed, while she'd been at work. Yes, it had been Christine's bikini he'd made Jane wear and, yes, he had persuaded her to have sex with him.

'I pulled out before climaxing, though,' he was careful to tell them.

They took him to Manly police station, where they questioned him again and typed up his answers. Surprisingly, he didn't dispute anything Jane had said, except a few minor details.

'I'm sorry I did what I did. I can't understand why I did it. There is something wrong with me, but I can't explain my actions,' he said, with no emotion.

Jane and her mother told the detectives that, although she wanted to save other girls from becoming his victims, she would not give evidence in court. A report on the case was prepared for the magistrate, including the details of his previous conviction six years earlier, but because Jane would not take the witness stand, he wasn't charged and the cops had to let him go.

WEDNESDAY 19 FEBRUARY 1969
UNION STREET, WEST RYDE
SYDNEY, AUSTRALIA

After Wilder admitted everything in front of Christine, the police organised a car to take Christine to her parents' house. She never saw her husband again, and five days later, with her mother and sister, she walked into Hornsby police station and told the startled officer on the front desk she believed her estranged husband could be the Wanda Beach killer, and she had information that could help. A detective interviewed all three women and wrote up a running sheet for the Wanda Beach investigation team. It detailed Wilder's violent temper, particularly if he was refused sex, his previous convictions from the gang-rape incident, and gave a description of him at age twenty-three, four years after the Wanda Beach murders: 177 centimetres tall, solid build, suntanned complexion, fair hair, blue eyes. The detective attached a mugshot of Wilder from his 1963 arrest when he was seventeen, as well as copies of all three statements. He wrote: 'Wilder is a "surfie" who frequents beaches . . . for most of his life Wilder has lived in the Meadowbank and Ryde area and it is possible may have known the murdered girls, although no evidence is at present available to substantiate this.'

In early May, another running sheet entry said considerable inquiries had been made to locate Wilder without success. It noted his wife, Christine, had begun divorce proceedings and gave details for her solicitor. The report ended: 'At this stage the matter cannot be carried further.'

Four months later, a detective added that he had been in touch with Christine's solicitor again and was told Wilder 'could be residing at 1 Rene Street, Ryde. This is believed to be the address of his parents'.

TUESDAY 11 NOVEMBER 1969
RENE STREET, EAST RYDE
SYDNEY, AUSTRALIA

Nearly nine months after Christine made her statement to police, claiming her husband was the Wanda Beach killer, a detective knocked on the door of the Wilder family home, a red-brick house in East Ryde surrounded by towering gum trees and overlooking the Lane Cove river. Wilder's mother, June, opened the door, holding a basket of washing. 'I'm looking for Christopher Wilder,' the detective said.

Wilder's mother didn't mince her words. 'He left in May. To start a new life in America.'

She shut the door in his face.

The Wanda Beach detectives were six months too late. The officer who had spoken to Christine when she'd first gone, with her mother and sister, to the police station in February had dutifully interviewed all three women, dutifully taken notes and dutifully sent through the details to be recorded in the Wanda case murder book. He did his job.

It is not clear what went wrong after that. Obviously, attempts were made to track down Wilder, but as they didn't get around to knocking on the door of his family home until nearly nine months later, those detectives were either hopelessly inadequate, frighteningly slow or, more probably, didn't take Christine's claims seriously. At best, they must have considered her allegations unbelievable; at worst, a fabrication.

For Christine to take the step of going to the police and telling them she was the victim of a violent and sadistic husband, and that she believed he was the perpetrator of one of the most heinous crimes in Australian history, was remarkably brave. Violence against a wife was not treated as a crime in the 1960s. Police and medical practitioners tended to turn a blind eye to such incidents, treating them as private family matters that they shouldn't get involved in. Some experts even went as far as suggesting the women were to blame and often provoked the abuse. There were certainly few services available for battered women and, ultimately, most women just suffered in silence. So, Christine's daring not only to speak up but also to accuse her husband of murder would have been unorthodox, to say the least.

Maybe, just maybe, if attitudes had been a little more enlightened, if there had been just one female officer on the Wanda investigation, then things might have turned out very differently.

2

FRESH START
(SAME OLD STORY)

It might have been a new country and a new life, but nothing about Wilder's dangerously warped personality had changed. Even before landing on US soil he had found a new victim. During the flight from Sydney to his stopover in Hawaii, he persuaded the father of an attractive teenage girl to swap seats with him, so he could talk to her about a career in modelling. He quickly convinced the naive teen to go into the aeroplane toilet, remove all her underwear and then come back and sit next to him. He didn't touch her, he didn't need to, it was the sense of control and dominance he exerted over her that was his elixir.

Wilder, now twenty-four years old, arrived in Miami with just a few dollars (that his father had reluctantly given him), a battered suitcase and plans to spend his days surfing. He soon realised, however, that despite the Beach Boys hit songs, the surf in Miami was mostly woeful, with rarely a decent wave breaking.

So, instead, Wilder knuckled down and focused on his career. 'I only went into business after I learned Florida didn't have surf,' he would later joke to friends.

Because of his strong carpentry skills, he found it easy to work. He had arrived in the middle of a huge property boom in Florida. There were many reasons the state became so popular during this period, including technological advances that made air conditioning widely affordable for the first time, making the hot climate more attractive to both the rich and retirees. This, alongside the growth of the leisure industry and the development of the interstate highway system, put Florida on the map as a desirable place to build a home. The various property companies perfected the art of land promotion, giving free trips to Florida where the potential customers were wined and dined and treated to a luxury stay in resort-style hotels. It was perfect territory for a young, ambitious Wilder, with an entrepreneurial, cocky confidence. During his first year he took whatever carpentry work he could and saved up his money, living in a succession of cheap-to-rent apartments.

His first business foray – investing in a topless bar in North Miami with a friend called Charlie – was not successful, but for a time he used it as a base to get free drinks and cheap sex. But when Wilder fell out with Charlie, and the partnership dissolved, he was left with nothing, except a beer belly, and was forced to dust off his tools and start out again as a self-employed carpenter. It proved to be the turning point for Wilder. He always gave customers a generous discount if they paid in cash, and he had soon established a reputation for hard work. He started to make good money, his apartments got bigger and the second-hand sports cars got sleeker and more expensive.

SATURDAY 13 MARCH 1971
POMPANO BEACH, FL
Confirmation that Wilder had not given up his proclivity for trawling beaches for young victims came less than two years after he

arrived in the US. Now twenty-six years old, he was picked up by
the police and charged with soliciting. He'd been on the prowl,
with stolen business cards in the top pocket of a shirt he had screen
printed himself, bearing the logo Barbizon Modeling. Barbizon
Modeling was a prestigious nationwide model agency (Ronald
Reagan, later to become US president, had once won the agency's Best Dressed Man in America award). Wilder did not work for
them and had no partnership or agreement with the company, but
the stolen brand gave him enough fake officialdom to entice young
women and girls and make them believe he could turn them into
the next Jean Shrimpton or Twiggy.

The 1960s and 1970s had been the first era of the cult of the
supermodel. Catwalk models and cover girls like Cybill Shepherd
(who started her career as a model after winning the Miss Teenage
Memphis contest in 1966) were becoming as popular as the major
screen icons. Many young teenage girls dreamed of being discovered
in a shopping mall or beauty pageant and Wilder had perfected his
modus operandi, to play on the aspirations of these beautiful young
women and girls. On that hot and sticky spring day at Pompano
Beach, Wilder targeted two teenage friends, luring them away to a
secluded spot. He followed his usual routine, photographing them
in their own clothes, then in skimpier outfits he'd brought with
him, until eventually he coerced them into posing naked. After their
ordeal the humiliated girls were brave enough to go to the police.
Wilder was picked up and charged with soliciting; however, the girls
were reluctant to testify in court and Wilder's lawyer managed to
negotiate a plea deal. He pleaded guilty to a misdemeanour charge of
disorderly conduct and escaped with a paltry $15 fine and an order
to pay just $10 in court costs. He had sexually harassed two teenage
girls, and pleaded guilty, but had got away with a slap on the wrist.

————————

So, although Wilder now had a criminal record in two countries, he still hadn't faced any serious punishment and none of his new friends or acquaintances in the US had any clue about his aberrant behaviour. He grew his carpentry business, started to develop his passion and interest in motor racing, and bought two properties, a flash home in Boynton Beach and a rural weekender in Loxahatchee.

It was in the seventies that Wilder developed his two most important relationships: with his best friend and business partner Lonnie 'Zeke' Kimbrell and his long-term girlfriend Victoria Darling.

Wilder met Kimbrell in 1976 when the latter was a superintendent project manager for a large construction company and hired Wilder as a carpenter. Born and raised in Alabama, Kimbrell had moved to Miami at the age of five but never lost his thick southern twang. He had a wicked sense of humour that went over the head of most and almost put paid to any friendship between the pair. The first time they met, Zeke insulted Wilder over his badly fitting toupee.

'What the fuck have you got on your head, man, what is that?!' he said, roaring with laughter.

Wilder took the ribbing on the chin, ditched the toupee, and the duo became buddies and, two years later, business partners when they set up a contracting business, Sawtel Construction, together. Kimbrell brought far more to the partnership as he was well known and popular in the construction game, and his address book was bulging with contacts for tradies and developers. Thanks primarily to these many contacts and Kimbrell's business savvy, the business grew quickly and successfully and they were soon employing up to seventy people.

Although Wilder had been hardworking and motivated in the first few years of the business partnership, he soon started to slack off, spending more and more time (and company profits) on car racing. The walls of Wilder's office at Sawtel were festooned with photographs of him racing his Porsche. Of course, there was no hint of his other hobby, no images of the pretty girls and young women he spent his weekends photographing.

Wilder had started dating Victoria Darling, an attractive, slim legal secretary, a few years earlier. They quickly set up home together and because of their shared passion for dogs, started a small business out of Wilder's rural property, breeding English setters. Wilder's divorce from Christine had been finalised in February 1972, so he was free to remarry, but he never proposed to Victoria. They had sex only sporadically and when they did, he could achieve orgasm only through violent domination. The relationship, which lasted for several years and was the longest Wilder had with a woman, was similar to his earlier short-lived marriage, founded on domestic abuse and bullying. Wilder didn't bother trying to stay faithful to Darling; in fact, if anything he became even more promiscuous during their on-off time together. He began spending a lot of money hiring prostitutes, sometimes two at a time from a local escort service, turning up to parties with one on either arm. His sexual perversions became so complex in 1979 that he voluntarily sought help at the South County Mental Health Center, in Delray Beach, which referred him to a sexual therapist, who would end up becoming one of the most defining characters in his life.

Ginger Bush was a former social worker turned psychotherapist, who operated her own one-woman practice in Boca Raton. The petite therapist, with her strawberry-blonde hair and striking makeup, found Wilder fascinating but daunting. Bush had a wide range of patients, from troubled child victims of sexual abuse to couples experiencing relationship problems in the bedroom, but none of them were quite like Wilder. The bubbly therapist would see the deeply disturbed and sadistic sex addict twice a week for almost five years.

The catalyst that had prompted Wilder to seek help was an affair that had started fairly routinely but had soon gone haywire. Wilder claimed to Bush that he had been seduced by a bookkeeper who worked for another building company. The relationship, he told her, had developed quickly into one of aggressive play-acting, with Wilder taking control. He had revelled in the role he created for himself as slave owner, ordering the woman to perform various degrading sexual acts. On one occasion he got her to perform a striptease for several workmen, getting his kicks from her total obedience. He became the ultimate authority on every aspect of her life, telling her what to wear, say and do. How willing the woman was in this perverted relationship isn't clear, but Wilder claimed to Bush that the relationship started to turn around, and it was she who eventually started taking control. Whether true or not, Wilder claimed that three months into their sex games she initiated sex with two of Wilder's employees and then taunted him with how much better in bed they had been. This sexual mocking by the woman had been unbearable for Wilder and only served to fuel his carefully concealed hatred of women in general.

Bush realised he was never without a woman in his life, and sometimes he had several at the same time, but she recognised he had no sense of loyalty, commitment or respect for any of them. She also knew that he posed a serious threat to them all.

At one stage she put her professional ethics to one side and tracked down one of the women Wilder was seeing. Susan Lambert,

an Australian divorcee with wealthy parents, had followed him from
Sydney out to Florida. Bush tried to persuade Lambert to walk away
from Wilder, but like most of the other women that Wilder wooed,
Lambert couldn't believe the charming man who took her on romantic dates to fancy restaurants and insisted on escorting her home
afterwards was a violent psychopath. Six weeks after she had ignored
Bush's warning, Lambert called the therapist. Wilder had savagely
sexually assaulted her, bashing her so viciously she was coughing up
blood from internal injuries. Lambert didn't press charges; she was
just happy to have escaped with her life. She thanked the therapist
for trying to warn her and disappeared very quickly.

Looking back, the question is: could Bush have done more to
stop Wilder? Was she just another in a long list of people being
manipulated by him? Interestingly, Wilder's friend Kimbrell
didn't have a lot of time for Bush or her methods. 'It wasn't a professional relationship at all,' he said later. 'Chris was always doing
stuff for her and her friends, doing favours. He thought she was
great, that she was his good friend helping him out, but to me
she was just telling him what she knew he wanted to hear, that
everything was okay.' Kimbrell was aware his friend was being
treated for sex addiction and had got into a couple of scrapes with
the law over what Wilder assured him were 'misunderstandings'
with young women, but he had no idea about the number and
seriousness of his crimes.

Certainly, the master puppeteer was still skilfully hiding his
true nature from most of those around him. He had become a regular at the La Noche nightclub near Hollywood Lakes, south of
Fort Lauderdale, where he liked to spend up big, drinking Kahlua-
and-cream cocktails in the VIP section, then dance with the young
models who hung out there. He would ply them with drinks then

drive them to his home in Boynton Beach and persuade them to be photographed in his DIY photo studio.

One woman who remembered Wilder well from that time, Vickie Smith, a 27-year-old fellow racing driver, thought he was harmless. She often went dancing with Wilder at the La Noche nightclub and they became regulars on Thursday nights. Despite their closeness, the two never dated. Smith was not stupid. She knew Wilder was a womaniser. 'He could recite the personal details of every good-looking woman that frequented the nightclub,' she told friends. But as far as Smith was concerned, Wilder was just that. She never saw the dark side of his nature. To her, Wilder was a good dancer and good company, often making her laugh with his cute Aussie accent. He was also the perfect gentleman. She claimed he was unfailingly polite and attentive, almost to the point of being old-fashioned, always opening doors and offering to help her out of cars.

SATURDAY 21 JUNE 1980
PALM BEACH MALL
WEST PALM BEACH, FL

Valerie and her friend Andrea, from Tennessee, were on holiday in West Palm Beach, Florida, when they popped into the Palm Beach Mall to do some shopping. They were both pretty girls, with brown hair and green eyes. At about 3 p.m. Wilder approached them with his usual spiel, telling them he was David Pearce, a talent scout from the Barbizon modelling school, and was interested in taking their photographs for a pizza advertisement he was shooting. He promised them $75 each and then walked them to a nearby restroom and told them if they wanted to be models, they shouldn't be shy and needed to remove their bras. When they came out of the bathroom, he made them walk around while he watched and directed, telling them, 'My eyes are the camera.' He took them to a couple of different locations, ending up in the car park of the mall, continually asking Valerie, 'What are you?' and making her repeat the reply, 'I am a Barbizon model.'

Later, he sent Andrea to buy pizza and Cokes, and when she returned, he got them to walk around while he sat in their car watching, the food on the back seat next to him. When they came back, he handed Valerie a slice of pizza and instructed her to take a big mouthful and chew it slowly, telling her it would be a big part of the ad. The girls, becoming more and more uncomfortable, did as they were told. Wilder then made Andrea drive to the back of the mall and wait while he took Valerie for a walk alone.

When he asked Valerie if she had a boyfriend and had ever had sex, she started to cry.

'Who are you?' he barked at her.

'A Barbizon model,' she answered a little groggily. The teenager told him she felt weird, as if she'd been drugged.

'Not much of a drug,' he told her sarcastically. Feeling his growing erection, he asked her to explain what she meant by 'weird'. Valerie said she felt like she was outside her body and her voice didn't sound like hers. He helped her into his pick-up truck, saying she could sit and wait until she felt better, but once they were inside, he drove behind a nearby building, parked and told her to take off her blouse.

'You want to be a Barbizon model, don't you?' he said as he removed her clothes. By this stage she was powerless to stop him.

'Don't worry, you're on drugs and will conk out in fifteen minutes,' he added, pulling his trousers down. He made her straddle him and give him French kisses. Valerie was semi-comatose.

'Now I want to get a little piece of your ass,' he told her. 'I want to fantasise about you for the next five years.'

When he'd finished raping her, he helped her put on her clothes then drove back to the mall and let her go in the car park to find Andrea.

The terrified girls went straight to the police and Wilder was arrested a couple of days later by Palm Beach detective Arthur Newcombe. Wilder quickly admitted everything to the astonished veteran cop. He sat in the sparse interrogation room while the detective smoked a cigarette, the typewriter clicking his replies, a grey cloud of smoke hugging the yellowing ceiling above his head. He told the detective that his business was his whole life, and he worked himself to the bone, 'but when the weekends roll around something came over me'. He said he'd attacked Valerie because he fancied her more, and claimed he had sexual problems and felt relieved to be admitting it all.

'Now I can get the help I need,' he told Newcombe.

It seemed like an open-and-shut case, but in court Wilder's lawyer, Nelson Bailey, outflanked the prosecution, arguing there was no evidence Valerie had been drugged. The defence claimed she had willingly taken off her blouse. There was a courtroom huddle between the prosecutor and Bailey, and it was agreed Wilder would plead guilty to a lesser charge of sexual battery. The prosecutor later argued that without eyewitnesses and any physical evidence, it came down to one person's word against the other's, and he thought he'd done well to get the result he did. Wilder got away with five years' probation. Under the terms of his probation he wasn't allowed to use false identities, misrepresent himself or leave Palm Beach county without permission. It was a minor inconvenience.

Once again, despite committing and admitting a horrendous sex crime, Wilder had escaped with little more than a slap on the wrist. The system, once again, had failed young women and allowed a predatory sexual deviant to escape justice and to continue offending.

Following the attack on the girls at the Palm Beach Mall, Wilder had been ordered to undergo weekly sex-therapy counselling. Ginger Bush, who he had already been seeing voluntarily, now became his court-appointed therapist. Within a few sessions he confessed to Bush he had drugged Valerie, putting a small dot of LSD in the pizza slice. He told her that he'd been lucky, the drugs must have left Valerie's system before the authorities tested her. 'A slice of good fortune,' he'd laughed. It was clear that Wilder was unrepentant, unabashed and merciless.

MONDAY 27 DECEMBER 1982
MANLY BEACH, SYDNEY
NSW, AUSTRALIA

Two years later and Wilder was back in Australia for a family holiday. After spending Christmas with his parents, who now lived at Sawtell on the NSW north coast, he drove down to Sydney in a hire car and checked into the Top of the Town motel in Kings Cross. The following day, Tuesday, he went over the Harbour Bridge back to his favourite beach, Manly, wearing shorts, T-shirt and a maroon baseball cap with 'Hawaii' written across the front, his dark brown hair falling just below his ears and his full beard having touches of grey at the edges.

Fifteen-year-old schoolgirls Amanda and Christine had gone to the beach with three boys, including Amanda's boyfriend, Rudi. It was a perfect Sydney summer's day; a gentle ocean breeze, a crisp azure sky without a cloud. The three boys left the girls to look for something to eat and when they hadn't returned by noon, Amanda and Christine wrapped sarongs around their bikinis and went to find food themselves. At the top of the sandstone steps opposite The Corso, Wilder made his approach. He'd spotted the girls when they had first arrived and had been waiting for an opportunity.

He told them he was from a photographic agency and asked if they would be interested in modelling for him in some commercials he was shooting. The girls giggled for a moment, looked at each other, then both nodded.

For the next two hours he drove them to a number of different locations on Sydney's north shore, making them change into stockings and high-heeled shoes, and then bullying both of them into posing topless for him. Afterwards, he blindfolded them and drove them to his hotel in Kings Cross. Driving up the ramp to the car park, one of the girls looked up and beneath her blindfold she caught a glimpse of a neon sign with the name of the hotel. Wilder took them one by one up to his room. He then forced Amanda into the bathroom and kept Christine in the bedroom and told both girls to take off their clothes.

'If you're good and do what I say, I won't make you have sex with me.'

He lay back on the bed holding the camera and made them undress him.

'I now want you to turn me on,' he said to Amanda, 'and put some feeling into it.'

He tried to give her a tongue kiss, but the brave schoolgirl resisted and forced her lips closed. He lost patience when she started to sob and told her to swap places with Christine, forcing her to French kiss him, then ordering them both to massage his feet while he masturbated.

He then blindfolded both girls and took them back down to his car separately and drove them to Central train station, but before letting them get out of the car he searched through their handbags and wrote down all their contact details and telephone numbers. He threatened that if they made any complaints or told anyone about him, he would send the photographs he'd taken to their parents. It was a blackmail threat he had used many times over the years.

Telling them he would be ringing their parents in the morning he said, 'I want to see you go now in a good mood. Get out, walk straight ahead and don't look back.'

They got home around 8 p.m. After initially both being too scared to tell their parents what had happened, one of the girls broke down when a police officer rang the house asking to speak to her father. The three boys who had accompanied the girls to the beach that morning had become worried when they saw Wilder driving them away in his car and had gone to Manly police station to report it. They had even made a note of the number plate on his rental car. It was very late that evening when Christine and Amanda told both sets of horrified parents the full story.

WEDNESDAY 29 DECEMBER 1982
MANLY POLICE STATION
SYDNEY, AUSTRALIA

Detective Sergeant Geoff Shelley interviewed the girls and later took them with Christine's father and another detective to retrace their movements with Wilder. It was 6.15 p.m. when they turned into Victoria Street in Kings Cross, and the girls directed them into a driveway at the Top of the Town motel. They drove up four levels of ramps to the motel parking area and found Wilder's hire vehicle, a bronze-coloured 1982 Ford Falcon sedan.

Shelley arranged for the girls to be taken home while he made inquiries at the reception desk and went up to room 114 on the eleventh floor. There was no answer to their knock, so the detective and his partner kept watch for forty minutes until Wilder turned up, and they followed him inside the room.

'Are you Chris Wilder?' said Shelley.

'Yes.'

Shelley asked him about Christine and Amanda.

'The girls allege you took photos of them. Where is the film?' asked the detective.

Wilder wouldn't look him in the eye. 'I was ashamed of myself last night and I threw it away,' he muttered. 'I tossed it in a bin outside.'

The detectives searched Wilder's camera bag and found two cameras, but there was no film in either one. They found the board shorts and T-shirt the girls had described him as wearing, as well as some running shoes.

'Where's the blindfold?' said Shelley.

'I threw it out with the film,' said Wilder, still not making eye contact.

Shelley kept firing questions. 'The girls allege you masturbated in front of them, is that right?'

'Yes, I'm sorry,' said Wilder.

'They say you made them kiss you, is that right?'

'Yes.'

'I've been told you took a series of photos with this camera of the girls in different positions here in the room. Is that right?'

'Yes.'

Whenever Shelley asked a clear and direct question, Wilder gave him a straight answer. Shelley decided to get him back to Manly police station to take a formal statement while forensic officers searched his room, clothing and camera equipment. It was 8.30 p.m. when Shelley got back to the station and walked into the interrogation room, sitting down opposite Wilder. The grey plastic chairs and the brown stained table were scuffed, scratched and full of dents. Shelley placed a brown folder down in front of him with the identification name tag, Christopher Bernard WILDER, DOB 13-3-1945, clearly visible. It was a thick file. Lighting up a cigarette, the amiable detective offered a smoke to Wilder, but he shook his head.

'No, thanks,' he said.

'When were you last in Australia?' said Shelley.

'About fifteen months ago on business,' he replied.

Shelley said he was going to ask more questions about the girls' allegations, but Wilder interrupted, 'Yes, but I want to see a lawyer before saying anything else.'

'In that case,' said Shelley, 'you will be charged with enticing the girls away for your advantage and with indecently assaulting them.'

THURSDAY 30 DECEMBER 1982
MANLY POLICE STATION
SYDNEY, AUSTRALIA

Wilder had a ticket to fly back to the US that Thursday, but instead he was stuck in jail, his passport confiscated. Three rolls of film discovered in his room were developed and revealed a large number of photographs of other naked girls in similar poses to those described by Christine and Amanda. None of the girls in the photos had contacted police or made complaints.

FRIDAY 28 JANUARY 1983
MANLY LOCAL COURT
SYDNEY, AUSTRALIA

After telling the court he had major business contracts that needed his attention, Wilder was freed, a month later, on $400000 bail, despite the objections of the prosecutor and police, and was allowed to return to the US. His father and uncle pledged their homes as collateral – $200000 lodged by way of deed on his parents' home, and a $150000 deed on his uncle's house. Wilder put up $50000 himself. His passport was returned and the case was adjourned for a committal hearing at Manly Court. Sitting in court watching proceedings was a young reporter for *The Sun*, Sydney's tabloid afternoon newspaper. Michael Robotham, who would become an international best-selling crime author, was captivated by Wilder that day in the courtroom and wrote about it: 'What struck me most was his charisma and charm. He didn't seem concerned by the charges. It was all a misunderstanding, a mistake that would soon be sorted out. He was beautifully dressed in expensive clothes. Well-spoken. Confident.'

Detective Shelley was furious with the decision to give Wilder bail. 'He was already on probation in the US. It's fairly evident that he was a dangerous criminal,' he said later.

When Wilder arrived back in Florida his probation officer, learning of his arrest in Australia, charged him with violating probation. Wilder surrendered, posted a $1000 bond and was released again. Immediately.

3

CHARY

He's a collector. That's the great dead thing in him.
— John Fowles, *The Collector*

**UNSUB; ROSARIO T GONZALEZ, 00:MM MIAMI FBI
FILE 7-1662**

SUNDAY 26 FEBRUARY 1984
HOMESTEAD, FL

'I love you, Chary, I'll talk to you tomorrow. Dream about me.'

Twenty-year-old Rosario Gonzalez, family nickname Chary, put the phone back in its cradle with the words of her fiancé making her heart skip a beat. She was so in love with Bill Londos it actually hurt. She smiled to herself. In just a few months they would be married, she would be Mrs Londos and then she could start making the first of their three babies. She enjoyed her part-time modelling, but, truthfully, being a mama was really all she wanted in life.

They had been talking over the details of the wedding: her dress was being hand-sewn; the furniture and the crockery were chosen.

Money was tight because Bill was only twenty-one and a student, and they still had to find the deposit for the hall where they were going to hold the wedding reception, but Chary was excited. Just three months and six days and four hours and five minutes to go, she laughed to herself. Two days ago, they'd celebrated the first anniversary of when they'd met.

Bill had fallen in love with her on the spot. He'd noticed her one day on campus and for the next three weeks waited on the same corner at the same time until he saw her again and could pluck up the courage to ask her out. Tall and handsome, with a sturdy physique and even sturdier mindset, he was a young man with enough drive and confidence to make a success of his life. He'd recently transferred to another college five hours north of Miami, but Chary still lived at home with her parents and younger sister, Lisette, in Homestead, a semi-rural community about 50 kilometres south of Miami.

Her family had fled Havana, Cuba, as refugees when she was seven years old, first to Spain, then after a couple of years to Massachusetts and finally to Florida. Chary's father, Blas, was deacon of the local church and her mother, Haydee, was a bookkeeper for a company that owned Channel 4, a local TV station. Chary and Lisette were very close. Chary was much more sociable, with a large circle of friends, while her sister was more shy and studious. Chary loved ballet and dancing, and followed the latest fashion trends and hairstyles, while Lisette, who had just turned eighteen, was much quieter and a bit of a tomboy, but they looked out for each other and were fiercely protective of their parents, neither of whom spoke English very well. The girls were religious about always calling to let them know where they were and what time they would be home, so they never had to worry.

At the weekend Chary, who was studying computer science at Miami Dade Community College, was a Sunday school teacher at her father's church. Slim and pretty with shoulder-length light blonde hair, she had won Florida's Miss Mannequin modelling contest for the previous two years, but she was just 167 centimetres and too short for the catwalk or a serious modelling career. Her big, almond-shaped hazel eyes and her dancer's elegance meant she got some fashion and promotional work through a local agency, but to help pay for the wedding she also worked part-time in a boutique at the local mall and had landed some temporary weekend work, distributing free aspirins for a sponsor at the Miami Grand Prix.

MIAMI, FL

A few hours after her chat with Bill, Chary jumped into her four-year-old blue Oldsmobile Cutlass to drive to downtown Miami for her shift at the Grand Prix. She parked near the Dupont Plaza Hotel and walked to the sponsors tent outside the Pavilion Hotel, arriving to pick up her samples shortly before her start time of 8.30 a.m. She was wearing beige ballet-slipper style shoes with her uniform of red shorts and a white T-shirt that had 'Mejoral' printed on the front. On her left hand was the diamond engagement ring Bill had bought, with money he'd saved from working nights at a service station. For the next four and a half hours Chary covered her patch on the south side of Bayfront Park, near the corner of Flagler Street and Biscayne Boulevard. It was only the second annual staging of the Budweiser Grand Prix and the hyped-up racing crowd was about 300000, double the size of the previous day.

On her way back to the tent for a lunch break, an off-duty Miami firefighter asked politely if he could take her photograph.

A smiling Chary perched on some sandstone steps and posed for him, clasping her hands around her knees, her curly hair tumbling down over her slender shoulders.

————

Wilder was feeling on top of the world. He'd barely slept at all last night, replaying yesterday's race in his mind until he could recount every single detail of his heroics on the track. His had only been a side bill race to the weekend's main event, but he didn't care. He'd started in twenty-first place on the grid and, 77 octane-fuelled kilometres later, had battled his sleek black Porsche 911 Turbo, in race number fifty-one, up four places to finish with a small allocation of the prize money. He planned to round off probably *the* best weekend of his life by adding a new butterfly to his collection. He'd recognised her yesterday at the racetrack and knew exactly where to look for her today.

He jumped in his pride-and-joy everyday car, a cream 1978 turbo-charged Porsche 911 Carrera, capable of a top speed of almost 240 kilometres per hour, and backed it out of his Boynton Beach home, a smart up-market bungalow backing onto the canal in Palm Beach County, which he'd bought for a knockdown $57 000 and then extensively refurbished.

After his usual steak-and-eggs breakfast at DJ's Diner, he hit the highway to Miami, put Eurythmics on the cassette player and floored the accelerator. He knew as he powered towards the city that he was breaking the conditions of his probation by leaving Palm Beach County without permission, but he did the same thing every weekend, driving thousands of kilometres, roaming Florida looking for attractive young women. His hours of operation were mid-morning to early afternoon, as he'd long ago worked out that young women were much less wary when a stranger approached them during daylight hours. He wasn't a bogeyman who came out at night; he was their worst nightmare who liked the sun on his back. He'd devised a strategy of targeting shopping malls 70 per cent of the time and popular beaches the other 30 per cent. Occasionally, he would try the beauty pageants, but today he was going to find his new 'plaything' at the races. It was after 10 a.m. when he pulled into the car park near the Bayfront Auditorium, deliberately parking across two spaces and ignoring the angry stares of other drivers. 'Morons,' he said under his breath, 'as if I'd leave a $60000 car like this somewhere it could get scraped by a shit-heap like yours.' He still had his racing credentials and his 'access all areas' pass from the previous day, and slinging his Pentax camera over his shoulder, he flashed the badge confidently at the man on the gate, who waved him through.

He'd first met Rosario Gonzalez at the Miss Mannequin pageant in October 1982, when she had been introduced to him by another contestant, Nora Arias, whom he had previously photographed. Rosario had won the event and he'd been there loitering with his camera, mixing with the other photographers. He'd given her his practised spiel and asked her to model for him, telling her she was very pretty and had 'so much potential'. He'd been instantly taken with her look of innocence and childlike naivety – he liked it when they looked really young – and as he talked to her, he fantasised about putting her hair into pigtails and keeping her captive in the secret torture room he'd built in his house.

'I think you could be the cover girl for a new magazine I'm working for,' he'd told her, seeing the excited look on her face, even though she had blushed at his flattery and shyly hidden her eyes beneath her curly bangs.

A few months later she had agreed to do the shoot with him. He'd got very excited planning for it, but when she arrived, she told him she'd rung her parents to let them know where she was and what she was doing. That had instantly put him in a bad mood, and he hadn't even bothered putting film in his camera. After pretending to take a few shots, he'd asked her to pose more provocatively, saying if she wanted to be a successful model, she had to do what he said. Next, he'd told her to start removing her clothes, that all models had to do nude shoots if they really wanted a modelling career. She had a big future, he'd told her, if she did what he said, but she was embarrassed and after a while became reluctant. He'd cut things short and had been glad to see the back of her.

Now it was payback time. He made his way steadily through the thronging crowds towards the race sponsors marquee area. He mingled for a while with some of the official photographers, including Robert Von Staden, a Pompano Beach freelancer for United Press International. He knew many of the press guys didn't particularly like him and thought he was a bit odd, carrying only one camera and lens.

'Who are you shooting for?' Von Staden asked Wilder.

'Just some start-up paper, man, you won't have heard of it.'

Before his race, the day before, Wilder had spent time in the Mejoral sponsors tent with Ted Martin, a professional photographer he hired from time to time to do studio shoots with girls, claiming he was talent-scouting for the big model agencies. He'd arranged to meet Martin again, at noon today, at the Budweiser overpass, but now regretted the plan. Usually, being around legitimate photographers gave him the cover of respectability he needed, but for his plan to succeed today, he needed to work alone. It was near to one o'clock, anyway. Hopefully Ted had given up on their rendezvous.

————

Chary was on her way to buy some *tostones* from a food truck near the underpass when he approached her. She was ravenous, having left home that morning without eating breakfast, and the fried banana chips were her favourite Cuban street-food snack.

'Hello, Chary, I thought it was you,' she heard someone say. She looked up and recognised him immediately. Her heart sank. It was the creepy guy she'd stupidly done a photo shoot with. She'd gone without telling her parents and had instantly regretted it.

'Oh, hello,' she replied, reluctantly. 'I'm working and just on my lunch break, so I can't stop,' she said, moving off. He stepped forward, blocking her path.

'I need you to come with me right now, do you understand?' he said, staring over her shoulder, his eyes cold. 'If you don't, I will send those photographs we did to your parents.'

Chary's world instantly collapsed. The thought of her father, a church deacon and the most gentle, kind and loving man, seeing those pictures filled her with horror. And what Bill would say if he found out, she couldn't bear thinking about.

'Why are you doing this?' Chary said to Wilder.

'My car is only a few minutes away. Come with me, I can show you the photographs, it won't take very long and if you do exactly what I say, I will give you all the negatives,' he told her, holding up a film canister for her to see. Chary knew she had no choice; she had to get those negatives and destroy them. He told her to walk slightly in front of him to one side and not to talk; that way, he said, 'no-one watching will know we are together'.

By 2.30 p.m., when Chary hadn't returned, the other girls became concerned and organised a search, but they couldn't find any sign of her. Her sweater was still in her locker along with her pay cheque. They'd seen her drop off her sample tray at lunchtime, to be restocked for the afternoon, and then grab her grey purse from her locker. She hadn't told them where she was going, and they just assumed she was meeting someone for lunch. One of the girls later recalled seeing Chary, still in her uniform, walking on a crossover towards Bayfront Park with a tall, bearded man slightly behind her.

Chary had told her parents she would be home around 5 p.m., depending on the traffic. By 7 p.m., when it was getting dark and she still hadn't shown up, they called the Pavilion Hotel to ask if the race was still going on. When they were told it had finished hours ago, they became so frantic they called Bill. He knew instinctively something was wrong. Chary wasn't the type of girl to go off without letting her parents know about it. He grabbed his car keys and drove straight back to Homestead. By the time he arrived it was almost 1 a.m. on Monday morning, Chary was still missing and her family were desperate. While he'd been driving, they had spent hours on the telephone ringing everyone they could think of, friends, family, hospitals and the Florida highway patrol in case she had been in an accident. Bill drove them all to the police station to report her missing. Normally it was at least twenty-four hours before police would begin investigating, but the family were so distraught, officers filled out a missing person's report on the spot. When they left the station, Bill drove Haydee and Lisette home while Chary's father and uncle drove to Miami and started searching the downtown race area. At 3 a.m. they found her car parked close to the Dupont Plaza Hotel. It was empty.

Witnesses later recalled seeing a Carrera driving too fast, heading north, on Florida's Turnpike, about 5 p.m. The driver appeared to be alone. At 6.30 p.m., the same night, a neighbour remembered waving to Wilder as he backed out of his garage, behind the wheel of another car he owned, a charcoal-grey Cadillac. Wilder had changed and showered and was on his way to dinner with friends. These friends recalled later that he had been relaxed during the meal but had made his excuses and left quite early, around 8.30 p.m.

'I want to get home and sit in the jacuzzi,' he'd told them, as soon as it was polite to leave.

MONDAY 27 FEBRUARY 1984
MIAMI POLICE DEPARTMENT, FL
Miami homicide detectives Harvey Wasserman and Jorge Morin were handed the missing person's case of Rosario Gonzalez on Monday morning, and by the late afternoon they were stumped. A missing girl with no history of running away, over 300000 potential suspects, many of whom were only in Miami for a few days to see the race, and no evidence anywhere of a crime. They interviewed Chary's family and friends and the other models who'd worked for Mejoral at the Grand Prix with her. There had been no ransom demand, and that seemed an unlikely motive anyway, as the family had little in the way of money, and no eyewitnesses to any kind of altercation.

Only a few hours after beginning their investigation, the detectives were right in the spotlight, with the case all over that evening's TV news on Channel 4, where Chary's mama worked. Haydee had rung the studio in tears, explaining why she wouldn't be at work, and the message had wound its way to the desk of the network's news editor. Within the hour the news chopper was landing in their back paddock at Homestead and Chary's family, with Bill alongside them, were being interviewed. The exclusive report went to air that night. -

TUESDAY 28 FEBRUARY 1984
GINGER BUSH'S OFFICE
BOCA RATON, FL

The next day Wilder attended his regular Tuesday morning session with Ginger Bush. Bush quizzed him about Rosario Gonzalez. She knew Wilder's sexual fantasies were becoming increasingly violent; that he was unable to obtain any sexual gratification unless he brutalised a woman first. She had seen the TV news story about the pretty woman who had gone missing while working at the Grand Prix. When Wilder revealed he had raced that weekend, she chastised him for breaking his parole conditions, asked him whether he had heard the story about the missing woman and challenged him outright if he knew Rosario. She knew that the best approach with Wilder was to be direct, as when confronted previously he had often confessed to police. This time he was clearly caught off-guard but quickly denied knowing anything about the missing girl. She suspected he was lying.

Wilder told her that he had severed all his female relationships in January and was following her advice and hiring prostitutes rather than picking up young girls on beaches or in shopping malls.

He said he was not having orgasms and had to hire a different girl every time, otherwise he became aggressive and physically violent. In the week before Rosario Gonzalez disappeared, he told Bush, he had used a local escort service twice and had become very threatening to one of the girls, telling her to leave because she was cold and nonchalant and he had been unable to get an erection. He blamed his performance problems on the anxiousness he felt about going back to Australia for his trial and having to face his parents and brothers, who considered him a fantasist.

WEDNESDAY 29 FEBRUARY 1984
BOYNTON BEACH, FL

For Detective Morin it was the usual dilemma: publicity could turn something up, but it could also put Chary's life in danger. With this case, and particularly now the story had broken on television, he believed it could only work in the investigation's favour to get as much coverage as possible. His partner, Wasserman, had given an interview with a reporter from the *Miami Herald* and the story ran in that day's final edition. Under the headline 'Police Press Search for Missing Model', Wasserman was quoted as saying, 'The Miami Police Department is investigating it as foul play. Hopefully, we're wrong. I pray we're wrong.'

The blitz coverage that followed, as other stations and newspapers scrambled to play catch-up, did produce leads, and more than 200 were followed up in the first week. The model who'd been the last to see Chary, with a bearded man walking close behind her on the overpass, was interviewed and helped police produce a photofit, which was released to the media. Then, as the days rolled by with no new developments, Chary's fiancé, Bill, asked to go up in the Channel 4 news chopper to look for possible dumping grounds near the highway. He also joined volunteers searching Alligator Alley in the Everglades. Chary's family, their friends and members of their church held a candlelit vigil and prayed for her safe return. The service was covered by the TV networks, and Chary's parents scrimped together enough money to offer a $5000 reward for information leading to their daughter's return.

The family begged the FBI for help, and an agent did a kidnap evaluation but found no evidence that gave the bureau jurisdiction over the case. Bill, along with Chary's parents, rang Miami Homicide every day to chase up news of their investigation, quickly growing impatient with the seemingly slow progress. Armed with a photograph of Chary, he went door knocking himself, accompanied by TV news crews, to try and find witnesses who may have seen her on the afternoon she disappeared. He struck a deal with a private investigator to take on the case, in return for mentions whenever Bill did media interviews.

Detective Wasserman interviewed a young girl who said she'd been approached at the Grand Prix by a well-dressed, bearded man, who told her she could be a model. He had shown her a business card and was carrying a camera. The bearded photographer was a good lead, but Chary's friend Nora hadn't come forward yet to tell detectives about the creepy man who had done a photo shoot with her and also with Chary. If she had, the bearded photographer would have become a top suspect. Instead, the Miami homicide detectives went back to square one.

Three weeks after Chary had disappeared, the investigation was in danger of grinding to a halt.

4

DEADLY PROPOSAL

**UNSUB; ELIZABETH ANN KENYON, VICTIM;
KIDNAPPING 00:MM, MIAMI FBI FILE 7-1664**

MONDAY 5 MARCH 1984
CORAL GABLES SENIOR HIGH SCHOOL
MIAMI, FL

Beth Kenyon came jogging out of the school entrance before the end-of-day bell and headed for her two-door brown Chrysler LeBaron convertible. Even if the flashy car, with distinctive New York plates, didn't attract admiring glances, Beth was the kind of woman who would turn heads. Local cop Mitch Fry, who was readying himself outside the front gate for the imminent mass student exodus, gave her a little wave and a shy smile. He was secretly a little bit sweet on Beth. The pair had become friends since Beth had started her first teaching job there last year, and they were always swapping 'war' stories about the daily dramas at Coral Gables High, in south Miami. It wasn't a poor neighbourhood by any means, but the drug tsunami swamping the city had seeped into the classrooms.

'Today was a quiet one, for a change,' she called out. 'I've got to fly, let's chat tomorrow.'

Mitch watched her as she slid in behind the wheel of the car, quickly backed out of her car space and, giving him a quick wave, catapulted forward into the afternoon traffic gathering outside the school. He was gawping at her so much, he would be able to tell detectives later exactly what she had been wearing: a silk pink blouse and skin-tight blue Jordache jeans, white shoes, white socks and a lot of makeup, a lot more than usual. It had highlighted her trademark dazzling smile.

'She'd seemed in a real hurry,' he told them.

Beth, full name Elizabeth Ann Kenyon, was twenty-three years old and could best be described as a classic beauty, with long brown hair that fell in soft curls, hazel eyes and a willowy elegance that made her seem both feminine and athletic. Her parents, Bill and Dolores, had done well for themselves from owning a string of convenience stores near where they lived in Lockport, New York State. They'd also bought a ranch-style summer house in Pompano Beach, about 60 kilometres north of Miami, to be near Beth, when she'd gone to the University of Miami after graduating high school in New York. Now all four of their children used it as a weekend retreat, especially when their parents flew in three times a year, for the summer, fall and winter holidays.

Dolores loved to spoil her kids, but Beth had been stubbornly independent and refused all offers of financial help, saying she didn't need her parents' money. After graduating from university, she was offered a job at Coral Gables teaching students with special needs. Beth loved helping kids, and she had been a volunteer teacher's aide before taking the job. She'd also done some modelling after she'd been Orange Bowl Princess and runner-up in the Miss Florida pageant, but she'd thrown herself into the teaching job rather than modelling, treating the latter more as a hobby. She was also the school cheerleading coach, which meant attending several games a week.

Teaching had, however, proved a lot more challenging than Beth had anticipated. In the past few months she'd helped save a suicidal student who had slit her wrists, stayed the night at the hospital rape centre beside another girl who had been assaulted, and been badly bruised breaking up a schoolyard fight. Beth confided in her mother how much she was struggling but told her she was going to stick it out until the end of the school year in June so she didn't let anyone down.

When her ex-boyfriend Chris Wilder had rung her to say there was a well-paid modelling shoot, if she was interested, she'd accepted in a heartbeat. She'd first met Chris at the Miss Miami beauty pageant when he'd offered to do a photo shoot with her and then taken her out to dinner at a French restaurant near her parents' weekend place in Pompano. They'd chatted about surfing and Australia while they ate crepes. Afterwards he'd driven her home and she'd told him she'd really enjoyed herself. He'd been the perfect gentleman, she'd told her mother. They went on a few more casual dates, including a day out watching him race and a meal with his business partner, Kimbrell, and Kimbrell's wife. Then, out of the blue, he'd shocked her by proposing marriage. She'd let him down as gently as she could.

'I've never even kissed the guy and he asked me to marry him,' she told her mother in amazement.

Dolores told police later that she had been relieved when her daughter had turned Wilder down. She recalled one time when they'd all had dinner together. He'd been incredibly polite and well-mannered and had even given Dolores a gift set of made-in-Australia napkins and placemats bordered with koalas and flowers.

Her husband, Bill, had been impressed with Wilder's manners, but she'd had a weird feeling about him, she told the detectives, even though she'd dubbed him 'Mr Personality plus' after the meal. At the time she couldn't put her finger on it, but she just knew she didn't like him.

Although things had been a little awkward between Beth and Wilder for the past year since she'd rejected his marriage proposal, Beth had welcomed his modelling offer as a nice distraction. She didn't know any more details, as Chris said he would tell her more when they met up. She drove a couple of blocks and pulled into the Shell service station where she regularly bought petrol and had taken her car recently when it developed a series of annoying brake and steering problems. Service station attendant Rickie Norman recognised the car immediately when she pulled up to the pumps. Beth, a regular who always made time for a chat, was peering into her compact mirror and dabbing at her lipstick when she asked him to please fill up with unleaded, before adding, 'no need to check under the bonnet, Rickie, I'm in a hurry'.

As he was pumping the gas, Rickie noticed a charcoal Cadillac Eldorado pull up behind Beth's car. There was a Eurythmics song pumping out of the stereo and the familiar lyrics to 'Somebody Told Me' died on the breeze as the engine stopped, and a shiny cowboy boot emerged from the driver's door and hit the concrete. The man that followed was tall and wearing a suit and a tie.

'Hi, Chris,' Beth called out to the guy, giving a little wave. 'I'm so glad to see you, I thought I was late,' she said, sounding flustered. 'Who will be taking the photographs?'

'I will,' the guy told her.

Rickie thought she looked a little disappointed.

'Do my hair and clothes look all right?' she asked the guy, looking down at her blouse.

'They're fine.'

Rickie thought he sounded impatient. The guy was a jerk, he decided. He put the nozzle back in the bowser and went to walk around the front of Beth's car to clean her windshield. She was rifling through her purse for a credit card, and when she saw him, she looked up, giving him a quick smile.

'Don't worry about that this time, Rickie.'

The douchebag in the suit looked at the pump display and shoved a $20 note at Rickie. 'That's for the lady's gas, we're late for the airport, okay.'

WILDER'S HOUSE
BOYNTON BEACH, FL

Nearly three hours later Dennis DeFranceschi, a buddy of Wilder's, who was on his racing team, was stopping by Wilder's house on Mission Hill Road, Boynton Beach, to drop off a set of keys. Dennis was always picking up or dropping off something at Wilder's place, such as a new car part or fresh racing shirts. It was a relaxed enough arrangement that Dennis would just let himself in after a quick warning knock on the door. Dennis owned a car repair shop where he supervised prepping Wilder's Porsche between races, and with their next event, at Sebring, less than three weeks away, he'd been hard at work with local mechanic Freddie Freimann trying to fix the various problems. He parked up on the grass verge outside Wilder's home and climbed out, but before he'd even managed to close his car door, Chris was bounding across the front lawn towards him. Dennis could see he looked nervous and was clearly upset.

'What's the matter, Chris?'

'Something big is going down, but I didn't really do it. You can't come in, Dennis, the dogs have had a big fight and broken the sliding door; it's a big mess inside.'

He looked frazzled. Dennis had never seen him like that before.

'Why don't I come in and give you a hand to clean up?' he said.

Wilder shook his head violently. 'I've arranged a repair man and a cleaner for tomorrow,' he said. 'Thanks for dropping off the keys. I'll come by the shop in the next day or so. I better get a move on,' he added and rushed back inside, closing the door quickly behind him.

Dennis told detectives later that it had been 'all a bit odd', but then, Chris was a bit of a weird guy at times. Dennis recalled the time he'd blurted out that he was going to be so famous one day and people would be writing books about him.

TUESDAY 6 MARCH 1984
GINGER BUSH'S OFFICE
BOCA RATON, FL

Wilder looked terrible, like he hadn't slept a wink. Ginger Bush was worried. The therapist had recently begun to wonder whether his fantasies were turning into reality. She'd brought up the Gonzalez girl last time he was here. He hadn't flinched, there was nothing concrete, nothing solid, nothing she could take to the cops, but she still felt uneasy. Today he looked like his nerves were jumping, like he'd drunk mugs of espresso, like shots, one after the other. He was wearing a long-sleeved shirt with the cuffs buttoned, and she wondered if he was covering something up, plus there was a bandaid between his thumb and forefinger, on his left hand. If she asked him about it, she was sure he would have an explanation ready. As soon as he sat down, she asked, 'What happened?'

'It's nothing,' he said.

She could tell he was trying to sound casual, but she saw the tenseness in the eyes.

'The dogs got into a fight and I got scratched trying to break it up. They even broke the glass in the back door, so I've got to get that fixed today, after we finish here.'

His words rushed out, staccato; he couldn't stop fidgeting and then quickly changed the subject to his upcoming trial in Australia. She let him talk. He was embarrassed about having to fly back, furious with his 'fucking mother', who wouldn't stop going on about it and how it was going to be in all the papers.

'Have they found the Gonzalez girl yet?' he asked, abruptly.

She knew he was watching for her reaction. Worried, or winding her up.

She suspected the former.

WILDER'S HOUSE
BOYNTON BEACH, FL

The two labourers were late. Normally when the boss wanted work done on his house, he threw them the keys and left them to let themselves in and get on with it, but this time, for some reason, Wilder was insistent on being there when they arrived. It was a last-minute rush job, an emergency, a broken patio window, he told them.

There was 'a hell of a lot of blood', they recalled later, and Wilder looked worn out and anxious. They could see he'd tried to sweep up a lot of the bigger shards of glass, but it was still a mess. The damage to the door and parquet flooring was extensive. There was a hole, about the size of an American football, quite high up in the glass about shoulder height.

'The dogs had a fight and one of them cut their paw really badly,' he said, nodding to the lounge where three long-haired English setters stood watching. One of the dogs had a bandage around its paw, but it hadn't been limping as they came in. The two labourers thought it looked more like the damage had been caused by someone's head going through the door, but they didn't get paid to ask questions, so they started measuring up, while Wilder paced up and down, sweating and flapping his arms around, waiting for the cleaning crew. They arrived minutes later, and the labourers could see Wilder start to relax. The cleaners would be busy, as there was a lot of congealed blood and staining around the smashed door, the slide tracks it ran on and the wooden floors. The labourers started packing up as Wilder was bossing the cleaning guys around, insisting they use a commercial-strength ammonia cleaner and watching intently, pointing out missed spots. One of the labourers noticed some scratches on Wilder's arms when the sleeves of his shirt rode up. As they were leaving, one of the cleaning crew tried to open the door to the bathroom that was off the pool deck. Wilder almost lost his shit, screaming at them, 'No, no, don't, not in there!'

A few days later, Wilder's regular cleaner would notice that the shower curtain in that pool bathroom was missing.

KENYON FAMILY BEACH HOUSE
POMPANO BEACH, FL

By noon that day Beth's older brother William Kenyon was beside himself. He'd been surprised the previous night when his sister hadn't shown up at their parent's holiday place, as they'd all agreed to get together because his baby daughter, Andrea, had just started to walk. Beth, who was also Andrea's godmother, had been excited when he'd told her on the phone. It was so unlike her not to turn up that first thing in the morning he'd rung to check on her, but her flatmate said Beth hadn't been home that night and she had no idea where she was. His mother, Dolores, had rung the school, but Beth hadn't turned up to work and hadn't rung in to say why. That's when William knew something was seriously wrong. He'd already called his sister's friends, and now he was working his way through the phone book ringing every hospital, his chest tightening as every hour ticked away.

Meanwhile Beth's father, Bill, was talking to the police, but it was proving to be a frustrating exercise. Dolores refused to leave the house in case her daughter called, so Bill went down to the Metro-Dade Public Safety Department himself to report his daughter missing. The police officer gave him a single sheet of paper to fill out, warning him that it was still too early to be treated as an active case. Sitting and praying by the phone, Dolores knew her daughter would never go off willingly without telling them. She had a nickname for Beth, 'Old Mother Hubbard', from the Mother Goose nursery rhyme, given to her because she was always so cautious. After a lunch that none of them could eat, William got out Beth's scrapbook and started going through all her photographs with his parents, to see if there was anyone they hadn't thought of, anyone she might be with. When Dolores saw a couple of Wilder, she remembered that Beth had told her on Sunday night that he'd offered her another modelling job. She called the Australian on his home number. After a few rings, the answering machine kicked in and Dolores left a message, telling him she was worried about Beth and asking him to please ring her.

MIAMI, FL
Mitch Fry knocked on the assistant principal's open door and popped his head in.

'You wanted to talk to me?' he said, smiling.

'Yes,' the assistant principal replied, 'have you heard from Beth at all? She hasn't turned up for classes this morning and we've not heard from her. Her parents are looking for her as well; she'd made arrangements to go and see them last night and never showed.'

The handsome young patrol cop frowned and said he hadn't seen Beth since she'd left school yesterday afternoon, but he'd start making some calls and see what he could find out. He went to the school office, pulled Beth's contact details and called her flatmate. Linda Cohen told him she was worried, Beth hadn't come home at all last night, hadn't called, and her parents were frantic. Mitch was starting to get spooked. He knew Beth would never go AWOL without letting anyone know, and she'd seemed her normal cheery self yesterday. As soon as his shift was over, he drove to Beth's apartment to check out her room. Her luggage bags were still there, and all her makeup and toiletries were still in the bathroom. Linda gave him Beth's contacts book, and he spent an hour on the phone working his way through the list. One was for a Chris Wilder; no-one answered, so he left a message, giving his name and number at the police station, saying that he was looking for Beth and asking for a call back. He called Beth's parents to let them know he would do what he could unofficially. Her dad was grateful and they promised to get in touch as soon as they heard anything.

SAWTEL CONSTRUCTION
BOYNTON BEACH, FL

That afternoon, Kimbrell and his secretary Frances were the only ones still at Sawtel Construction. Wilder had been losing interest in the day-to-day running of the business, but he still popped in most afternoons, mostly just to shoot the shit. Today he was smiling and bouncing along as usual, singing a Janis Joplin song, 'Mercedes Benz'. It was a standing joke between the three of them, but Frances was probably the only one of them who still found it particularly funny.

'What happened to you?' she said, pointing at a plaster on Wilder's hand.

'Just the dogs fighting,' he replied, waving off any other questions.

KENYON FAMILY BEACH HOUSE
POMPANO BEACH, FL

Bill Kenyon had been trying all day to get the local police department to take his daughter's disappearance seriously but kept hitting the same barrier, that she'd only been missing for a little over twenty-four hours and her file was way down the list of priorities. Uptight and anxious, the quietly spoken businessman was watching the news on TV when he heard another report about the girl, Rosario Gonzalez, who had disappeared at the recent Miami Grand Prix. He remembered talking about her with his son the night before, before Beth had gone missing. William had remarked on how much the girl had looked like Beth. It rattled Bill. He needed to do something. He might not have any influence in Miami, but he could trump that with some real heavyweight political connections elsewhere. He called his friend Congressman John LaFalce in New York and told him everything. The next day LaFalce put Bill in contact with fellow Democrat Bob Graham, the governor of Florida. Graham had been born in Coral Gables not far from the high school and was very interested in the story of a young teacher, from a good home, who had disappeared in mysterious circumstances. He said he would put in a call to the director of police at Metro-Dade, but in the meantime, he knew someone else who would be able to help, a father and son private-detective agency. The father, Kenneth Whittaker Sr, was a former FBI agent.

THURSDAY 8 MARCH 1984
PALM BEACH, FL

Tom Neighbors was a detective who liked the comforts of home. On quiet days he preferred to go and eat with his wife, Dana, rather than grab a greasy counter lunch somewhere or order in pizza at the office. He'd been in the Palm Beach sheriff's department for eight years and had worked in a bunch of different units, but primarily missing persons and homicide. Today had been one of those quiet days, so about 1 p.m. he took off home for some lunch.

As he pulled up outside his neat and tidy weatherboard, he rec-ognised Wilder's white Porsche in the driveway. Wilder was one of Dana's regular customers. She ran an embroidery and monogram-ming service from home, and for the past year she'd been sewing all the names and logos on his racing suits and the black silk shirts his pit crew wore. Tom knew that whenever Chris called in, he usually stayed a while, he and Dana chatting like a couple of old women, nattering on about nothing as far as Tom could make out. He knew Dana enjoyed it when Chris called round with a new order, because he paid promptly in cash and chatted to her like one of her girl-friends. He knows how to talk to a woman, Dana had told him many times.

Tom liked the big Aussie, too. He was the type of bloke you'd want your daughter to bring home, he thought: polite, good look-ing, successful. Tom parked on the street, got out of his unmarked detective car, took off his coat and put it on the back seat. When he wore it, which was regulation out of the office, his service weapon and handcuffs couldn't be seen. Now they jiggled against his hip in full view as he walked up the side of the house and in through the open kitchen door. Chris always had a friendly chat with Tom about what was in the news and the racing business, but today when he walked in, Tom sensed a pall come over the general chit-chat. Dana was laughing and smiled at him, reaching to give him a kiss, but he got the feeling Chris was suddenly anxious to leave. He seemed a bit uptight and wouldn't make eye contact.

'Hi, Tom, how are things?'

'Bit on the slow side, thank goodness,' Tom told him, as Chris got up and headed for the door. Tom prided himself on being observant and an excellent judge of character, 'a cop's sixth sense', he called it. Often when he met someone for the first time and wasn't sure about them, he'd pull their files when he got back to the office, and invariably they had a record. It had never occurred to him to do that with Chris.

WHITTAKER INVESTIGATIVE CONSULTANTS
NORTH MIAMI, FL

If the police weren't going to get off their backsides and look for his daughter, Bill Kenyon would pay someone to do it for him. The self-made millionaire didn't care how they did it, or what it cost, he just wanted Beth found as quickly as possible. He knew time was running out; he'd been expecting a ransom demand ever since she had gone missing, but it hadn't come.

Governor Graham had told him if anyone could find some-one in Miami, it was the Whittakers. Kenneth Whittaker Sr was a tough-as-nails recently retired former special agent, who'd run the Miami office of the FBI for J Edgar Hoover. He was a lawyer and was based in the same office building as his son Ken Jr, who headed up a private detective agency, which they'd set up together, staffed by ex-FBI agents and former marines. The governor knew them well and had put a call through asking if they would help some new friends of his with the possible disappearance of their daughter. 'Although she dates a lot of guys and comes from a lot of money and has travelled, it's very unlikely she would be gone for this long if something isn't wrong,' he told them.

Bill and Dolores came to the offices of Whittaker Investigative Consultants to meet Ken Jr and the team who would be looking for their daughter. They sat under a large framed portrait of Hoover while they told Ken all about their daughter and what they knew of her recent movements. On the wall opposite was a photograph of Kenneth Sr being blessed by the Pope, alongside original FBI fingerprint cards and photographs of notorious gangsters such as John Dillinger and Pretty Boy Floyd. The massive oak desk dominating the room was crammed full of signed gridiron footballs and photographs of Miami's major sporting legends. Ken Jr, wearing a button-down white shirt with no tie, was tall and solidly built with sandy-coloured hair and brown eyes. He had a disarming, boyish smile, Dolores thought.

At twenty-eight years old, Ken Jr was building a very successful career after a somewhat rocky beginning. He'd started out as a cop in Miami but turned in his badge after a couple of close shaves on the street, deciding it didn't make good sense to risk his life a third time for a $20000 basic salary. He really wanted to follow in his father's footsteps and join the FBI, but two broken hips playing ball in high school meant he couldn't pass the medical. He tried law school at Michigan State University, but he couldn't settle back into a classroom environment and returned to Miami with no job and a tough decision to make.

His father and a bunch of other senior agents had just retired from the agency and had a lot of plans to go fishing until he put a proposal to them. He would work under them for however long it took to learn investigative skills and the art of surveillance. They could give him every shit job that came along, and he'd do the coffee run every morning, so long as they taught him every skill they had. After two years of cutting his teeth, he had been ready to step up and take over the private-detective side of the business, and his father was able to concentrate on practising law. Now they worked out of two large side-by-side offices and took calls for help from the state's governor.

Ken Jr felt an immediate connection to Beth and the Kenyon family. He was also from a large family, in his case the eldest of six, and his mother, like Dolores, was a devout Catholic. Bill Kenyon wrote out a cheque to cover several days of the $1000 daily fee and said he wanted him on the case 24/7 and to receive regular reports. Dolores didn't talk much during the meeting, mostly pulling at a tissue she was grasping in her hand with her head down, holding things together as best she could. Ken decided to start with Beth's flatmate. The Kenyons had brought a photo of Beth with them, and Ken took a copy with him when he went down to his car, which was parked at the back of the building. The two-seater Datsun 280ZX sports car was his pride and joy even though he knew it was really a poor man's Corvette, the real car of his dreams. An hour later, standing in the middle of Beth Kenyon's messy bedroom, the afternoon sunshine streaming in through the plantation shutters, with her clothes strewn everywhere, it was impossible to tell if there had been a struggle, Beth had left in a hurry or she was just untidy. He chatted to her rattled flatmate as they went through her wardrobe together.

'Are any of her clothes gone, bikinis or winter clothes? Anything that might suggest she was headed to the beach or the snow for some skiing?'

'She would have told me if she was going away,' Linda insisted, but looked carefully and admitted that some of Beth's holiday stuff might be missing.

He made a note to get Bill Murphy, one of his senior investigators, to check all flights to upmarket warm-weather locations on the night Beth had gone missing.

Linda told him about a Coral Gables cop who had called round. She handed Ken the card he'd left her, as well as Beth's little black contacts book and her most recent photograph album. Before he left, Ken Jr checked Beth's jewellery. Dolores Kenyon had told him her daughter had a favourite lucky ring that she never went away without. It didn't take him long to find it on Beth's dressing table, hanging on her ring tree. It had been seventy-two hours since Beth had gone missing. Most cases like Beth's ended up happily enough, with the girls coming home a few hours or days later, tail between their legs, shamefaced and sorry, but he got the feeling that this case was different.

When he got back to the office he started flicking through Beth's little black book. He recognised a whole bunch of familiar names, local celebrities, athletes and business bigwigs around town, guys Beth had either dated or met at functions. One of them was a good buddy of his, Miami Dolphins linebacker AJ Duhe, and when he called him up, he struck paydirt. AJ's wife, Frances, the 1980 Orange Bowl Queen, was a friend of Beth's, hence the listing. Frances spent quite some time on the phone with Ken going through all the names, telling him which guys Beth had dated most recently, what she'd said about them, which ones, if any, she might have considered going away with on a whim. Before hanging up, Frances told him about Beth's teaching job at the high school and how she'd been finding it difficult. Ken put a call through to the Coral Gables assistant principal and caught him before he'd left for the day, asking if he could come around in the morning and speak to the kids in Beth's classes and the girls on her cheerleading squad.

'Of course,' he replied, 'I'll make the arrangements.'

Next, he called Mitch Fry and arranged to meet the young patrol cop the next day as well. Bill Murphy, a tough, straight-talking former FBI special agent, bustled into Ken's office and told him there was one flight the afternoon Beth disappeared that might fit the bill – Bahamas from Fort Lauderdale airport. The two men drove out to the airport forty minutes away and started checking cars at either end of the parking lots. An hour later they met roughly in the middle and had found no sign of the LeBaron convertible. It was late when Ken got home to his apartment, but he put a call in to his father and brought him up to speed with what he'd been doing. Kenneth Sr told his son to get some sleep and he'd ring Bill Kenyon and give him a progress report.

At the Pompano Beach house, it had been a few hours since the phone had rung and Dolores leaped up to answer it on the kitchen extension before the second ring kicked in. It was Chris Wilder returning her call from Tuesday.

'I'm sorry I didn't call sooner, I've been away for a few days,' he said, speaking slowly.

'Have you seen Beth recently?' Dolores asked him.

'No, it would be more than a month since we last went to dinner. Why? Is anything the matter?'

Dolores told him quickly about Beth. Wilder seemed uninterested, and she could tell he was impatient to end the call. She was disappointed he knew nothing and couldn't help. She was also mindful not to tie the phone up in case one of the Whittakers was calling with news, so she quickly ended the call.

FRIDAY 9 MARCH 1984
CORAL GABLES SENIOR HIGH SCHOOL
MIAMI, FL

Ken Whittaker Jr drove down to Coral Gables early to beat the worst of the rush-hour traffic. He met up with Mitch Fry outside the school gates and handed him a large steaming cup of strong black coffee. Mitch told him about the moment he'd watched Beth drive off from school the day she'd disappeared.

'The police still aren't treating Beth's case as an active investigation, so I'm working it off the books,' he said. 'I know a few people around, who dated Beth. I'm reaching out to them and chasing down leads.'

They compared notes on their separate visits to Beth's apartment and then Ken headed for the sports fields. He heard the cheerleaders before he saw them. The Cavaliers, with their recognisable crimson and grey school colours, were one of the state's most famous squads, participating in the very first Orange Bowl in 1935. Ken talked with several of the team about Beth, and it was clear the rookie teacher was popular, well respected and a positive role model for the girls. They told him she'd seemed a bit preoccupied on that Monday but hadn't told them why. Just as he was leaving, one girl stepped forward shyly.

'I don't know if it is important, but she kept having weird stuff happening to her car recently.'

She had taken it to the Shell service station, just down the road. Ken, who'd intended to canvass local businesses and restaurants with a photo of Beth anyway, walked the several blocks down to the service station on Bird Road. He could tell immediately that the pump attendant was a bit of a character. Ken took out a photo of Beth.

Rickie smiled. 'That's Beth, we do her car for her,' he said.

'Was she here on Monday afternoon?'

Rickie nodded. 'Why do you need to know?'

Ken showed him his private-eye ID and told Rickie that Beth had gone missing.

Rickie looked shaken. 'She's a really nice lady, one of our nicest regulars,' he said.

'Tell me about when she was here that day.'

'It was pretty normal, I was pumping her some gas and chatting to her, but then this dude parks up behind her and walks over, all gruff and in a hurry.

'He said, "Look, we're running late for the airport, just pump the gas, okay" and then he gave me $20 to pay for it.'

Ken went to his car and took out Beth's photo album that Linda had given him. He turned over every page slowly, asking Rickie to look through it with him and see if he recognised anyone. On the very last page was a photo of Beth with a bearded man in a white shirt taken on Derby Day at the historic Hialeah Park horse racing track.

'That's him,' Rickie almost shouted, pointing to the photo.

'Are you sure?' said Ken.

'He walked right towards me, man, I could identify him,' replied the attendant confidently. 'He was driving a mid-tone Cadillac Eldorado.'

'I might need you once I track this guy down to see if you can make positive identification, face to face,' Ken told him.

Ken drove back to the office as quickly as he could, working the lead over in his head. He now had a face for the man Beth was last seen with, but he needed a name. He rang Linda Cohen and Frances Duhe and asked them if they knew who Beth's date had been at the Derby Day races.

'That was Chris Wilder,' said Linda. 'Beth told me that he'd once suggested she could make a lot of money if she went to Australia with him and did some nude modelling.'

Frances also confirmed the identity. 'Wilder proposed marriage to her, but he's a lot older and Beth's family persuaded her to stop seeing him. He's Australian and I think they were worried he would take her to live there.'

Ken updated his father, and they arranged to meet up in the office the next morning. Before he left for home, he called Bill Kenyon to bring him up to speed. Bill had a lead too. He'd rung Miami airport security and Beth's licence plate had shown up.

'They don't know exactly where it's parked, though,' Bill said.

Ken put down the phone and shouted across to his investigator Bill Murphy. 'We're going to Miami airport this time.'

There were five multi-storey parking lots at Miami International Airport, and Ken told Bill to start at building one while he drove around to five and started there. Forty minutes later, Ken found Beth's vehicle in the far corner of Level M, backed up right against the wall. He'd almost driven past it and had to reverse back, as there was no licence plate on the front and it was impossible to see the rear one. He knew from her dad that Beth's car had a New York licence plate and that she kept a spare key in a small magnetic box hidden inside the front bumper. When he ran his fingertips along the length of chrome, he found it. He popped the trunk first and found Beth's licence plate among a jumble of clothes, school books and *Saturday*

Night Fever videos. He knew now this was serious and rang Metro-Dade detectives, but they weren't particularly impressed and told him it still didn't prove there had been a crime. They argued she could have removed the plate herself because she didn't want anyone to know she'd gone off with a boyfriend. Ken sighed heavily; he knew they were wrong. He stopped off at a pizza place on the way home, and by the time he was sitting down in his favourite armchair with a bottle of cold Budweiser it was gone midnight. He churned over in his mind exactly what he was going to say to Wilder the next morning.

5

CONFRONTATION

Ken walked through the open door into his father's office, sat down in the plush padded green chair across from him and told him about the car. Kenneth Whittaker Sr knew they needed to tread carefully. If something had happened to Beth, by ringing Wilder they could be tipping off the main suspect in the case. For the past two decades and more, Kenneth Sr had been on the law enforcement side of this argument, and he would have been vehemently against any outside interference in a live case, but the police department still hadn't started treating Beth's disappearance as a serious investigation. The governor himself had asked them to take the case, which carried a lot of weight. Their loyalty was to the family, and they wanted to find Beth.

'Let's do it together; we'll put it on speaker. Let me do the talking.'

The phone rang fourteen times. They were about to give up when it was picked up.

'This is Chris,' said a voice that had a slight Australian accent and a faint lisp.

'Chris, this is Ken Whittaker and Kenneth Whittaker Sr, former FBI Miami chief here, have you got a minute?'

'What's this about?' replied Wilder, guarded.

'Chris, I'm an attorney representing the Kenyon family and we're conducting an inquiry into Beth's whereabouts. I know you know Beth, correct?'

'Yes, I do know her, I used to date her. We ended the relationship. I moved on, she moved on,' Wilder said, revealing a touch of belligerence. 'I spoke to Mrs Kenyon and told her all this and assured her I had no idea where she was.'

'Have you seen Beth lately?' said the veteran investigator.

'No, I haven't seen her for more than a month. We stopped dating six months ago. Her family didn't want me to keep seeing her and I honoured their wishes.'

The father and son investigators looked at each other across the table. They'd caught him in a lie.

'I don't know anything,' Wilder continued.

'Whoa, whoa, whoa, Chris, it isn't that easy,' Ken interrupted him. 'I've got an eyewitness that puts you with her on Monday afternoon around 3 p.m. He picked you out of a photo line-up.'

'That's fucking bullshit, it can't be,' said Wilder, almost shouting. 'I can categorically deny that. This is all a mistake,' he added, furious now. 'I haven't seen Beth in a long time. You've got fucking nothing on me, this is all bullshit.'

'Okay, Chris, I hear you,' said Kenneth Sr, trying to calm things down. 'If you know anything about where she is, her parents are very distraught, so, please, I would encourage you to talk.'

'I have no information, I didn't help her, I didn't see her,' Wilder spat back.

'Okay, then,' said Ken, 'would you cooperate with me and consent to a line-up if I can put one together, so our witness can confirm or deny it? If he identifies you, though, then you and I, we've got a problem.'

There was silence for a moment.

'I would cooperate if that is the best way to resolve this,' said Wilder, clearly caught off-guard.

'I'll call you tomorrow to fix up a time,' said Ken.

'Before you go, Chris,' said Kenneth Sr, 'would you mind ringing her parents and letting them know what you've just told me?'

'I fucking will,' said Wilder, slamming down the phone.

Ken turned off the speaker and turned to his father. 'This guy is bullshitting.'

GINGER BUSH'S HOUSE
BOYNTON BEACH, FL

Ginger Bush was just back from doing the weekly shopping when the phone rang. Wilder. She knew it wouldn't be good news. Whenever Chris Wilder rang her at home it meant he was either in more trouble or else he needed her to talk him down from whatever agitated state he'd worked himself into. Just recently it had been his upcoming trial in Australia; as the date drew nearer, he had been increasingly apprehensive about it.

Before she'd even managed to say, 'Hello, Chris,' he was swearing and blabbering about private investigators contacting him at home. He was highly strung, and it took Bush a while to make sense of what he was saying. He was finally able to explain that the parents of missing woman Beth Kenyon had hired a pushy former

FBI agent, who was accusing him over the woman's disappearance. They wanted him to take part in a 'line-up' to see if an eyewitness could pick him out as being with her on the afternoon she vanished.

'This is crazy, Ginger,' he said, his voice a couple of octaves higher than normal. 'I didn't do anything to Beth but they're trying to pin this on me.'

Bush told him to cooperate with whatever the private detectives needed him to do. 'If you had nothing to do with her disappearance then you have nothing to worry about,' she reassured him. By the end of the call he was calmer and told her he'd see her next Tuesday, as normal.

KENYON FAMILY BEACH HOUSE
POMPANO BEACH, FL

Bill Kenyon was chain-smoking several packets of cigarettes a day and had hardly slept since Beth disappeared. Ken Whittaker had called earlier and revealed how they had caught Wilder in a lie about being at the petrol station with Beth. Bill was a self-made man at the height of his business career. The 56-year-old was used to getting his own way and giving orders that his staff carried out without challenge or question, so his lack of control over the police was making him angry. He felt like he was failing his daughter. At 7 p.m. he decided to go for a ride, clear his head and meet an old friend of Beth's, who had offered to help, so when Wilder called the house, it was Dolores who answered the phone. She could tell straight away that Wilder was angry.

'I like you, I like Beth,' Wilder told her. 'Why is this man Whittaker calling me?'

She tried to explain that everyone associated with Beth was

being investigated, but Wilder cut her short and asked to speak to Bill. When she said he was out, he ended the call abruptly.

An hour later, Bill was home when Wilder called again.

'Mr Kenyon, I don't know what this is all about,' said Wilder, claiming he'd been in his office working at the time the private detectives were alleging he was at the garage with Beth.

'It's a case of mistaken identity,' he said.

Bill knew he was lying, but Ken Whittaker had warned him earlier to stay calm if talking to Wilder, because Ken had made arrangements to see Wilder the next day and didn't want him to cancel. After the call, Bill called the private detectives to discuss their next steps. He wanted them to put Wilder under 24-hour surveillance, but Ken told him it would need four guys on twelve-hour shifts at $75 a hour each, making it close to $4000 a day with expenses. Beth's brother William was sitting with his father, itching to get out of the house and do something proactive to help.

'I'm coming down,' he suddenly announced. 'I'll watch him tonight, and first chance I get, I'm going to confront him and make him talk.'

Ken argued against the plan. 'It'll just screw up the investigation,' he said.

He pointed out that surveillance was a real skill and Wilder's house was a difficult one to watch, adding it could also be dangerous, but Bill Kenyon, sharing his son's frustration, said they would go together.

GINGER BUSH'S HOUSE
BOYNTON BEACH, FL

That evening, Wilder called Ginger Bush with another update. He said he had spoken to Beth's parents and told them he hadn't seen her for weeks and had nothing to do with her disappearance. The therapist made a note that he was in a lot more control than he had been earlier. He told her the investigators no longer wanted to search his house, but they still wanted to bring a witness up from Miami to see if they could identify him as the man with Beth when she was last seen. The investigator, Wilder told Bush, had said Beth's brother wanted to drive up to Boynton Beach and 'beat his ass'.

WILDER'S HOUSE
BOYNTON BEACH, FL

Dolores made Bill and William a thermos of strong coffee. They each gave her a hug and a promise not to return without some answers. Bill, without even agonising over it, got his .38 revolver, made sure it was fully loaded and put it in the glove box. By the time they turned off the highway at Boynton Beach thirty minutes later, they had discussed several options and worked out a rough plan. They would watch Wilder's house for as long as it took to confirm he was home, and then decide their next move.

His was the last bungalow on the right-hand side of the road, just before a small bridge over a canal. They parked on the other side of the bridge and kept watch for more an hour. Ken had been right, it was a difficult place to conduct surveillance on because any strange car, not parked on a driveway, stood out and attracted attention from curious residents. A few times they felt so conspicuous, they went for a drive around the neighbourhood before returning. On their way back the third time, they were approaching the house when the curtains were suddenly pulled to the side, and Wilder's face was at the window staring back at them. Bill, who was still driving, panicked for a moment and hit the accelerator. He sped over the bridge and, after a couple of hundred metres, pulled over onto the grass verge and stopped. His hands were shaking so much, when he took them off the steering wheel, he had to clench his fingers to try and relieve some of the tension. He took a deep breath and looked over at his son.

William had taken the gun out of the glove box and was holding it in his lap. 'I'm going in. I'll point the gun at his head until he tells us where Beth is. The Whittakers have done what we paid them to do, they identified who was responsible for taking Beth. If the police won't do anything to help, then we'll have to do it ourselves.'

There was a part of Bill that wanted to agree, but he couldn't risk losing his eldest son as well as his oldest daughter. 'They've got new evidence. Now the police will finally get their asses into gear and pick Wilder up for questioning.'

William shook his head, frustrated.

'Put the gun away, son.'

William did as he was told. He was convinced they were passing up the best chance of finding Beth, but he was worried about his father. Bill hadn't slept properly for days, napping fully dressed in an armchair, in case a call came in about Beth. He wasn't eating, either, and was smoking so many cigarettes he sounded awful. It was 11 p.m. when they arrived home, Dolores waiting for them on the porch, a huge look of relief on her face when they pulled into the driveway. Inside, Bill immediately reached for the phone and, despite the late hour, called Mitch Fry. He filled him in quickly about the day's events.

'What should we do? Should I have somebody watch Wilder's house round the clock?'

The patrol cop didn't hesitate. 'You have the money, you have a private detective, he has the manpower, watch the house.'

Bill then called Kenneth Whittaker next and said he wanted

to talk to him and his son about surveillance on Wilder, and ten minutes later, they all hooked into a conference call. Kenneth Sr was concerned they could still be jumping to the wrong conclusion and advised holding off on starting full-time surveillance until after Ken Jr met with Wilder in the morning, when they would have more information. He was in full agreement, though, that Wilder looked like their man and had a hell of a lot of explaining to do.

SUNDAY 11 MARCH 1984
WILDER'S HOUSE
BOYNTON BEACH, FL

Ken Whittaker wasn't taking any chances for the showdown meeting with Wilder. He had a concealed weapon permit, and although he didn't normally wear his gun, on this occasion he strapped it onto his hip. He also had backup, Mike Fornelo, a giant of a man and former US special forces, who had served two tours in Vietnam and was also armed. He was not someone people would pick a fight with, even a guy like Wilder. Ken had rung the pump attendant the night before, and Rickie had been a little reluctant about driving to Boynton Beach and back on a Sunday, so Ken had told him he would make arrangements with Wilder for a line-up on Monday or Tuesday.

The two private detectives arrived outside Wilder's house fifteen minutes early, at 7.45 a.m., with most of the neighbourhood still sleeping behind their neatly trimmed lawns and white picket fences, but they didn't bother to wait and walked up Wilder's driveway to the cacophony of several dogs barking loudly from inside. Ken knocked several times, but apart from the three dogs, which he could see when he peered in the front bay window, there was no other movement. He was about to turn around and tell Mike they should grab some coffee and breakfast and try again later, when the door suddenly opened.

'Hello!' said Mike, a big grin on his face.

While Ken had been knocking and peering in the front windows, Mike had gone up the side of the property, jumped the fence and let himself in around at the back, stopping just long enough to calm down the dogs. What they were doing was illegal, but Ken didn't hesitate, stepping inside and closing the door behind him. They divided the house up between them and searched everywhere. In the garage, Ken, a car enthusiast, admired the black racing car with 'Wilder Racing' detailed on the side. The Porsche's hood was up and it was clear the engine had blown and was being stripped down. There was a black helmet on the workbench with 'Chris Wilder' stencilled on it above the visor. The garage and the house were immaculate, even more spotless than a show home. Mike couldn't get over the garbage bins: every one throughout the house was cleaner than his apartment, he told Ken. They searched the master bedroom with the king-size waterbed and a jacuzzi next to it on the deck, and Ken saw references to Wilder's Australian heritage everywhere, from the ceramic kangaroo planter to the large photograph of a koala on the wall. The swimming pool had a kangaroo and a koala in a tree painted on the sides, and on the bottom a map of Australia in different colours. In one of the smaller bedrooms they found photographic equipment, a reflector and white backdrop set up for a shoot. On the dresser Ken discovered several stacks of 5 x 7 inch photographs of young girls, many in swimming costumes, a few topless, an awkward bashfulness in their eyes as they tried to cover their breasts from the camera. The topless shots were a little to the side of the other pile and Ken put them in his pocket. He was taking a risk – it would be obvious to Wilder when he returned that someone had been inside and taken them – but the investigator felt a bad vibe about the house. He reckoned if Beth was missing, there might well be others and they could be in the photos. After about twenty minutes the two men let themselves out the front door and went back to their car, which was parked at the side of Wilder's house on a patch of grass, next to a small bridge over the canal. Ken took out his fancy new mobile phone, one of the first ever Motorolas, so new that even police officers or FBI special agents hadn't been issued with them yet. Ken sat down in the back seat with the phone and put a call in to an old college buddy of his, who was a detective at Boynton Beach police department.

'Can you tell me anything about a Christopher Wilder?' Ken asked him, after they'd got through the usual catch-up banter.

'Shit, Ken, what do you want with him?' he replied. 'We've got a real thick file on that sonofabitch, you'd better get over here.'

The major crimes detective told him to 'bring coffee' as he hung up.

A couple of hours later, Ken and Mike walked out of Boynton Beach police station knowing they were onto something big. Wilder, they discovered, had a serious criminal past. He was facing kidnap and rape charges in Australia and was due to fly back in a couple of weeks for his trial. He also had a record in Florida, a conviction for attempted sexual battery against a young girl, which meant he was on five years' probation. If he hadn't been given permission to attend the Grand Prix, then he was in violation and could be arrested. Wilder, they had learned, also had a misdemeanour offence for pretending to be a photographer in order to get two girls to pose naked, and he'd been acquitted of raping another young girl, whom he'd met while working for her parents.

KEN WHITTAKER'S HOUSE

NORTH MIAMI BEACH, FL

The whole of the drive back, something kept nagging away at Ken. He turned over everything he'd seen inside Wilder's house, but he was sure he was missing something. When he got home, he was still frustrated he couldn't put his finger on what was bugging him, so he pulled out his working file on the case and spread it all out on the dining room table. His girlfriend, a model and former Miss Florida pageant finalist, dropped in to see him.

'I know him, I remember that beard,' she said, pointing at the photo of Wilder at the races. 'He was at the pageant and tried to solicit a bunch of the girls to take topless photos. He was quite aggressive. He claimed he was a famous photographer, but the organisers warned all the contestants to stay clear of him, because he wasn't official.'

That's when it clicked into place, and the private eye realised what had been right in front of him when he was in Wilder's garage. He thought back to the Porsche, the helmet with Wilder's name on it, the Grand Prix and a model called Rosario Gonzalez, who'd gone missing and whose story was showing on the TV news every night. She had disappeared, just like Beth. Now, with the information he'd learned at the police station, Ken was convinced the two cases had to be connected. Wilder was the link.

He called Miami Homicide asking to speak to one of the lead detectives on the Rosario Gonzalez case and was transferred to the desk of Detective Morin. Ken explained who he was and told the detective his theory about the two cases. He laid it all out, how Wilder had a violent past of assaulting girls after posing as a photographer, and had probably broken the terms of his probation by driving in the race, which was enough to bring him in for questioning. He even relayed what his girlfriend had said about Wilder being aggressive and trying to solicit young girls.

Morin was tired, hungry and knee deep in paperwork. A potential witness had seen a girl in a pair of red shorts matching Chary's description running away from a Chevrolet on the turnpike, while being chased by two men. Spread over Morin's desk were printouts of more than a thousand Chevrolet drivers who owned models containing the same combination of three numbers and letters in the registration. It was laborious work whittling down the list, and he was determined to finish before heading home that night. Still, he listened to everything the private eye told him, making notes as he did so. He didn't know anything about the Kenyon case, so he was a little cautious in his response.

'I've got thousands of leads, Ken,' he told him. 'There were drivers and crews from all over the world and my girl might have gone off with any of them. We're chasing them all down and this is another one I will add to the list. I'll put his name down and check it out.'

'Listen,' said Ken, 'this is really solid. Talk to Boynton Beach detectives about this guy Wilder, they'll tell you all about him.'

MIAMI POLICE STATION
MIAMI, FL

Morin thanked Ken Whittaker for the information and promised him he'd get onto it as soon as he could, which he did, later ringing Metro-Dade Homicide to speak to the detective handling the Beth Kenyon investigation. Unfortunately, when he put in the call the file had not been escalated and was still stuck with Missing Persons.

Before he left for the night, Morin called the Gonzalez family and asked if any of them had heard the name Christopher Wilder before. They hadn't.

TOM NEIGHBORS' HOUSE
PALM BEACH, FL

Wearing white shorts and an expensive designer sweater, Wilder had left home early that morning to avoid the meeting with the private detectives. He went for breakfast and then spent the day driving around the popular local beaches and malls looking for pretty girls to photograph. By late afternoon he decided it was safe to return home. On the way he stopped off at Dana Neighbors' house with some more patches to sew onto his racing suit, in time for the Sebring event that was coming up, but left quickly when he spotted Tom firing up the barbecue. Tom joked to his wife that Chris always seemed to be in a hurry whenever he was at home.

KEN WHITTAKER'S HOUSE
NORTH MIAMI BEACH, FL

Ken Whittaker had called Wilder's home number repeatedly all evening without success. Before going to bed, he called Mike Fornelo and Bill Murphy and told them to go up to Boynton Beach in the morning and stake out Wilder's business address, which was a lot easier to watch than his home. Ken told them that if Wilder turned up, they should have a go at him for ducking the meeting they had organised.

'Get him on the phone so I can talk to him,' he told them.

6

THE PAST
IS NEVER BURIED

MONDAY 12 MARCH 1984

CORAL GABLES POLICE STATION

MIAMI, FL

Mitch Fry had been stewing all night over what Bill Kenyon had told him about Wilder, how he'd lied about being with Beth at the garage. The patrolman decided to run a records check on Wilder and discovered the same information Ken Whittaker had. He also knew about the Rosario Gonzalez case and thought there could be a connection, so he rang Metro-Dade Homicide. When he took the call, Detective Wasserman hadn't yet spoken to Morin about his conversation the previous day with Ken Whittaker. He listened intently to what Fry told him.

'All the hairs on the back of my neck stood up on end and I got a cold chill,' was how the detective later described his reaction to hearing the young cop's information.

Fry told him how frustrating it was that Beth Kenyon's case was still bogged down in Missing Persons and hadn't been assigned a detective yet. Wasserman made two calls. The first was to a Palm

Beach detective he knew. He asked him what they had on Wilder. 'The guy is a psycho, he's capable of anything,' said the detective, not even having to check his files.

The second was to Metro-Dade police department to speak to whoever was running the Beth Kenyon investigation. A week after the young teacher had disappeared, Wasserman was told no-one in Homicide had been assigned the file yet.

BOYNTON BEACH POLICE STATION
BOYNTON BEACH, FL

Bill and William Kenyon had received the update from Ken Whittaker about Wilder's criminal history, and his strong belief that Beth's case was linked to Rosario Gonzalez, so they drove straight up to Boynton Beach police station. Ken paged Mike Fornelo and Bill Murphy and arranged for them to go into the station with the Kenyons. He figured the more pressure that could be applied the better. Lieutenant John Hollihan confirmed to the four men that Wilder was due to return to Australia at the end of the month for trial on kidnap and rape charges, and that he was currently on $400000 bail from the Australian courts.

The news was a bombshell for Beth's father and brother. William was outraged and demanded that Wilder be arrested immediately, but Hollihan explained his hands were tied, as they hadn't received any notification from Metro-Dade police that his sister was even missing, and there was no evidence of a crime in Palm Beach County for them to act on. Bill could sense all hope of finding his daughter vanishing before his eyes. He'd now dealt with three different police departments, Miami, Metro-Dade and Palm Beach. They all had different pieces of the same jigsaw, but they hadn't been communicating with each other, despite all his pleading phone calls day after day. He was a broken man. Beth had been missing a week, the Gonzalez girl for fifteen days now, and in his heart he knew the chances of his daughter still being alive were bleak, at best. There were loud voices in the room, suddenly, and the noise brought him back from his deep and dark thoughts. He looked up and feared his son was about to get himself arrested, he was so upset. He stood up, putting his hand on William's shoulder, and told him they were wasting their time. He needed to get out of that room quickly before one of them said or did something silly.

As soon as he was out of the station and could find a phone, he put a call in to the FBI office in Miami and begged them to take over the case, but he was told they had no federal jurisdiction that would allow that. He put the phone down, steaming and determined to apply as much pressure as possible to force a change of mind.

Bill Murphy called Ken Whittaker and filled him in. Ken told him they should stake out Wilder's office as planned and keep the Kenyons a good distance away, in case Wilder turned up. By lunchtime the two private detectives were in position, and Bill and William were watching with binoculars from a vantage point across a field next to a drive-through car wash.

SAWTEL CONSTRUCTION
BOYNTON BEACH, FL

At 3.30 p.m. Wilder turned up at work in his Carrera, and by the time he was walking through the entrance doors, Mike and Bill were only one step behind him and barrelled their way into his office, ignoring Wilder's protests.

'My boss needs to talk to you,' Mike said to Wilder. 'You failed to show as arranged to meet with us yesterday.'

'Who are you guys?' said Wilder angrily. 'I don't have to put up with this, I don't have to talk to anyone.'

'Sit down,' said Bill Murphy. 'I'm going to get my boss on the fucking phone and you are going to talk to him.'

'Why are you even questioning me?' said Wilder.

'Why wouldn't we, with a record like yours,' said Mike pointedly.

Wilder's heavily suntanned face went pale.

Bill punched Ken's office number into the phone on Wilder's desk, and when it was answered he hit the speakerphone button.

'What the fuck, Chris?' Ken bellowed. 'You didn't show up yesterday. I drive all the way up there and, what the fuck, you had my number, but you didn't call me?'

'I had things I needed to do yesterday,' Wilder replied, belligerent.

'Come on, Chris,' said Ken, 'you told me you liked Beth, you wanted a relationship with her, and now I'm investigating her disappearance, you're not even giving me the time of day – especially as I have a witness who saw you with her, the last time she was seen alive. He even noticed your accent, Chris, that's how sure he is.'

'That's bullshit,' said Wilder, furious.

'Well now I really have an issue,' Ken continued, 'because when you failed to show up, I went over and saw my buddy in Boynton Beach police, and you've got one serious history, Chris.' Ken couldn't see Wilder's face, but the absence of any comeback told him he'd hit the mark. 'Where were you last Monday?'

Wilder's business partner and secretary listened, stunned.

Wilder finally found his voice. 'Zeke, Monday, we were at a meeting with the client, right, in the early afternoon, correct?'

'That's right,' Ken heard a voice in the background say, fainter than the others.

'Shut the fuck up,' boomed Mike. 'Mr Whittaker will ask the questions, don't you lead your buddy here.'

'Okay, Chris,' said Ken, 'give me the name of the client you met that day, because I have you in Coral Gables at three o'clock, and I need to validate that alibi.'

'No, no, no, I'm telling you I was at a meeting, Zeke will vouch for me,' implored Wilder.

'He was with me,' said Kimbrell in a quiet voice. 'He couldn't have been in Miami.'

Ken ignored him. 'Chris, he's your partner, of course he's gonna vouch for you. Why don't you just level with me, man, you know where she's at, why don't you just tell me?'

'This is bullshit,' said Wilder, erupting again. 'You're not going to nail me for whatever this is.'

'I've got some serious concerns now, Chris, especially since my visit to Boynton Beach PD, you've got a record here and you've got issues in Australia —'

'I'll take care of that,' Wilder butted in. 'I gotta go back to Australia, that will all be taken care of, don't worry about that, Mr Whittaker,' he said, calmer now, wheedling.

'Well, I am worried about it,' said Ken, 'because I have a girl missing that you dated, I have an eyewitness that puts you with her on the day she went missing and now I have this other girl as well. I know you raced at the Grand Prix and you went back the next day and then she went missing. I think you took Beth,' said Ken, deliberately speaking slowly now, 'and I think you took Rosario Gonzalez as well.'

Wilder exploded. 'That's fucking bullshit. I don't know what you're talking about. I was working here when you say I was at the garage with Beth, and I don't know this other girl. You're trying to pin this all on me and it's fucking wrong.'

'Okay, can you account for your time on that weekend Rosario went missing, that Saturday and Sunday?' said Ken.

'I'm Australian, we like to let our hair down a bit and get a little crazy at the weekend,' Wilder said. 'I'm a crazy Aussie who likes to have a good time. I race cars and go water skiing and play about on speedboats. You're not going to nail any of this on me.'

Mike and Bill stood intimidatingly on either side of Wilder's desk, blocking his way in case he tried to run.

'I have parents that are concerned, Chris, and I need to get to the bottom of this. I want to go ahead with the line-up and come up there tomorrow with a detective and the gas station attendant who saw you with Beth. If you're not the man, then I move on; I have a list of people that she could have gone off with skiing, down to the islands, so you should do this.'

'I wasn't anywhere near Miami on that Monday,' said Wilder.

'Remember who you're dealing with here,' said Ken. 'I told you about my dad, the former FBI chief, well, he's got juice, so every time you look outside your house or go to your office there might be someone in your trees, or in a van across the road, watching you. That'll be us, Chris.'

'Fuck you,' said Wilder, cutting the connection and telling Mike and Bill to get out of his office.

GINGER BUSH'S HOUSE
BOYNTON BEACH, FL

At 6.30 p.m. Wilder left a frantic message on Ginger Bush's voice-mail, saying he was afraid of the private investigator, who had several men keeping him under surveillance. When Bush rang him back, Wilder was so strung out she was worried about his state of mind. He was babbling about his trial in Australia and worried his probation would be revoked because he'd raced in the Miami Grand Prix. The therapist advised him to contact his Palm Beach attorney, Barry Cohen, in case there was any move to rescind his probation arrangements.

TUESDAY 13 MARCH 1984
HIALEAH, FL

Detectives Morin and Wasserman might have wanted to follow up on the tips about Wilder, but instead they had to spend the day with eight colleagues, and an FBI agent, chasing down a man trying to extort money from Rosario Gonzalez's family.

GINGER BUSH'S OFFICE
BOCA RATON, FL

Wilder spent the morning of his thirty-ninth birthday in a therapy session with Ginger Bush, angrily railing against everyone he said was making his life intolerable, and the private investigator, harassing him for no reason.

'Beth's car turned up at the airport, so clearly, she must have gone away with someone,' he told Ginger.

The therapist made a note. Wilder told her about the witness they wanted to bring up to Boynton Beach to identify him, but he was too afraid of the private detectives to go ahead with it. 'I haven't seen Beth for at least five weeks.'

Before leaving, Wilder asked Ginger if they could confirm another session for Thursday.

She booked him in, writing in her notes that he was 'a powder keg ready to explode'.

METRO-DADE HOMICIDE UNIT
MIAMI, FL

Metro-Dade detective Ray Nazario was a twenty-year-plus veteran of the force. A stocky and pugnacious-looking cop, he'd seen it all and a little bit more in his long career, during which he'd investigated several hundred homicides. Dade County was the official murder capital of the nation in 1984. One magazine later dubbed it '*Miami Vice* without the music'. The streets were awash with bodies, drug-related shootouts and an influx of criminals from Cuban prisons, who had fled to Florida in the early eighties. Which is why the taciturn detective had been so surprised the previous afternoon when he was given the Beth Kenyon missing person file and assigned four other detectives to help him out. He was told to make the case a priority. Nazario figured the department was, for some unknown reason, getting heat to start an investigation. The hunch was confirmed when a bit later he got a call from Ken Whittaker, who filled him in quickly on everything they knew about Wilder.

Nazario was angry they had already approached Wilder.

'Just humour me, go and see Rickie at the gas station,' said Whittaker. 'You can bring Wilder in on the probation violation.'

But Nazario was old school; he wasn't a cop who played hunches. 'I don't see any evidence you have found here. It's not a crime to pay for a beautiful woman's gas.'

Whittaker tried one more time, but Nazario had made up his mind. He didn't rate the work Whittaker had done, refused to rely on any of his information, particularly the photo identification from the pump attendant, dismissing it as contaminated evidence because Whittaker had shown him one photograph and not a proper line-up. He was sceptical about the car at the airport too.

Beth could have parked it there herself and jumped on a flight with a boyfriend.

Beth's father was devastated when Whittaker told him about the detective's reaction. He later told reporters, 'If anybody asked me how they should handle a situation like this, I'd say take it into your own hands. Don't count on the police for anything. They were negligent and unresponsive.'

When Whittaker told his father that Nazario was a card-punching jerk, Kenneth Sr reached for the phone. 'Time to ring the FBI.'

BOYNTON BEACH, FL

Wilder and Zeke Kimbrell bought a second-hand car for the business, a Chrysler New Yorker with a blue vinyl roof and scuffed blue interiors, stained in places. Zeke thought it was for their estimator so he could visit clients. Wilder, though, had other plans, but he didn't confide in his partner. The registration plate, QUM 978, was loose and had to be screwed back in place before Wilder drove it away.

KENYON BEACH HOUSE
POMPANO BEACH, FL

Bill and Dolores Kenyon's political lobbying had brought results. New York congressman John LaFalce, New York senator Al D'Amato and former governor of Wisconsin Lee Sherman Dreyfus had all pressed the FBI to intervene in their daughter's case, and now the Kenyons were told the bureau were going to work closely with Metro-Dade police and would be handling all out-of-area leads and inquiries. They were told the special agent liaison officer would be contacting them soon to arrange a meeting.

BOYNTON BEACH PIZZERIA
BOYNTON BEACH, FL

Wilder was paranoid after the conversations with Whittaker and told Kimbrell, in the car park of the pizzeria in Boynton Beach, that he was taking off. Kimbrell told detectives later that he'd never seen Chris as anxious or out of control.

METRO-DADE HOMICIDE
MIAMI, FL

Ray Nazario issued the first press release on the disappearance of Beth Kenyon, his contempt for Ken Whittaker obvious in the brief statement. 'The investigation is being pursued as a missing person's case. There is no evidence available at this time to suggest any criminal activity or foul play,' the detective emphasised.

7

STINK EYE

WEDNESDAY 14 MARCH 1984
FBI MIAMI FIELD OFFICE
MIAMI, FL

FBI special agent John Hanlon was in the middle of making plans to leave the bureau when he copped what would become the biggest case of his career. The 46-year-old New York–born investigator had just sat the bar exam in Fort Lauderdale and had his future mapped out. To put his three kids through college, he was going to turn in his badge at fifty and become a federal court prosecutor. The call the day before to drive down to the FBI's Miami office for a new assignment hadn't fazed him too much. Hanlon had been an agent for twenty-one years, the last four in Florida, and was one of those lawmen who blended in, could pass unnoticed in any crowd, a fed who preferred to listen rather than throw his weight around. Urbane and charming, medium build with greying temples and a dry sense of humour, he was a natural raconteur, which boded well for his intended career change to the courtroom, where he wanted to carry on being the good guy making the bad guys dance.

Since moving to Florida, he'd been working mainly undercover in combating major art fraud. He had posed as a hotshot art thief in one sting that had prevented the heist of $25 million worth of works by Degas, Monet, Manet and Rubens from a museum in Connecticut. His new assignment didn't seem like the type of case that would 'get him on the balls of his feet'.

The bureau had been getting a lot of calls about a missing teacher, Beth Kenyon, who'd vanished shortly after leaving the high school where she worked in Coral Gables. There had been no extortion demand, though her parents were wealthy business-people, but Metro-Dade police department had a lot of leads they needed help chasing down, and he was to be their liaison agent. Almost immediately, he was also given the same task for another missing girl, Rosario Gonzalez, which was being handled by the Miami police department. Another special agent had initially been given that case, but he was a SWAT and security expert and was drafted to Los Angeles to prepare for the Olympic Games, which were only three months away.

Hanlon knew immediately that the Kenyon case was going to be a hot potato, because of the bad history between Metro-Dade police and the FBI. The bureau had conducted a secret two-year corruption investigation into the force's homicide unit in the early eighties, and six of the thirty-five detectives were relieved of duty, with nine more transferred to the patrol section, for alleg-edly collaborating with Mario Escandar, Miami's major drugs kingpin. As a result, eighteen months previously, four homicide detectives had been jailed after Escandar cut a deal to testify for the prosecution, referring to the shamed officers as 'my young men of iron', and detailing how they snorted cocaine and trafficked the drug for him. Now Hanlon was being tasked with working alongside the corrupt detectives' former colleagues. He decided to tackle the problem head on, and face to face. He drove over to south Miami and dropped in on the homicide unit in person. If he expected the stink eye, he was right; his reception was chilly, to say the least. But he'd also broken the ice, and he earned grudging respect for going.

Back at the FBI office on Biscayne Boulevard, he got a call from Kenneth Whittaker Sr, his former boss. There wasn't a great deal of warmth between the two men, but Hanlon polished his gold-rimmed aviator glasses and listened respectfully to Whittaker's request for a meeting with his son Ken.

While there were none of the fireworks that had peppered Ken Whittaker's conversation with Nazario, the meeting was still an awkward affair. Ken Whittaker took Hanlon through everything they had discovered about Wilder and his background, including how they had spoken to him twice and accused him of knowing something about Beth's disappearance. Ken Whittaker told him he thought Nazario was a fool.

'Can your guys rattle Wilder's cage by knocking on his door?'

Hanlon was more than capable of putting on a show when he needed to, but said, 'I'm not going to squeeze police to pick up Wilder. There are no federal laws that have been broken from what I can see. I am there to assist the two police departments, but they call the shots.'

Hanlon was a dad himself, with two sons and a daughter, and had enormous sympathy for the Kenyons, but, in his opinion, hiring the private investigators hadn't achieved anything but scaring Wilder. He got the Whittakers to back off and hand all their material over to Metro-Dade Homicide.

Ken Whittaker called the Kenyons.

'I sugarcoated it,' he told his father after the call. 'I told them we gave all the facts to the FBI and they were going to go back and see what they could do.'

In the meantime, with the Whittakers effectively run out of Boynton Beach, and neither Metro-Dade nor Miami homicide departments prepared to do it, no-one was watching Christopher Wilder.

8

HI. THIS IS EDNA.

WEDNESDAY 14 MARCH 1984
MIAMI HERALD **NEWSROOM**
MIAMI, FL

If Miami was the murder capital of the world, the Queen of Homicide crime reporters was Edna Buchanan. Feisty and fearless, no murder, no matter how gruesome or run of the mill, was considered complete until she was ducking under the police tape, clutching her notebook in her hand. Forty-something, with shoulder-length blonde hair, Edna grew up in Paterson, New Jersey, where she used to read the New York tabloids out loud to her Polish grandmother, and was tougher than many detectives, as well as being quirky and funny. She had her own unique writing style that everyone in Miami recognised, and she was not afraid to go alone into tough neighbourhoods, where her colleagues rarely ventured. Married twice, first to a reporter and then to a cop, Edna had taken over the crime beat on the *Herald* more than a decade earlier, after a spell when no-one was keen to do it full time.

In the early eighties, at the start of the Cocaine Cowboys era, when the Colombians and the Cubans were waging war for control of the drug trade, Edna's editors told her to cover just the major homicide of the day. Edna had other ideas, believing it was such a historic time in the history of the city, she should cover every single murder for a year: black, white, immigrant, it didn't matter. She got all 637 into the paper and won a Pulitzer Prize.

Only a few months earlier, Dade's murder rate had hit new heights with fourteen people killed in separate events and five critically hurt within five days. Edna reported:

> In the latest wave of violence, a teenager's throat was cut and her body dumped in a canal, a former airline stewardess was garroted and left with a pair of scissors stuck between her shoulder blades, four innocent bystanders were shot in a bar-room gun battle, an 80-year-old man surprised a burglar and was battered to death with a hammer, an angry young woman, who 'felt used', beat her date to death with the dumbbells he used to keep fit and a robbery victim was shot dead as he ran for help.

Most cops would break out in hives when they got a call with the greeting, 'Hi, this is Edna. What's going on over there?' The Metro-Dade police chief had even blocked off the homicide squad with an electronically controlled entrance to try and prevent her getting in. Detectives dubbed the barrier the 'Edna Buchanan door'.

It didn't stop her.

One of Edna's secrets was to call into the Miami and Metro-Dade homicide departments at the weekend when the top brass were all on the golf course, and she could read all the missing person's reports. That's how she had first heard and wrote about Chary. She'd interviewed Chary's parents and talked to her fiancé, Bill. Now, Nazario was telling her about his new case, a missing school teacher called Beth Kenyon. Edna later discovered both girls were models; both were beautiful, both had suddenly disappeared and both had no reason to disappear. Edna rang Beth's parents and they put her in touch with Ken Whittaker.

She remembered later, 'The minute I heard about Beth Kenyon, in a different jurisdiction, I knew – like I knew my name, like I knew the sun was going to rise tomorrow. Without a doubt. They had both been snatched.'

Even though her deadline was looming, Edna called her contact at Miami Homicide and told him there was another case like Rosario Gonzalez, another young girl and model missing, but he didn't buy it.

'You see conspiracies everywhere, Edna,' he told her. 'You have way too much imagination.'

The next day's *Miami Herald* carried Edna's story under the headline, 'Baffling Disappearances of Two Women May Be Linked'. She reported: 'Both women are strikingly beautiful and each seems to have vanished without a trace, perplexed police said Wednesday. Kenyon has modeled clothes and bathing suits and appeared on an advertising poster. Gonzalez, 20, won modeling contests.'

The story said detectives had failed to find a man who may have been walking with Chary when she was last seen, and that Beth had been seen speaking to a man in a service station on the day she vanished.

THURSDAY 15 MARCH 1984
GINGER BUSH'S OFFICE
BOCA RATON, FL

Wilder didn't show up for his extra therapy session on the Thursday. In fact, Ginger Bush would never see Wilder, soon to become her most infamous client, ever again. Her phone in the following weeks would often ring, and when she answered no-one would speak, but she could hear breathing and knew someone was there.

9

PLAYING HOOKY

THURSDAY 15 MARCH 1984
502 BUTLER AVENUE
DAYTONA BEACH, FL

Colleen Emily Orsborn was a rebellious fifteen-year-old and quite a handful for her mother, Frances. The petite and pretty teen with sandy brown hair and hazel eyes was the baby in the family, with three sisters and two brothers. Her parents had recently separated, and when her father walked out, Colleen, the only one still living at home, had shouldered the responsibility of looking after her mum, who was battling the early stages of emphysema.

A bright and sassy girl, Colleen's grades began to suffer, and she'd recently had to change schools because of ongoing behaviour problems. A couple of times, she'd spent a night or two away from home. She and her mum often rowed, but mostly over silly stuff, and despite the problems they still loved and looked out for each other. Money was tight and Frances, despite her sickness, still had to work. That morning, before leaving for work, she had managed to get Colleen up and ready for school, but knew she would be too late for the school bus, so pressed some money into her daughter's hand, kissed her on the cheek, gave her a quick hug, and told her to behave herself at school.

As soon as her mum left, Colleen, who weighed less than 45 kilograms and was 160 centimetres tall, changed out of her daggy school uniform and slipped into a hot-pink bikini that matched her pink nail polish. There was a music festival on at the Daytona Beach Bandshell next to the boardwalk and a concert later by the 'rad' alternative rock band REM. The little studio apartment she shared with her mum was only three blocks back from the beach.

METRO-DADE POLICE DEPARTMENT
MIAMI, FL

The meeting in the office of Metro-Dade captain Bob McCarthy was a powerful who's who of Miami lawmen. Around the table with McCarthy sat the head of Metro-Dade's homicide division, Major John Farrell, and Ray Nazario, one of his most senior detectives, Miami homicide detective Harvey Wasserman, as well as special agents John Hanlon and Erwin Mall of the FBI.

Rosario Gonzalez had been missing for eighteen days and Beth Kenyon for ten, and they had come together to work out how to proceed on the two investigations. While publicly the word from both police departments was they were looking at multiple suspects, the fact they had come together in the same room confirmed that Wilder was their main focus.

John Hanlon informed the police officers that the FBI's view was that primary jurisdiction for both cases lay with them, but that the bureau had a 'vital interest' in being kept up to speed with all developments. He went further, saying he offered 'total and complete support to you guys and will conduct any and all investigations you request'. Everyone nodded and agreed.

It was decided that the FBI would obtain airline flight information, get up-to-date background checks on Wilder through Interpol and retrieve telephone records from Wilder's home and business as well as toll logs for his registered vehicles.

Unfortunately, Wilder had already fled, and as their meeting was breaking up, he was cruising the streets near one of the state's most famous beaches, already looking for a new victim.

DAYTONA BEACH, FL

Daytona Beach was bracing itself for the Spring Break invasion of hyped-up college teens hellbent on having the party of a lifetime. The influx had already started, and by the weekend every single one of the city's 20000 hotel rooms would be full, many sleeping five or six each. Many of the area's businesses would do 75 per cent of their annual trade in the next three weeks. The white sand would be crammed with pretty girls in bikinis, flirting with boys, drinking beer and playing music on giant 'boom boxes'.

Wilder knew Daytona well; he would often go there in his Porsche and take it for a drive around the race circuit, do a few practice laps, especially before a race. It had only been a few weeks since he'd raced in the 24-hour event there with Dennis DeFranceschi and Buz McCall. He'd stayed in the Golden Eagle Motor Inn, and on the first night over dinner at Valle's Steak House, he'd hit on a waitress and at the end of the meal given her a pit lane pass. The tiny twenty-year-old, with long dark hair, watched him practise the following day and later that night went back to his room. Next morning, however, he'd freaked her out by going down on one knee and proposing marriage, telling her he had everything in life except a beautiful woman to look after him and begging her to go back to Boynton Beach with him and be his princess. The waitress had been so creeped out by his behaviour she'd immediately fled, never returning any of his calls, and even leaving her job at the restaurant.

WILD OLIVE AVENUE
DAYTONA BEACH, FL

At just past nine o'clock on that Thursday morning, one of Colleen's friends, Angela Graham, was sitting under the shade of a giant oak tree, watching her boyfriend shoot hoops at the old basketball court on Wild Olive Avenue. The girls had made loose arrangements to ditch school that day and hang out at the beach together. There were only a couple of days left before the holidays and a lot of local kids were playing hooky. It was already warm, and Angela was tapping her feet to the distant thump of a ghetto-blaster, when a blue-and-white sedan with a vinyl roof pulled up alongside her. The driver had a neatly clipped beard and was wearing mirrored sunglasses and an expensive watch. He beckoned Angela over to his car, told her he was a photographer, that she had a nice figure and he would like to take her picture. Staring at her breasts, he told her she had a lot of potential and if she posed for him, in a nearby abandoned school, he would pay her $100. Angela wasn't tempted even when he offered to share some marijuana with her. When her boyfriend shouted over to her, the driver backed off, telling her he would be back later with more money, in case she changed her mind.

HOWARD JOHNSON MOTOR LODGE
DAYTONA BEACH, FL

At 2 p.m. that day Wilder checked in to the Howard Johnson Motor Lodge near Interstate 95, using his own Visa card. It was a large motel with more than one hundred rooms, and no-one would later be able to recall the man who stayed in room 165. Receipts revealed he ate alone in the attached restaurant, ordering a steak dinner with all the trimmings, but nobody remembered seeing him. At some point that evening he checked in with his message service and listened to Edna Buchanan asking him to call her back about an article she was writing. Her voice was light and friendly as she explained how she was working on a story about two missing girls, Rosario Gonzalez and Beth Kenyon, and she wanted to give him the opportunity to comment. She said she understood he was the last person to see both women and there were a couple of questions she wanted to ask him. She left her name and phone number. He never returned her call.

502 BUTLER AVENUE
DAYTONA BEACH, FL

When Colleen didn't return home that night, her mum thought at first she may have gone to stay with one of her friends and did a ring round, but none of them had seen her. When she found out Colleen hadn't gone to school that day, she got really concerned and the next day, with her eldest daughter, Margaret, a clerk in the local sheriff's office, she contacted police. The officer insisted on waiting the standard forty-eight hours before filing a missing person's report, which, because it was the weekend, meant it was four days later, 19 March, before Colleen's details joined the missing person files. Despite Margaret telling him that Colleen's brother and his wife had just had a baby, and how excited her sister was to become an aunty, the officer dealing with her paperwork wrote, 'runaway, missing juvenile' at the top of the file, relegating it to low priority and pushing it towards the bottom of the pile.

The initial police responses to the disappearance of many of Wilder's victims exposed sloppy police work and systemic attitudinal problems. Even though Wilder was now operating in the 1980s, a much more enlightened era than when he had first started his catalogue of crimes, the police, sheriff departments and the FBI were still very male dominated. There was also a lack of proper training or development of what today are considered core skills for law enforcement, such as emotional intelligence. Inevitably, this meant old-school detectives being too quick and ready to dismiss family concerns, too easily persuaded that the various victims were just more run-of-the-mill runaways, who would turn up eventually, safe and sound. The paperwork was dutifully done, but in most cases Wilder got away with his crimes because too many did too little, too late. It had been too easy to suspect Beth Kenyon had skipped town with a boyfriend, Rosario Gonzalez had got cold feet about her upcoming wedding, and Colleen Orsborn had run away from a tough situation at home.

FRIDAY 16 MARCH 1984
HOWARD JOHNSON MOTOR LODGE
DAYTONA BEACH, FL

Wilder checked out early, before the newspapers arrived in reception, and headed south-west on Interstate 4 towards Orlando. The *Miami Herald* had another article by Edna Buchanan under the headline 'Race Driver May Be Link to Missing Models':

A thin thread may link two missing aspiring models who vanished without a trace nine days apart, police said Thursday.

It is detectives' only lead.

A self-described 'modeling agent' who knew Elizabeth (Beth) Kenyon, 23, is believed to have been the last person seen with her on March 5, the day she disappeared. The same Boynton Beach man drove a race car at the Grand Prix, from which Rosario Gonzalez, 20, disappeared Feb. 26. [. . .] The man, in his 30s, 'is somebody we're looking at,' a Miami homicide detective said Thursday.

Detective Ray Nazario was quoted: 'We don't know if the victims are alive or dead, I'm still considering everybody a suspect.'

Ken Whittaker Jr was also interviewed and although Wilder wasn't named, Whittaker revealed that Beth had introduced the wanted man to her parents, who he said were both distraught.

ROUTE 27
LAKE WALES, FL

A day after Colleen Orsborn went missing, on Route 27, in Lake Wales, a 45-minute drive south of the spot where her body would eventually be found, Wilder stopped at 11 a.m. to buy petrol at a Texaco service station. He bought a copy of the *Miami Herald* and started panicking. Even though he thought the cops had been as slow as wet cement so far, he was definitely in the spotlight now. He was struggling to breathe, biting down hard on his nails, his skin clammy, sweat dripping down his armpits and back. He needed to get back on the road quickly; it was always the best remedy when he felt tense and needed to relax.

MIAMI HOMICIDE UNIT
MIAMI, FL

Rosario Gonzalez's family read the article as well and rang the detectives to demand that Wilder be arrested and taken in for questioning. Chary's sister, Lisette, who helped translate the call, was given several assurances that Wilder was under surveillance, that they knew he had a plane ticket back to Australia and were watching him night and day. She was told to inform her parents they had nothing to worry about.

SEBRING INTERNATIONAL RACEWAY
SEBRING, FL

Wilder parked outside the Sebring International Raceway, where he was scheduled to be racing his next event in eight days' time. He'd been looking forward to the race, had arranged for Dana Neighbors to embroider new personalised shirts for himself and the pit crew, and helped Dennis fix up the engine, but he knew he wouldn't be racing now.

Kimbrell was at work when Wilder called him.

'It's Chris. I'm in Tallahassee,' he lied, paranoid the cops could be listening in. 'I'm in fucking big trouble, Zeke, big fucking trouble.'

'Is it true, what's in the *Herald*?' Kimbrell asked.

'It's all bullshit,' Wilder said. 'I had nothing to do with any of it. I can't go home, they have it under surveillance. After that fucking story, everyone in Boynton Beach thinks it's me that bitch is writing about. My ass is grass but I'm not going to jail, I'm not going to do it.'

He was choking up.

'Come to my place,' said Kimbrell. 'If you didn't have anything to do with those girls who disappeared, and I believe you, come back now and I will help you to sort it out.'

CAR REPAIR SHOP
DELRAY BEACH, FL

On his way to Kimbrell's house, Wilder realised he would pass near Dennis DeFranceschi's repair shop. He started to sweat and his stomach began to tighten. He took a couple of deep breaths, put on his favourite Eurythmics tape and started singing along to the lyrics from 'Regrets' until he pulled up outside the shop. It was well after 8 p.m. Dennis would recall later that Wilder stood there staring at the Porsche, his eyes red-rimmed, brimming with tears. He'd never seen the controlling neat freak so emotional.

'Thanks for everything, guys, but this is goodbye,' said Wilder, not looking at Dennis or mechanic Freddie Freimann directly. 'I won't see you again, I won't be in touch again, and I don't want you to try and contact me. When I walk out of here, I don't want you to follow me, either, and look at the car I'm leaving in. I don't want you to get involved in what's happening.'

Dennis and Freddie were speechless. They'd both seen the *Herald* that morning and gossiped about it most of the night. Of course, they'd worked out it was referring to Wilder, but weren't sure what to say or how to react. Wilder started walking away. When he got to the doors he turned around and added, 'This probably won't end well.'

KIMBRELL'S HOUSE
DELRAY BEACH, FL

Wilder was still emotional when he arrived at Kimbrell's house just after 10 p.m. He'd driven around after leaving the repair shop and made sure Kimbrell's place wasn't being watched by cops. By the time they were sitting down at the dining table, coffees in front of them, Wilder admitted he'd broken his probation by racing at the Grand Prix, but he told Kimbrell that he was getting blamed for something he didn't do. He told him he was going to take off for good, go to Mexico, where an old client had invited him to stay.

'If you know anything about the missing girls, you should tell me now,' Kimbrell argued.

'They just want a fall guy, someone to take the rap.'

Kimbrell had always known his business partner was full of 'bullshit' about most things. He knew Wilder's two flashy rings were actually cubic zirconia, not diamonds, that his property and race cars all carried large debt. He even knew that his partner had been fleecing the company they had set up together.

When Kimbrell and Wilder had first set up Sawtel Construction, Wilder had made his then girlfriend, Victoria Darling, the company secretary. It was a smart move that effectively meant Wilder controlled the company, always able to count on Darling's vote or signature to outflank Kimbrell when he needed to. The company was successful and grew quickly, but Wilder was creaming off the top by approaching clients himself and giving them a discount if they paid him in cash. Kimbrell wasn't stupid. He quickly figured out what his partner had been doing, confronted him and then hired his own wife as the company accountant to monitor the books. Kimbrell had long forgiven Wilder, believing he was just a lonely guy, who did it all to impress women. What he didn't know or believe, even as the evidence started mounting up, was that his friend of many years was actually a psychopath who had already kidnapped and killed three women.

Wilder's exit strategy was in place. Kimbrell was his power of attorney so he would keep the business. He knew the police would trace him through credit card receipts, so he borrowed Kimbrell's. He was already carrying $10000 in cash and had plans to withdraw more when he was clear of Miami. He shook Kimbrell's hand in silence, unable to look him in the eye, and climbed into his car. As he drove off, the Eurythmic's song 'Regrets' blared out once more from the speakers.

10

THE CAPTAIN'S DAUGHTER

**UNSUB; THERESA W FERGUSON, 00:MM MIAMI
FILE 7-1669**

SATURDAY 17 MARCH 1984
LOXAHATCHEE, FL

Wilder spent the night at Loxahatchee in a basic mobile trailer he kept there, next to the kennels, in the middle of the pond cypress. He'd used it as a photographic studio on a few occasions, and it was remote and difficult to find. When the first rays of sunlight appeared, he drove over to Boynton Beach and, after half a dozen drives past the house to check if anyone was watching, he parked, went inside and quickly filled a suitcase with clothes, then fussed over his briefcase, which was brown with rigid sides and a silver handle. Inside, most of the soft leather lining was obscured by the smorgasbord of items he'd carefully packed into the various compartments and pockets. When he was finished sorting it out, he stepped back and admired the neatness of his handiwork. It contained his two passports, the US one he travelled on and his lapsed

Australian one, $10000 in carefully stacked $100 banknotes, a roll of silver duct tape, a wide assortment of business cards, mirrored sunglasses, a blindfold and handcuffs, hairbrush, large double-bladed knife, the revolver he'd bought from the local gun shop a year ago, his favourite marked-up copy of *The Collector*, his contacts book, several *Playboy* magazines, lengths of thin white rope and a pair of scissors. Despite his anxiousness to get on the road and away from the house, he lingered a moment on the back deck, taking in the jacuzzi adjacent to his bedroom, the map of Australia on the bottom of the pool and the speedboat that was bobbing about in the water tied up to the small pontoon. He walked briskly to his car, where the dogs sat panting and wagging their tails, and put the briefcase in the boot alongside a rolled-up sleeping bag and a DIY electric-shock device, which was coiled and secured with a velcro fastener.

He didn't dare have a last breakfast at DJ's Grill, it was far too close to Boynton Beach police station, so he went a few kilometres before turning into another drive-through near the highway. In Loxahatchee, as soon as he had the dogs settled in the kennels, he didn't hang around long and hit the road again, heading north. A couple of hours and 200 kilometres later, he pulled off Interstate 95, turned right towards the ocean on State Road 528, and in less than half an hour was checking into the Holiday Inn, his favourite hotel chain, on West Cocoa Beach. He unpacked, went down to the bar and ordered a St Patrick's Day Tom Collins cocktail. He took his first sip and started plotting his next victim.

MIAMI, FL
Meanwhile, the police were re-interviewing and taking statements from all the people Ken Whittaker and Mitch Fry had already

spoken to, while John Hanlon at the FBI was receiving reports and background history on Wilder. They were happy the paperwork was flowing nicely between the agencies, and they were building up a strong dossier of evidence against Wilder.

SUNDAY 18 MARCH 1984
SATELLITE BEACH, FL

Theresa Wait Ferguson, aged twenty-one, had spent Sunday morning in the backyard working on her tan while reading a couple of her favourite fashion magazines and a chapter of the latest Stephen King novel. With her long brown hair, big brown eyes and great body, Theresa got attention from men wherever she went. Born in Massachusetts, she had been a baby when she'd moved to nearby Indian Harbour with her mother, after her parents' divorce. A couple of years later her mother, Frances, remarried and her stepfather, Don, was now captain of the local police department. Theresa was a dreamer and was always making plans for the future and her career as a fashion model. After graduating from Satellite High School, she had landed a job with the founders of a local start-up company, which specialised in silk-screen T-shirts, and was now the quality control supervisor. She had a boyfriend, Dan Bednarz, who'd recently given her a 'promise' ring. They were crazy about each other and talked about heading to the Big Apple together as soon as he graduated from the Florida Institute of Technology. The plan was that Dan would find a job with one of the big marketing firms, while Theresa would enrol in the Wilfred Academy of Hair and Beauty Culture.

Indian Harbour was a sleepy beach town that got a few week-end visitors but never drew a crowd, except when there was a big space-rocket launch at Cape Canaveral a few kilometres up the road. Normally on a Sunday, the attractive young couple met for breakfast at the Blueberry Muffin Restaurant in Indialantic, a ten-minute drive south, but Dan was away on a Spring Break holiday with his mates and wouldn't be back till the afternoon. Theresa had arranged to go shopping with two of her closest girlfriends, Kirsten and Sam, and at 11 a.m. she interrupted her mother in the shower to tell her she was heading off. She drove her 1977 Pontiac Sunbird over to Kirsten's house, but Kirsten was too hungover from clubbing the night before to even make it out of bed. Theresa gave up on her and drove over to Sam's house, but she was at the doctor's. Her mother told her that Sam, who worked with Theresa at the T-shirt company, had hurt her eye after goofing around with a football. Theresa wrote Sam a quick note to tell her she'd see her at work the next day and then drove off to go shopping alone at the Merritt Square Mall, on Merritt Island. She parked just before 1 p.m. and walked off into the mall, wearing a burgundy blouse, blue jeans and her favourite boots.

CANAVERAL PIER
COCOA BEACH, FL
Wilder had treated himself to breakfast in his room, and once he'd checked the newspapers, watched the news on TV and showered, he was ready to go prowling. Carrying his Pentax and stocked up with stolen business cards, he headed for Canaveral Pier looking to find some pretty college students enjoying their Spring Break. It wasn't long before he targeted two girls walking along the pier in their bikinis. He walked up to them confidently, claimed he was a professional photographer, on assignment for a local surfing store, and asked if they would be interested in modelling for him. He needed swimsuit models to pose in fur coats. He told them they

had a lot of potential and he could pay them $250 plus $25 for every photo chosen by the client. The girls just giggled, told him they really weren't interested and walked on. It was another rejection, more humiliation, and it put him in a bad mood. He was more than a little paranoid now about being reported and, worried the girls might alert security or the local police patrol about him, he decided to cut his losses and go to the nearby shopping mall instead.

MERRITT SQUARE MALL
MERRITT ISLAND, FL

Theresa, who had parked outside JCPenney, had spent a good hour and a half shopping and decided it was time to head home. She knew Dan would be back shortly from Fort Lauderdale and she was eager to see him again. She'd bought a new outfit, Calvin Klein jeans and a pink blouse, which she'd kept on after trying them on and paying for them. As she headed to the car, another shopper, following behind her, couldn't stop herself from staring. She thought Theresa, with her long legs and silky hair, walked like one of those catwalk models you saw on TV. She would tell detectives later that she noticed a well-dressed man, with a neatly groomed beard and thinning hair, approach the beautiful young woman and start talking to her. The man was smiling and holding a camera. As she walked past them, she saw that the girl, who was wearing a pretty blouse that showed off her figure and tan perfectly, was wearing a gold chain around her neck and a small diamond ring on her left hand. The man seemed to be doing most of the talking, and she heard him mention a 'great modelling opportunity'.

———————

Theresa's eyes almost popped out of her head when the fashion photographer said he thought she had lots of potential. She immediately agreed to go to his car to check out his portfolios. When she realised his car was parked right next to hers, she laughed at the coincidence. The photographer said he'd like to do a quick shoot with her at a nearby beach for a local surfing store.

'It won't take long, and I will bring you straight back to your car,' he said enthusiastically. 'If you come with me, we can chat on the way about your modelling career, I have so many contacts in the industry that could help you.'

It was the height of the supermodel era. Girls like Theresa would have had posters of the likes of Elle Macpherson and Christie Brinkley plastered all over their bedroom walls.

Theresa didn't even think twice, all those lessons from her step-dad about accepting lifts from strangers forgotten, her head full of how her modelling dream was about to come true.

COCOA BEACH, FL

One hour after an excited Theresa jumped into Wilder's Chrysler and left the mall, the phone rang at the Texaco service station in Cocoa Beach. Bill Brady picked up and heard a man say nervously, 'My car's got stuck in the sand and I need a tow.'

It was Wilder.

'I'm only visiting up here,' he explained, 'and I got a bit lost. I pulled off the road and hit some soft sand.'

Wilder told Bill he'd walked about ten minutes to find the payphone, which was just off State Road A1A near Canaveral Groves, half an hour from the mall. Bill knew the spot; it was quite remote and a favourite lovers lane rendezvous. He'd pulled quite a few embarrassed couples from the sludgy sand over the years, and only ten days ago police had recovered the skeletal remains of a young female in the same area. Bill told the caller it would take him a good forty minutes to get over there in his truck. He saw the driver waiting for him by the side of the road and turned off on a dirt trail, into a grove of trees. The Chrysler, parked where it couldn't be seen by passing vehicles, was buried in the sand to below its hubcaps. There was no sign of anyone else, which Bill thought was odd considering the popularity of the location with couples, but the man was well dressed and pleasant enough. Bill didn't need access to the boot of the Chrysler to make the tow, but he recalled later how he'd rested his hands on it, when he'd fixed the chain to the back axle. Wilder paid with a credit card in the name of LK Kimbrell.

'Thanks, Mr Kimbrell,' Bill said, handing it back after taking an imprint.

Wilder wished Bill a nice day, quickly got behind the wheel and drove off, heading north. Wilder spent a second night at the Holiday Inn registered as LK Kimbrell. No-one remembered him entering or leaving the room and no-one remembered seeing him with anyone.

That night Wilder called his parents in Australia, full of pretence and fake bravado. He didn't really want to talk to them, but he regularly called them on Sunday nights, and he didn't want them to start fussing if he missed the call. They had no idea about his current situation, and he didn't enlighten them. He assured his father he had his plane ticket to Australia and would be arriving on 31 March, well in time for his trial, which was due to start the following week. His parents were excited because he would also be home for their wedding anniversary on 15 April. Wilder didn't contradict them, but he knew he wouldn't be celebrating with them.

It was doubtful he would go back to Australia, and even if he did, he wouldn't be going to their anniversary party.

MERRITT SQUARE MALL
MERRITT ISLAND, FL

Dan Bednarz had first tried calling Theresa at 2 p.m. when he got back from Fort Lauderdale, and when she hadn't arrived home by 5 p.m., he was as worried as her parents. He told her stepfather he would check all the places Theresa might have gone with a friend for a drink or a meal, while Don went to the mall and looked for her car. It was 10.30 p.m. when Don Ferguson, still in his captain's uniform, found his stepdaughter's Sunbird where she had parked it outside JCPenney. It was locked, and on the back seat he could see a jumble of her clothes. A short while later, Dan turned up and the two men sat watching the car in case Theresa turned up. Don left at midnight, but Dan stayed in the deserted lot until 4.30 a.m.

MONDAY 19 MARCH 1984
HOLIDAY INN
WEST COCOA BEACH, FL

Wilder skipped breakfast at the motel in favour of an early start. He didn't bother to check on Theresa, who had been hogtied in the boot of the car since he'd picked her up at the mall. The FBI would never find out for sure why Wilder didn't take Theresa into the motel and sexually abuse her, but they did establish that he had hogtied her so tightly, the weight of her legs on the rope around her neck had strangled her to death. Was that an accident? Was he trying to dump her when he got stuck in the sand? Or was he getting a thrill out of the tow-truck driver not knowing she was in the boot?

Did he get to the motel, intent on taking her inside to abuse her, only to discover she was already dead?

Whatever the case, that morning Wilder drove west on State Road 528 until he hit Interstate 4 and then went south-west and took the exit for Haines City, in Polk County, 110 kilometres from the motel. After a few minutes, he took a turn on to Deen Still Road, little more than a dirt road running east-west between US Route 27 and State Road 33. The cicadas were screeching in the marshes, the huge cypress trees doing little to block the hot spring sun. Wilder parked on a small bridge running over one of the small alligator- and snake-infested creeks. Checking there was no-one around, he opened the boot, dragged Theresa's body out, lifted and dropped her into the muddy water.

Afterwards, he drove straight on to the North Carolina National Bank in Tampa, where he cashed a $280 personal check at the drive-in teller. He was captured on CCTV, behind the wheel, wearing a crisp white shirt, coolly completing the transaction as though he didn't have a care in the world. Fifteen minutes later, after waiting to see if police responded to any call-out, he went into the bank and cashed a check for $4250, which left just $800 in his account. He now had around $15000 stashed in his briefcase.

He filled the Chrysler up with petrol and headed north until he pulled into the La Quinta Motor Inn in Tallahassee four hours later. The hilly tree-lined state capital, famed for its gracious old plantation homes and charming southern hospitality, was the largest city in the Florida Panhandle region. Wilder chose the motel for its proximity to the Governor's Square shopping mall, a short drive away. He paid for a room with Kimbrell's credit card and gave the reception clerk the registration of a car he'd stolen the plates from in Orlando, a couple of months earlier.

PALM BEACH PROBATION SERVICE
PALM BEACH, FL

Edna Buchanan's story on the previous Friday had pushed police into finally taking action. A week after Ken Whittaker had asked detectives to pick up Wilder on a probation violation, Metro-Dade police finally notified Palm Beach County that he had raced in the Miami Grand Prix. A probation supervisor confirmed Wilder did not have permission to attend, and that they would approach the judge for a warrant to pick him up. Detectives reassured the Gonzalez and Kenyon families that Wilder would be taken in for questioning either that day or the next.

They were wrong. By the time they would get a warrant and knock on his door three days later, on 22 March, Wilder would have already been on the run for five days. Edna Buchanan wanted to know why the detectives hadn't taken up Whittaker's suggestion straight away, or at least put Wilder under surveillance.

Metro-Dade homicide captain Bob McCarthy, who had hosted the meeting of lawmen the previous Thursday, claimed, 'We had nothing to pick him up on. I wouldn't authorize sending a homicide team all the way up to Palm Beach County to sit on surveillance. Nobody had any reason to believe Mr Wilder was anybody but an honest hardworking businessman known to Elizabeth Kenyon and the family. I don't believe I have to justify what my men have done. I can understand the concerns of Mr and Mrs Kenyon, but we have a thing called civil rights. Just because he dated a man's daughter doesn't mean we can rush out and pick him up.'

Nazario backed up his boss. 'I couldn't accuse him [Wilder] of abduction, I couldn't accuse him of kidnapping. I could bring him back here and put him under the lights, but this is 1984. We don't do that. In this business you don't deal only with the deceased but with the life of the potential subject – because he could get the electric chair for first-degree murder. We had no proof that he was a maniac.'

Their answers, as thin as ancient parchment, would be little comfort to Haydee and Blas Gonzalez, and Bill and Dolores Kenyon, and they would give no solace to Frances Orsborn.

11

MODUS OPERANDI

When you draw something it lives and when you photograph it it dies.
— John Fowles, *The Collector*

UNSUB; LINDA E GROBER, 00:MM TAMPA FBI FILE 7-899

TUESDAY 20 MARCH 1984
GOVERNOR'S SQUARE
TALLAHASSEE, FL

She was the most beautiful so far. He'd chosen well and congratu-
lated himself for passing on the earlier possibilities, lengthening his
stride, closing the gap, just a few steps, close enough to touch her.
Slender and tiny, she would be light as a feather.

––––––

Linda Grober was smiling, bouncing along to the song 'Down
Under' by Australian band Men at Work blasting from one of the
stores. The Governor's Square shopping mall was only a few minutes from the university campus and the apartment she shared with

her girlfriends, and it was a trip she had done a hundred times. The nineteen-year-old, slim and lithesome with a stunning face, big blue eyes and deeply bronzed limbs, was a creature of habit and had a favourite spot where she liked to park, seven spaces from the main entrance. She got out of the car and headed for the basement section of Maas Brothers, where she was hoping to get a present for Eddie, for their five-and-a-half-year anniversary. A photo album, to fill with snapshots of all their best moments. Her sorority sisters had teased her about that this morning, laughed at her for still celebrating the half-year anniversaries, but Eddie was such a romantic. 'I love that about him,' she thought. She couldn't believe how quickly the years had gone; she'd been with Eddie since she was fourteen years old, but she was still besotted with him. Her first and only one.

She knew she should really be studying, as she was in her sophomore year of veterinary science at Florida State University, but although she loved animals and was desperate to work with them, she was having too much fun to be a grade-A student. If she wasn't hanging out with Eddie, she was off surfing or partying with her girlfriends and smoking a bit of pot. Her mum and dad would be cross with her if they knew. Linda grimaced sheepishly to herself. Born in Oslo, Norway, she had moved with her wealthy parents to America when she was a toddler. She'd never wanted for anything. Her life was pretty damn perfect, she knew that. She had her own car and enough money so she didn't have to work her way through college, and her doting dad was a total pushover. Although careless about her privileged lifestyle, she was, however, generous to a fault and fiercely loyal to Eddie and her many friends.

———

She heard the steel-tipped heels of his cowboy boots against the polished marble tiles as she was reaching up for a greeting card.

'Excuse me, I'm a fashion photographer looking for a fresh new face for an assignment I'm doing for a major magazine,' he said quietly, a hint of a lisp. 'I think you're just the one I'm looking for.'

He paused and smiled for a moment, not too close, not threatening her space. He was wearing a hand-tailored dark pinstriped suit with a maroon tie, and his moustache and beard were neatly clipped. The large diamond ring on the pinkie finger of his left hand, the gold watch on his wrist and the Pentax camera hanging casually from his shoulder completed the look: confident, professional, successful and respectable.

'I think you definitely have what it takes to make a really good model,' he added, nodding slightly to emphasise the point. 'It's a really fantastic opportunity and it wouldn't take very long at all. I can see that you have so much potential.'

It was a perfect pitch, honed over the best part of two decades. He hadn't met a pretty girl yet who didn't get all dreamy at the thought of a modelling career. He'd once told Ginger Bush that he had an 85 to 90 per cent success rate, and it hadn't been an empty boast. If there was still a minor fault after all this time, it was that he never quite managed to maintain eye contact.

'We could do the test shoot nearby,' he added, producing a business card he'd stolen from an exhibition by a local photographer and holding it out to show her. 'As you can see, my studio isn't far away. It wouldn't take very long, and I will pay you very well for your time,' he added.

'That's very kind, but I'm really not interested in modelling,' she replied. 'My boyfriend wouldn't like it if I did. Anyway, I'm a surfer and I don't shave my legs.'

He didn't push it, just gave her a few more compliments and left her alone.

The second approach came a short while later, as she walked between stores, her blonde curls falling over her face. He looked sheepish, embarrassed to be troubling her again.

'I was thinking, if you'd reconsider I could drive you to the park up the road and photograph you there,' he said. 'You have the perfect figure and face for what the magazine is looking for. It will be the easiest $25 you ever make, and I could give you four hours' work every week for $25 an hour.'

She was midway through repeating how she really wasn't interested when a thought struck her, and she mentioned she had two very beautiful roommates who might model for him if he was interested. She called them from a nearby payphone. He waited patiently as she left a quick message and then walked back over, apologising that her friends weren't home. She wished him luck and said goodbye. He smiled, shrugged his shoulders as if to say, 'Oh well, you can't win them all' and walked off with a slight wave. Then he waited. He was good at waiting and, later, as she headed back to her car he began to follow.

Linda was rummaging in her handbag for her car keys when she noticed him again, just behind her in the car park. She freaked out, just a little. She'd laughed to herself when he first approached her – she was such a midget, as if she could be a catwalk star. It had been a bit creepy, but he'd been super polite and well dressed, and they were in the middle of a store with sales staff and customers. She hadn't been that perturbed, not really, not even when he'd come up to her again outside the store. He was just a balding, everyday guy with a voice that was very soft and quiet, gentle almost. But now he was back and she felt a pang of panic.

'Hi there, again,' he said as if bumping into an old friend. 'What a lucky coincidence, I'm parked right next to you.'

He'd watched her arrive earlier and eased the nondescript Chrysler sedan he was driving into the empty parking space next to hers before approaching her in the mall. It was a big old clunker, eleven years old, but he'd deliberately chosen it because it blended in so well and didn't attract attention like his beloved Porsche Carrera, or his black racing Porsche that he'd driven in the recent Miami Grand Prix.

The man was chattering away, but Linda hadn't been listening, her mind had been whirring. Should she try and make a run for it? She tuned in again.

'Of course, I only do fashion work,' he said, his head tipped on one side, smiling, disarming.

It reassured her a little.

'I've got some magazine covers that I've done, in the car. Why don't you check them out?' he said, opening the boot of the car and pulling out a briefcase.

He saw her hesitate and glance around. There was no-one. He opened the lid, like a door-to-door salesman, and told her to have a look inside. She gingerly moved forward and peered in. It was tidy, papers neatly stacked. She noticed a passport with 'Australia' stamped on the front in gold lettering, then she was doubled over, in agony.

He'd driven his clenched fist into the pit of her stomach. He hadn't had much room to swing but he was muscular, and it was a sucker punch. She was gasping and wheezing, desperately trying to suck air back into her lungs when the second blow came. This time he hit her in the face, on her cheek under her left eye. As she began to crumple to the floor, he reached out and grabbed her by the arms to stop her hitting the ground, then pushed her into the back of the car.

There was a moment of dizzy confusion as Linda started to wake up. She was lying on her back, spread-eagled across the back seat of a moving car. It smelt like dog. She felt an overwhelming wave of nausea and started to pull herself up, groaning. The car braked abruptly and she was thrown against the front seats. She tried to get up, but she felt disorientated, and then the rear door was flung open and he was looming over her.

She started burbling, a hundred miles an hour. 'Please let me go, please don't hurt me, if it's money you want, my dad is wealthy, I'll write you a cheque now for a million dollars . . . I'll do whatever you need me to do, just don't hurt me.'

'Shut up, and don't talk again,' he barked at her.

His voice was harsh, not at all like it had been back at the mall. He stuffed a cloth gag into her mouth, tore off a length of duct tape and then placed the ends roughly on either side of her mouth, using both hands to press down hard, so her head was forced back-wards into the blue seat cushion. She wanted to struggle but it was futile; he was far too powerful and there was very little room to manoeuvre. Linda remembered a movie she'd watched with Eddie, about a girl who had been kidnapped and sold into prostitution, and she started panicking, wriggling maniacally, kicking out with her feet in a stomping motion. She tried to scream, but the tape meant she could only muster a muffled whimper. He smacked her hard across the cheek several times and snapped, 'Keep doing that and I will really hurt you, I might even kill you, I've done it before.'

The tone in his voice was enough. She stopped thrashing, her whole body going limp.

'Now you're going to cooperate while I tie you up, do you understand me?' he asked.

She nodded once to show him she understood. She didn't know where she was, or how long she had been unconscious, or what this crazy, strange man was going to do. He'd shown no interest when she'd mentioned money. She knew that wasn't good.

'Keep it together,' Linda told herself. 'Keep cool, engage with him, don't fight.'

He used pre-cut lengths of white rope to tie her arms behind her back at the elbows and wrists, then tied her ankles to her wrists tightly with more rope, forcing her back to arch. Even though she was skinny and very flexible, it was an unnatural position and she knew it would become very painful, very quickly. Then he ripped off two more pieces of duct tape and put them over her eyes. The sudden blindness terrified her most of all. Picking her up like she was little more than a toothpick, he pulled her out of the back seat and threw her down into the boot, slamming the lid shut.

She felt the car do a quick U-turn, the tyres spinning in the loose soil. The rain that had been threatening all day finally began to fall, heavy drops that made a steady thumping sound against the boot.

————

His favourite tape was jutting out of the cassette player, and he reached down, pushed it in and cranked up the volume. The *Touch* album by the Eurythmics had been released a few months earlier, and the band were about to kick start their US tour with an appearance on *Late Night with David Letterman* that evening, which he planned on watching. He was obsessed with their music and played it whenever he drove. He started to tap the steering wheel as the chords of the album's opening track reverberated inside the car. He felt on top of the world, determined to put the stress of the last few days behind him.

He parked in a quiet spot not far from the shopping mall. He'd remembered the phone message the girl had left her flatmates and knew that as soon as she was reported missing, the cops would check it out. He needed to move her car. The rain had eased and after he cut the engine he heard the girl thumping inside the boot. He got out of the car calmly and, after looking around to make sure there was no-one watching, lifted the lid.

Linda had been distraught in the blackness of the trunk, horrified at the thought he would park somewhere and abandon her to die, but with the duct tape still over her eyes, the silence as he opened the boot was even more petrifying. She froze, desperately trying to show her submission, that she got it, she'd learned her lesson, she'd keep quiet.

He punched her in the side of the face, then used his thumb and forefinger to pinch her nostrils together and close off her air supply. With the duct tape across the mouth, she couldn't breathe.

'This is your fault,' he whispered in her ear, his hot, stale breath washing over her.

She panicked, started thrashing around, but he kept hold of her and she realised this was it, this was how she was going to die. She thought briefly about the pathologist, who would examine her body and see the tatty knickers she'd thrown on that morning.

'That was your last warning,' he bellowed in her ear this time, taking away his hand, as she snorted in air and choked down saliva.

He tightened her bindings even more. 'I'm leaving a tape recorder on the back seat of the car. If I find you've made a single sound, I'll know about it, and it won't be good for you.'

Linda felt a whoosh of air against her cheek as he closed the boot. She took a few ratcheting-up breaths and felt a spreading warm sensation between her legs. She'd wet herself. The music suddenly kicked back in, but not as loudly this time. She'd listened to him singing along to 'Here Comes the Rain Again' time and time again while they had been driving, but now a new Eurythmics song was playing. The lyrics to 'Sweet Dreams (Are Made of This)', filled the stifling, tepid air as she lay, quiet, still, tears pooling in her eyes behind the tape.

———

He took Linda's key from her handbag and headed towards the mall, walking slowly, checking carefully, in case someone was watching the car. He went into the mall bathrooms to wash his hands thoroughly and, ten minutes later, was driving her car through the exit. He drove slowly for a couple of blocks and then pulled up across the street from a cocktail bar with a garish pink neon sign over the door. He jumped out, locked the car, jogged through a gap in the late afternoon traffic and went inside. He didn't drink much as a rule, but whenever he did, he only ever ordered one of two things, a White Russian or a Tom Collins. The bar hadn't yet filled up with the after-work crowd, and he flirted with the waitress while watching her mix his Kahlua, vodka and cream. She passed him the White Russian with a shy smile. Not as hot as the girl in the car, he decided, but on another day, he would have been interested. He spent twenty minutes chatting with her and nursing the cocktail, but his eyes rarely strayed from the front window where he had a clear view of the road outside, which led to the mall entrance nearby. He hadn't seen a cop car or heard so much as a single siren. He paid for his drink, went to wash his hands again and then left, making sure to give the waitress a small tip. He drove Linda's car to a nearby bank, with a parking area at the side, and left it in the farthest corner so the plates couldn't be seen from the street. He dropped the key down a kerbside drain and walked briskly back to his Chrysler.

———————

Linda heard him come back, get into the car and start driving. She was now in a lot of discomfort and pain: her stomach was sore, the side of her face throbbed, her throat was stiff and her right arm had gone completely numb. She had no idea what this insane man was planning to do with her. She pictured her body, dumped in a ditch covered with weeds and vegetation. Her parents, who were in the middle of a divorce, would be torn even further apart. She knew they would blame each other. She began praying. As he drove along, Linda started, perversely, thinking of the car boot as her sanctuary. If he was driving, he wasn't harming her.

Three times she heard him pull up and pump small amounts of petrol into the car. She could hear other car doors closing, people speaking and once even a car radio playing country music. He was taking a risk; did he get a thrill out of watching the other drivers walk right past his car on their way to and from the cashier, not suspecting a thing? She knew she should start kicking the boot again, try and make noise, get help, but she didn't dare, the thought of the punishment too appalling. When they were moving, she could tell by the bumps and potholes that he was driving on minor roads. He regularly stopped and checked on her. She quickly realised if she did what he wanted without hesitation, Mr Harsh disappeared and Mr Nice emerged.

At one stop he took the tape off her eyes and mouth and offered her some food and water. Her lips were sore and swollen from the duct tape and she was painfully thirsty, but was worried he'd laced it with something, so only pretended to take a sip. 'I can't feel my arm,' she said.

He repositioned her gently. 'Is that better?'

At the next check-up, when he saw her lips turning blue with cold, he got a blanket, which smelled like dog, from the back seat and wrapped it around her. Every time he checked on her, he was like a programmed robot: methodically repeating the procedure of re-applying the duct tape on her eyes and mouth, then testing all the knots on her bindings twice before closing the boot. She wondered how many other girls there had been.

I 2

SCENT OF SUCCESS

It was perhaps the biggest single decision of Wilder's life. He'd parked in a small clearing off the hard shoulder of the road 30 kilometres north of Tallahassee at the junction where Concord Bainbridge Road joined US Route 27. It was already dark, but the moon was full above the giant pylons that disappeared into the scrubland littered with broken glass and discarded take-away wrappers. Twenty minutes' drive further was the small town of Bainbridge in south-west Georgia, located on the banks of the Flint River, which fed into the giant Lake Seminole reservoir, famous for large bass fishing and duck and goose hunting. The car engine was switched off, and he was staring straight ahead through the wind-screen. He'd even forgotten about the girl for the moment. He sat slumped forward in the driver's seat with his left forearm resting on the steering wheel, while he systematically chewed away at the nails on his right hand. He'd been a chronic nail-biter since his early teens, the shrinks always made a big fuss about that, and at times of stress he would bite them so hard they were left red and tender. Times like now.

Less than 300 metres away, he could make out the road sign marking the boundary line separating the states of Florida and Georgia. It was just a line on a map to most people, but for him it marked the point of no return.

He'd been mulling over his options for the past ten minutes, getting steadily more hyper. He was tensing up, taking shallow breaths, perspiration forming on his brow. His abdomen was bloated as a result of the colitis he'd suffered from since his teenage years, and the spasms of pain were really strong this time. He used the handle on the side of the seat to lower the backrest, and then the lever at the front to move the cushion as far back as possible. He was a tall man, and he still had to bend his legs to fit his knees under the steering column, but he had at least taken some of the pressure off his stomach, and he felt more comfortable.

Should he turn back now, dispose of the girl and go back home? Tough it out with the media and cops? The newspapers would soon get fed up of writing about the missing girls, and the cops hadn't even got around to questioning him yet. He'd been too careful, too clever. Without any bodies, the idiots had nothing on him. The *Miami Herald* had reported he'd raced in the Grand Prix the day before that Gonzalez slut went missing, and that was a problem. By leaving Palm Beach County without seeking permission from his parole officer, he was in violation of his conditions and could be picked up. He'd broken parole a dozen times before – hell, every time he raced his car at Daytona or Sebring, he'd done it – but it was always worth it. Even if he wasn't arrested for breaking parole, he was supposed to be flying back to Australia next week to stand trial for kidnapping those two silly bitches he'd picked up at Manly Beach on his last trip back home. He should never have let them go.

In his briefcase were the plane tickets for him to return to Sydney. He'd told his parents he was flying back via San Francisco, but it was a lie and he wouldn't speak to either of them again. Fuck them both anyway, the shit they'd put him through. In the fading light, with dusk fast approaching, he realised he'd switched to chomping the nails on his left hand, the ones on his right all bitten to the quick. Re-focusing on the signpost up ahead, he knew his only other option was to keep on going, but abduction across state lines was a federal crime and that meant the FBI. He'd run rings around the local cops for years, but the FBI, that was a whole different story.

'Well here we are, what's it to be, shit or bust?' he said to himself, smiling, imitating the voice of his TV cult hero JR Ewing from *Dallas*. He knew the answer, of course, he always had, really, and he reached forward and turned the ignition key. For the past year he'd told a few of his racing teammates they would read about him on the front page of every newspaper one day, that he would be the most famous man in America and on every TV news bulletin. He knew they all thought he was just fooling around and daydreaming about winning a big car race. He re-adjusted his seat, put on his sunglasses, pulled on his leather racing gloves with the Porsche logo, gunned the engine and surged forward in a spin of wheels. Seconds later, he was speeding past the road marker, whistling the Ray Charles song 'Georgia on My Mind' as he did so. His head was full of images of the girl again, and he was so looking forward to rewarding himself with 'play time' that evening.

———

Linda was cold, exhausted, hungry and wired. She had been in the boot of the car now for so long, she had resigned herself to never getting out, to being imprisoned in there until it became her grave. It had been a while since he had even been to check on her and she didn't know what that meant, whether it was good or bad. Every time they stopped, and she heard the car door open, she thought he was coming to kill her. Her nerves were frayed and to hold it together as they drove along, she had forced herself to replay everything back in her mind since he'd first spoken to her in the mall. She'd burned a mental image of his face into her memory, in case she ever got out of this. She imagined herself sitting with one of those police artists she'd seen on TV and re-creating his tanned face, from the wispy V-shaped tuft of light brown hair in the middle of his balding head, to the thick, groomed triangular moustache, full beard and sideburns, and thick eyebrows above those flat eyes.

The car was stopping again, and she could tell they were no longer on the highway. There were no passing cars. He turned off the engine. She heard the clunk of the driver's door. She held her breath, wondering if this was it. She felt a sudden breeze on her cheek and then his hand ripping off the duct tape over her eyes. She looked over his shoulder at the dark sky. She had no idea where they were or what time it was, and for a fleeting moment she thought of Eddie and her flatmates and what they had been doing since discovering her missing.

'I want you to do exactly what I say, do you understand? Nod if you do.'

She nodded, eager to please him. He was holding a large brown suitcase, and he bent down and placed it on the ground against the rear bumper.

'If you do exactly as I say, you have nothing to fear, but if you cause any trouble then it will be different, and I won't protect you from the others,' he told her.

'Others?' she thought to herself, panicking. 'There's others?'

He ripped off the tape across her mouth while staring somewhere over her shoulder and said, 'You will cooperate with me now or you will die here. Say "Yes, sir" if you understand.'

'Yes, sir,' she managed, in a very quiet voice. It was unsettling that he didn't want to look her in the eye.

'Good. Now who do you belong to?'

'You, sir,' she replied, immediately.

'That's right,' he spat back triumphantly, 'your pussy is mine.'

He untied the rope connecting her ankles to her wrists, and the relief at relaxing the strain on her back was immediate.

'I'm going to lift the suitcase into the boot and you will climb inside,' he told her.

It was all happening so fast, she wasn't sure she'd heard him right. Had he really said he wanted her to climb into the suitcase? She knew it was best not to complain or to provoke him by being anything but completely compliant, so she didn't resist when he pushed her sideways and put the case down next to her in the space he'd created.

'Get in,' he said, unzipping the lid all the way around and opening it.

She lifted her ankles over the edge of the case and shuffled across on her bum. He grabbed her by the elbows and lifted her in, turning her on her side. To fit she had to bend her knees so her legs were underneath her, in a kind of Z shape. She was petrified and couldn't work out what he was doing, or why. Was he going to zip her inside and throw her into a river somewhere so she would sink and drown? For the next few minutes, he got progressively more impatient as he forced her into a variety of different positions, but despite her small stature he couldn't get the zipper to close past her shoulders if she lay on her side, or past her knees if she was on her back.

'Get out,' he finally barked at her in exasperation, and she didn't need a second invitation. She could tell he was angry his plan hadn't worked, but he didn't seem to blame her, which was a relief. She watched as he picked up the case, raised it above his head and flung it into some bushes nearby.

'Stay exactly where you are and don't make a sound,' he told her.

He walked around the side of the car, out of her sight briefly, returning with a rolled-up dark blue sleeping bag secured with a belt. He undid the belt and rolled the bag out next to her, zipping it open.

'Get in,' he said.

He made her bring her hands, which were tied behind her, around to her front by bringing them under her bottom and then down her legs and over her feet. She then lay on her back while he zipped the sleeping bag closed about halfway up, trapping her legs inside.

———

'I'm going to pick you up and put you in the front seat,' he told the girl. 'Remember, I'll only stop the others having sex with you if you do exactly what I say.'

When he was behind the wheel, he turned to face her, replaced the duct tape over her mouth and eyes and said, 'I'm going to zip the sleeping bag up and over your head, sit still and don't move.'

The Glen Oaks Motel, 5 kilometres south of Bainbridge, was set back about 40 metres from the highway with no adjoining property on either side. He got there quickly, and leaving the car in the dark shadows as far from the reception as he could, he registered under the name of LK Kimbriell Jr, deliberately misspelling the name of his business partner, and paid cash. He listed the stolen plates as the rego number, wrote down Cadillac in the space for model of car, and gave a false home address in Charlotte, North Carolina. He got into the car and, switching on the side lights only, drove slowly past a parked semi-trailer and pulled into the very end space opposite his room. He left the girl sitting in the passenger seat again, while he prepared things. He opened the room door, flicked the light switch and then made a couple of trips to carry his briefcase, an overnight suitcase and the girl's handbag into the room, placing them inside the door, neatly lined up. He closed the curtains on the window overlooking the car park, turned on the television and flicked through the channels until he found what he was looking for. He then put his black briefcase on the side table next to the bed furthest from the door, opened it up and took out an air freshener, which he sprayed liberally around the room.

Then he went to the bathroom, opened one of the four sachets of soap, and washed his hands vigorously. As well as his escalating sexual perversions, Wilder during this period also suffered increasingly from obsessive-compulsive disorder (OCD). He'd always insisted on his homes, office and cars being excessively tidy and clean. His neurotic need to repeatedly wash his hands was another symptom and would get worse at stressful times. He dropped the soap and wrapper into the waste bin, took great care to dry his hands, and then folded the towel perfectly and hung it back exactly halfway over the rail. His last act was to go to his briefcase again, take out a small atomiser bottle of perfume and spray a fine mist over the bed. The scent was *Tatiana* by model and fashion designer Diane von Furstenberg, a one-time princess. It was the perfume he bought for his mother.

Satisfied with his preparations, he went outside and opened the passenger car door, took off the seatbelt restraining the girl and, putting his head against the silky fabric of the sleeping bag right next to her ear, said, 'Do exactly what I say or I will kill you. Swing your legs round and I will pull you upright.'

She followed his instructions, and as she lifted and twisted her legs, he gripped and yanked the top of the sleeping bag so that she was able to stand up. Almost in the same movement, he crouched slightly and flipped her over his shoulder into a fireman's lift. It was three strides into the door and then another five to the second of two double beds, where he dropped her backwards onto the striped quilted bedcover. Five hours after driving out of the mall, he finally had her where he wanted her. He zipped the sleeping bag open the whole way and then ripped off the tape covering her eyes. She blinked repeatedly, trying to adjust to the light.

'The others might be here soon,' he told her. 'If you don't co-operate, I won't stop them having sex with you. If you're any good, you'll be sent to South America to be sold. They pay a lot of money for pretty blonde American bitches like you down there.'

Linda felt him launch her off his shoulder and as she fell backwards, it flashed through her mind that he'd thrown her off a cliff or a building. She braced herself for the impact, but contact came quickly, it was soft, and her body relaxed, bouncing into the air. It was a mattress. She was in a bedroom. She heard the zipper, the fabric of the sleeping bag no longer against her face. He ripped off the pieces of tape across her eyes, doing it crudely and removing clumps of her eyebrows in the process. The white light, dazzling from above the bed, hurt her eyes. The room was seedy, with the lumpy mattress and bare brick and concrete walls. It was like an underground bunker. She felt buried and trapped. There was a TV on a desktop halfway along the opposite wall that was playing a bunch of advertisements quite loudly, and a door to what she guessed was a bathroom in the corner. He was talking to her again and giving her instructions.

'I'm going to undress you. Don't move or you will be punished.' He paused for a second, then added, 'If you don't do what I want you to do, I'll bring you to the brink of death.'

Linda closed her eyes, and her whole body went into defence mode and tensed up. It took every ounce of self-control she had not to wrench herself away as his large hands moved firmly up and down her stomach, and pressed hard over both her breasts, his fingers digging into her nipples, before he began removing her clothes. When he bent to take off her underwear, she felt his hot breath wash over her and became so nauseous she almost threw up. He gave orders as he undressed her, 'lift your leg', 'arch your back', but the whole time Linda kept her eyes clamped tightly shut. When he took off her bra, he bit down on her breast hard, and it was only because of the tape across her mouth that she didn't scream.

'Relax and look like you're enjoying it,' he ordered her.

She did her best to fake enjoyment, but she knew if she opened her eyes and watched him, she would start crying and not be able to stop. Lastly, he removed the two rings she was wearing, a gold one with three little sapphires surrounded by tiny diamond chips, and a pearl ring she wore on her pinkie finger. He placed them on a small table by the far wall next to her clothes, which he'd folded carefully as he removed them.

'Now lie back and be still,' he told her.

She looked rigidly at the ceiling, trying to imagine herself somewhere else, anywhere but this seedy, yucky motel room with this monster, who was now at the foot of the bed, undressing. She looked across at his naked body. He was grossly hairy, especially his back and chest, and he seemed like a giant to her, with big, brawny arms. He was very methodical and neat in the way he removed his suit and tie, putting them on wooden hangers and placing them in the wardrobe along with his shirt, carefully spacing each hanger the same distance apart. He put his cowboy boots together and placed them down precisely on the floor of the wardrobe, pointing outward.

He started asking her a series of questions, telling her to nod or shake her head in reply.

'Do you have a boyfriend, are you a virgin, are you on the pill?'

She considered lying but decided it might make things even worse. He must have been satisfied with her answers, because once he had finished sorting his clothes, he stopped talking. He was naked except for a chunky gold chain around his neck and a pair of gold bikini-style briefs that hugged his waist tightly, emphasising the beginning of a paunch.

He took off his briefs.

———

Linda had remained rigid while he had been touching himself. She'd closed her eyes and tried to zone out but it had been hard to completely block his fast, shallow breathing and low groans. She could feel him staring at her breasts while doing it, and she would have vomited but for the tape over her mouth. When he suddenly stopped, she steeled herself for what might come next, but he just got off the bed, threatened her that she had to be better next time and went into the bathroom. She could hear him running water in the basin, and the tinkling made her suddenly desperate to pee.

When he came back in the room and started fiddling with a coil of rope, she waved her arms, signalling she wanted to say something. He yanked the tape back from her mouth, the last bit quick and fast. She bit her lip and tried to keep her voice as calm as possible, even though he'd hurt her, and her heart was bursting out of her chest.

'I need to go to the bathroom,' she said, pointing with both arms out in front of her, her wrists still tied together.

'Who owns you now?' he asked, his eyes burning with excitement.

'You, sir,' she said quickly through gritted teeth.

He pulled a hairbrush out of his briefcase and grabbed her hands, pulled her forward and onto her feet, and led her to the bathroom. He stood aside and gave her a shove through the door, which he kept open, standing in the doorway. Reaching to put the brush on the vanity in front of the mirror he told her, 'Be quick, clean yourself up and brush your hair.' He stood back, watching. Linda had never peed in front of a man before, but she didn't dare ask him to turn around. Afterwards, she looked into the mirror above the basin and was horrified by her appearance. It wasn't her dishevelled and matted hair or the drained lifeless look in her eyes that stunned her, but the bruising and swelling around her nose and left side of her face where he'd punched, smacked and pinched her. She splashed water on herself and patted at the swelling on her cheek, using a starchy face towel to dab away at a few specks of blood. It stung badly, and she put the towel down. She picked up the brush

ABOVE LEFT: Wilder as a young boy
(supplied by Channel 9)

ABOVE RIGHT: Wilder as a young man
on holiday in Australia *(supplied by
Channel 9)*

MIDDLE LEFT: Best friends Marianne
Schmidt and Christine Sharrock
(supplied by Schmidt family)

BELOW: Wanda Beach, where Marianne
and Christine were murdered *(shot and
supplied by Marianne's brother Hans)*

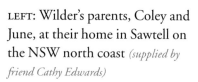

LEFT: Wilder's parents, Coley and June, at their home in Sawtell on the NSW north coast *(supplied by friend Cathy Edwards)*

RIGHT: Wilder's best friend and business partner, Zeke Kimbrell *(supplied by FBI Agent John Hanlon)*

Wilder's psychotherapist Ginger Bush *(Joe Raedle/Getty Images)*

Kenneth Whittaker Snr and his son Ken Whittaker Jnr, the private detectives who confronted Wilder about missing women *(supplied by Ken Whittaker)*

Crime reporter Edna Buchanan at her desk in the newsroom at the *Miami Herald* *(Paul Harris/Getty Images)*

FBI Special Agent John Hanlon, who led the manhunt for Wilder *(supplied by John Hanlon)*

Palm Beach detective Tom Neighbors thought Wilder was a friend until he went on the run *(supplied by Tom Neighbors)*

Rosario 'Chary' Gonzalez with her fiancé, Bill Londos *(supplied by her family)*

Rosario Gonzalez modelling shot

(supplied by her family)

Missing poster for Rosario Gonzalez

(supplied by her family)

Final photograph of Rosario Gonzalez taken minutes before her abduction at the Miami Grand Prix *(supplied by her family)*

Colleen Orsborn *(supplied by her family)*

Michelle Korfman *(supplied by FBI Agent John Hanlon)*

Young mother Beth Dodge, Wilder's final murder victim *(supplied by FBI Agent John Hanlon)*

High school teacher Beth Kenyon, killed after she turned down Wilder's marriage proposal *(supplied by FBI Agent John Hanlon)*

Survivor Linda Grober was shopping for a present for her boyfriend, Eddie, when Wilder abducted her *(supplied by Linda)*

Linda was a university student at the time *(supplied by Linda)*

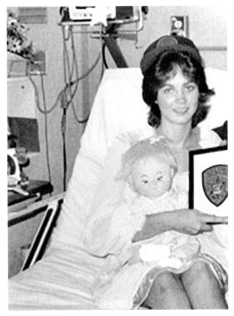

Survivor Dawnette Wilt in hospital after escaping from Wilder *(supplied by FBI Agent John Hanlon and the Miami History Museum)*

Teenager Tina Risico spent ten days as a Wilder 'butterfly' and is the only girl he allowed to go free *(supplied by FBI Agent John Hanlon and the Miami History Museum)*

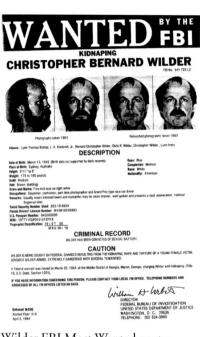

Wilder FBI Most Wanted poster

(supplied by FBI Agent John Hanlon)

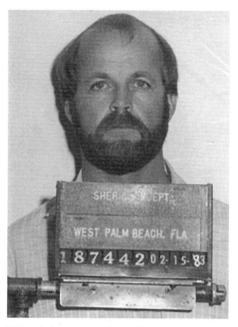

West Palm Beach Sheriff's Department arrest photo of Christopher Wilder

(supplied by West Palm Beach detective Tom Neighbors)

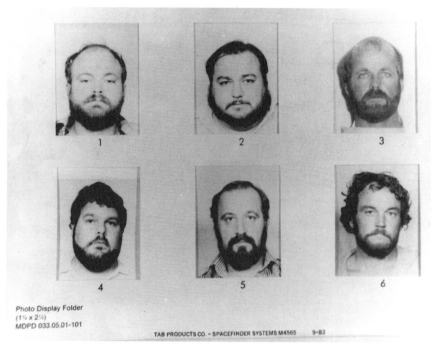

FBI and police suspect photo line-up; Wilder is number 3 *(supplied by FBI Agent John Hanlon)*

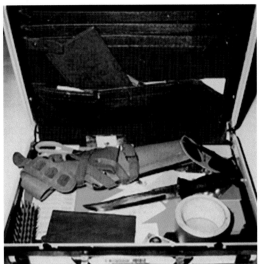

Wilder's 'kill kit' briefcase *(supplied by FBI Agent John Hanlon)*

The knife used to stab Dawnette Wilt *(supplied by FBI Agent John Hanlon)*

Wilder caught on bank CCTV shortly after dumping Theresa Ferguson's body *(supplied by FBI Agent John Hanlon)*

Scene at the Getty Service station in Colebrook, New Hampshire following Wilder's death in Beth Dodge's Pontiac Firebird *(supplied by FBI Agent John Hanlon)*

Rosario Gonzalez   Beth Kenyon   Colleen Orsborn   Terry Ferguson

Linda Grober   Terry Walden   Suzanne Logan   Sheryl Bonaventura

Michelle Korfman   Tina Risico   Dawnette Wilt   Beth Dodge

Wilder's twelve victims in his final forty-seven days – only three survived: Linda, Tina and Dawnette *(supplied by FBI Agent John Hanlon)*

and tried running it through her hair, but it jagged on the tangles and knots. He came in and grabbed the brush and slowly began brushing her hair himself. She blanched, standing transfixed, watching him in the mirror. He was almost trancelike, as if reliving some previous experience. When he was satisfied, he painstakingly removed all the loose hairs from the bristles, carefully put them into the wastebasket, and washed his hands once more, unwrapping a new bar of soap.

'Okay. That's enough, get back to the bed,' he told her.

Everything was about to get much worse.

When he'd plugged one end of an electric cable into the power point, he stood up and stared at the teenager lying naked on the bed. The device was his invention – well, strictly speaking, it had been his father's, but he had adapted it, made it into his very own torture machine. A 120-volt shock would get instant obedience. The cable was about 4.5 metres long, with a plug at one end and a small box switch in the middle. At the other end the wires split and the copper endings were exposed. He told the girl she was going to experience exactly what he had when he was even younger than her, and that the pain would last for ten seconds if she was good, but if she made any noise or tried to resist he'd shock her for thirty seconds. Pulling off two strips of duct tape he used them to attach the unsheathed wire ends to her two big toes, then got onto the bed and lay down next to her, holding the switch in his hands.

'Start massaging my thighs, make it good and don't make a sound,' he said.

Raising herself up slowly, she knelt by his side, placed her hands on the outside of his right thigh, and began rubbing in a small circular motion with the tips of her fingers. She saw him flick the switch a split second before the shock wave hit her, a surging, piercing sensation throughout her entire body. Her toes felt like

they were touching a piece of red-hot vibrating metal. Her mus-
cles compressed involuntarily and began to twitch. He had given
her a generous ten seconds, counting 'one thousand, two thousand,
three thousand', all the way to eleven before switching it off.

She collapsed back on her heels making a half-cry, half-grunt
sound.

'Do it again and do it with feeling this time,' he ordered her.
'I want it to look and feel like you're enjoying it. If you don't then
it'll be thirty seconds next time, do you understand?'

She nodded slowly, still not looking up, and he hit the switch
again. When he finally flicked the switch off, he waited a moment
before speaking.

'I said, do you understand?'

The girl, breathing rapidly, quickly replied 'yes' in a croaky
voice.

'Close your eyes and keep them closed,' he told her.

He reached for a bottle of superglue he'd put on the bedside
table earlier and began to squeeze globs of the mixture on her eyelids. She didn't try and pull away, not with him so close and the
switch within his reach on the bed, but she tried flexing the mus-
cles around her eyes hoping he wouldn't notice and mete out more
punishment. Her vision was heavily blurred with all the sticky
gunk, but when he lowered his hands with their disgusting nails,
there was a tiny slit in the lid of her right eye that she could partially
see through. She felt him get off the bed and disappear somewhere.
A moment later she heard the unmistakable sound of a hairdryer
being switched on. She had some vision in one eye but for the
next couple of minutes he ordered her to close both eyes tightly
and lie still while he blasted warm air onto the glue hardening on
her lashes. When he'd finished and was putting the dryer on the

bedside table, she took the opportunity while he was distracted to try and force her eyelids open. She was partially successful, able at least to make out blurry shapes.

For the next two and a half hours Linda was tortured, molested, raped and humiliated with sick games of sexual submission. If she displeased him, or gave the impression she wasn't enjoying herself, he took sadistic pleasure from shocking her. This took place on her fingers, toes and even her nipples. The burns, and the teeth marks where he bit her breasts, left scars, welts and pockmarks over much of her body. He would stop occasionally to watch the TV. Linda started to see it as her ally. He seemed to forget about her while he watched. It was her only respite. It gave her time to think about her predicament and how she might survive.

He would change channels frequently, and when the opening music to the TV show *Dallas*, which she recognised, began playing, his interest peaked. He hadn't said much at all to her for a while, but now he was explaining why he liked the program so much.

'Good old JR Ewing, he doesn't take any shit from anyone, especially women,' he told her gleefully.

She listened, confused, while he began quoting him. 'The world is littered with the bodies of people that tried to stick it to ole JR Ewing!' he repeated, and then another, which made him laugh out loud: 'Never tell the truth when a good lie'll do!'

When *Dallas* was over and he had raped her a second time, he got himself a snack and a soft drink. He didn't appear to be in any hurry to stop abusing her, and he flicked through the channels again on the TV until he found something he was interested in. It was a telemovie with lots of young women in bikinis dancing and gyrating to music. Re-attaching the electrodes on her pinkie fingers, he told her to stand.

'Now copy the girls on the television,' he told her. 'I own you, remember, dance sexy like you mean it, or . . .' He didn't have to finish the sentence; Linda knew he was referring to the torture device and that he would instantly press the switch if she didn't comply with his every demand.

She started moving her hips to the music, holding her arms out in front of her and moving her head from side to side slowly, her blonde hair falling over her face. He was lying back propped up against the pillows with the switch in his hands as she danced for him by the side of the bed. She'd worked out that if she showed him she was suffering or in pain, it excited him and he would try to inflict more of it. She willed herself to be totally compliant, but to express no emotion. He picked up the hairbrush again and held it out.

'Brush your hair slowly while you dance,' he told her.

13

ROLL THE DICE

Linda had reached the point where she couldn't take any more. She had been violated, abused and humiliated, and no longer cared if she lived or died.

'If I'm going to die, I want it to be on my terms,' she thought. 'I don't, won't, can't, survive any more of this.'

The tipping point came when he returned from the bathroom with a razor blade and told her when the TV show finished, he was going to shave her pussy. She had just enough vision to make out that he was staring down at her groin, then looking up to her face expecting to see her react. She bit down on the inside of her lip again to keep a hold on herself, but she was totally freaked out.

'I'm either going to die or I'm going to get out, but that is not happening,' she told herself, looking at the razor blade while she continued to dance and brush her hair as he instructed her. After a while she turned her head and, through the slit in her glued lashes, could see that he wasn't even paying attention to her, he was so absorbed in the television again. The electric cable he'd tortured her with for hours now was plugged into the wall right in front of her, and she knew this was the moment.

The second double bed was between her and the door to the motel room, and she would never make it past him, not in her present condition. The bathroom door was only a few steps away, though, and that had a lock on the inside. She leaped forward, jerked the plug out of the socket and hurled it and the hairbrush at him while she lunged at the bathroom door. She didn't make it. She was slowed down by the wires stuck to her fingers, and he had reacted fast to her movement and batted away the plug and the brush with one hand, while jumping off the bed and grabbing her shoulder with the other. Linda felt him spin her around, and she used every reserve of strength she had left to try and fight him off, pushing back with her arms and kicking her legs out as wildly and as hard as she could. He pushed her down onto the carpet in the space between the bed and the bathroom door, trying to overpower her and smother her flailing limbs. Like two wrestlers, they grappled and grunted. He was obviously much stronger, but Linda managed to hit him a couple of times. He reached onto the bed, snatched up the hairdryer and brought it crashing down three times on the side of her head as hard as he could. The first two were glancing blows, but the third split Linda's scalp, blood splattering everywhere. She had a flashback to a childhood memory of 'play dead' games she used to play with her dad. Playing it now with this sadist, she knew she was gambling with her life. Linda could feel a terrible throbbing pain in her head and guessed that she was bleeding badly. Thinking he had bashed her into submission, he released his hold, leaving her arms suddenly free. Straight away, she raised them up and jammed her straightened fingers towards where she hoped his eyes were. She hit the target, and he gave a sudden yelp and pulled himself violently backwards, clawing at his face.

'Fucking bitch!' he shouted, rubbing his eyes and blinking furiously. Linda pushed up off the ground and stumbled and fell through the bathroom door. She slammed it shut and flicked the catch as quickly as possible, then heard a thud as he hit the door on the other side. She collapsed onto the floor and began screaming as long and loud as she could. He was kicking the door and rattling the handle, but it held. When she stopped screaming, breathless, there was an eerie silence for a moment. Then she heard his voice.

'Open this now and come out or I will kill you.'

'No,' she shouted back and began screaming again.

She didn't stop until her voice started to crack. She was kneeling on the floor, frozen with fear he was going to come for her and get through that door somehow. Another movie crashed into her mind, *Three Days of the Condor*, a thriller that had scared the wits out of her. She remembered vividly the scene where a man thought he'd escaped a gunman, who had been attempting to kill him, by locking himself in a bathroom, only to die immediately when the gunman shot him through the door. Linda jumped straight into the bathtub and lay down flat. She stayed that way, intermittently screaming and banging with her palms on the bath and the wall, for at least half an hour. She couldn't understand why no-one came. She heard him moving around for a while after she first locked herself in, but then there was silence.

'He's waiting for me to open the door,' she told herself. 'He's lying in wait, just pretending to have gone away.'

She picked at the glue on her eyelashes; it was so painful she had to stop as soon as she'd restored reasonable vision to both eyes, which were now red, raw and puffy. She started to feel light headed, the red droplets of blood trickling down the side of the bathtub, forming a sticky red puddle. Her father was a surgeon and the club doctor for the New York Mets baseball team. She'd picked up enough over the years to know that she was weak, sleepy and shivering because she'd lost too much blood and gone into shock. Sooner or later, she realised, she had to open the door and try to get help or she could very well bleed out and die right there in the bath. She climbed out as quietly as she could and tiptoed her way to the door, pressing her ear to the wood. She strained to hear, but all she could make out was the TV playing. After a huge intake of breath to prepare herself, she slowly turned the catch and then opened the door, bracing herself for him to suddenly pounce on her with a knife or something. Nothing happened, and when she had opened it fully, she saw that the room was empty. He had taken everything, including her clothes. She looked around frantically, but every single trace of her was gone, her handbag and purse, her clothes and shoes, even her two rings. She hadn't eaten or drunk anything for hours. Like a struggling marathon runner, she'd hit a wall and was now bone-weary. She locked the door to the room, terrified he would come back. He'd told her about other men. She couldn't take a chance knocking on another door. She couldn't trust anyone, but she needed to raise the alarm. She couldn't go running around outside naked and covered in blood. She pulled back the covers on the clean bed, grabbed hold of the frayed cotton top sheet and wrapped it around herself. She checked out the window. His car wasn't there. She timidly stepped out of the room.

————

Truckie Billy Parrish thought he'd seen and heard it all during his years on the road, but this night at the Glen Oaks Motel took the cake. He'd been dozing in his room, in front of the TV, when a domestic had started up in one of the nearby rooms. A woman, screaming the place down, shouting and banging on the walls. He didn't know if she was high on drugs or what, but it went on and on, and in the end, Billy just couldn't bear to listen to it any longer. He decided he might as well get an early start and quickly packed up his stuff. He was walking across the parking lot towards his eighteen-wheeler truck when he came face to face with a man.

'He was buck naked, scurrying out of the door of the room where that woman had been screaming like a banshee,' Billy would later recall. 'He was carrying an armful of clothes and a briefcase, and as he went past me, he turned and said, "Sorry, man."'

The man trotted off to a car parked nearby, opened the passenger door and dumped everything inside. As Billy hauled himself up into his cab, he heard the car's boot slam and then another door open and close. Moments later the man, still naked, was behind the wheel of the car, speeding off.

Billy shook his head and sighed, then spent the next few minutes plotting his route. He fired up the truck's engine, the smoke belching from the chimney vent, and started doing a U-turn in the lot when he spotted a young blonde girl, completely dishevelled, wrapped in a bedsheet, creeping out of the same room the man had come from. Billy momentarily caught her eye then got out of there as fast as he could.

14

SURVIVOR

WEDNESDAY 21 MARCH 1984
GLEN OAKS MOTEL
BAINBRIDGE, GA

She didn't know what to do next. The truck driver had ignored her, and now she was pretty sure she was hallucinating because of blood loss, exhaustion and trauma. Wild thoughts were swirling around in her head that the motel was some kind of staging area for a prostitution ring, and the men he'd threatened her with would be coming to collect her at any moment. Her muddled brain was processing things in slow motion, she couldn't think straight, all she knew was she had to get away from that room. In desperation she began shouting, 'Help me, please, somebody please help me!' as loud as she could manage. Nobody came. She stumbled around a corner, and though her vision was still affected by the now hardened lumps of glue caked around her eyelashes, she could make out a small swimming pool surrounded by tables and chairs. Next to the pool was a door with a bright yellow light over a sign that said 'Reception'.

Clutching the bedsheet tightly around her shoulders, she limped along as quickly as her bare feet would allow, her big toes red and sore with bits of duct tape hanging off them from the electric-shock torture machine he'd hooked her up to. She reached the door, the sheet trailing on the ground behind her, and turned the handle. It was locked. She was confused and tried again, but it didn't budge. She could see lights on inside, and a couple of shapes moving around, and started banging on the glass. 'Open the door, please, I need help!' she shouted, using one hand to block out the glow from the overhead light as she peered through the window. There was what looked like a young Indian couple with a small child standing behind the reception desk, looking back at her.

'Open the door,' she repeated loudly, but the nervous-looking man shook his head several times, turning between her and his wife, who was holding the child on her hip.

'Open this fucking door!' Linda bellowed. 'I need to call the police, it's an emergency.'

The man stepped forward nearer to the glass and she could just about discern he was wearing a badge that said 'Night Manager'. He looked unsure what to do, confronted with an agitated girl, wrapped in a sheet and bleeding from a head wound, shouting and carrying on like she was high, or something.

'There is a payphone about half a mile up the road,' he told her, pointing his finger over her right shoulder.

It was the breaking point for Linda. Tucking the two ends of the sheet together and jamming them under her chin, she got hold of one of the plastic pool chairs and lifted it up.

'I'll smash this fucking window right now if you don't let me use the phone,' she said, setting herself to swing the chair and glaring at him in a way she hoped was intimidating.

'Okay, okay,' he replied, looking scared and waving his hands up and down as if appealing for her to calm down. He turned and said something she couldn't hear to his wife.

'Where is this, where am I?' Linda asked them as she watched the man take a phone book from the reception desk, open it quickly and begin searching. The couple huddled over the book, ignoring her question. He was flipping the pages and saying something to his wife, and the pair of them kept looking up and giving her worrying glances. The man eventually spoke up and said they were looking for the number of the local hospital, but Linda lost it again and screamed, 'Fuck, just call the police, please.' This time they did.

She was trembling and panic-stricken that other members of the kidnap gang might arrive at any moment, and she begged the night manager to open the door and let her in. Finally, he relented, but he refused to be locked in with her and insisted on leaving the reception door open. A few minutes later, the unmistakable sound of a police siren could be heard in the distance getting louder, and then Linda looked up from the couch where she was huddled and saw the reflection of a flashing blue light bouncing off the water in the pool.

––––––––––

When chief deputy of the Decatur County sheriff's office Jim Morris arrived on the scene, he could see the night manager waiting outside the motel reception, looking agitated. Morris stepped out of his cruiser, put on his hat, hitched his gun belt higher on his waist and, after a quick introduction, signalled for the night manager to lead the way. As they walked, the manager described how a naked girl had barged her way into his reception. His words burbled out so quickly, it was difficult to make sense of what he was saying. Jim, a solid, no-nonsense career cop into his seventh year in the job, knew immediately the injured and mussed-up girl in front of him was not the usual motel victim, bashed by a low-life boyfriend or husband. This girl had been through something altogether different. He took off his hat, sat down next to her and quickly rang Dispatch, telling them to send an ambulance. He didn't press her for any details except her name, address and a contact number for someone he could call. The girl, who said her name was Linda Grober, gave him the phone number of her apartment and the name of two girlfriends who lived with her there; she also gave him the details of her boyfriend, Eddie. He chatted to her quietly, trying to comfort her, but he could tell she still didn't feel safe. She was shaking, telling him over and over that a man had kidnapped her and tortured her.

Morris checked out the room where the girl said she'd been held. He found blood on the carpet and wall, as well as several pieces of duct tape. As soon as he saw the blood, he called for a forensics team. There was nothing in the room that looked like it belonged to the girl, but in the bathroom were a couple of Porsche racing shirts, and a pair of dirty men's socks, embroidered with kangaroos. The man had given a bogus ID when he'd checked in – the car registration number was stolen and the home address was false. The girl claimed she had no idea who he was. The forensics team would take fingerprints, but it was a motel room so there would be lots to sort through. It would take time.

BAINBRIDGE MEMORIAL HOSPITAL
BAINBRIDGE, GA

Linda wondered if the cop was part of the ruse. The night manager and his family had disappeared. Was it a trap? The parking lot started filling up with cars and cops, an ambulance arrived and medics put her on a stretcher, covered her with blankets and connected her up to a drip. It was less than a ten-minute drive to the Bainbridge Memorial Hospital, but for Linda, strapped into the gurney, unable to move and being driven along the highway, it was like she was back in the boot of his car. By the time they pulled into the ambulance bay outside the emergency centre, Linda's bones were rattling and her body was shutting down fast.

Once in a hospital bed, Linda was struggling to cope. She had this idea in her head that she'd be going home later that night, would be back to uni in the morning and would never have to tell her parents what had happened. But everyone was fussing around her, examining her wounds, doing tests and asking if she wanted anything to drink. The paramedics who'd brought her in, the doctors and nurses in the ER, and the police officers milling around at the door, they talked in whispers and kept looking over in her direction, but no-one seemed to know what to say to her.

At that very moment, the curtain dangling halfway around her bed was pulled aside and a nurse with a cheeky smile bustled in, took one look around the room, and then at Linda, and said to her in a thick southern drawl, 'Now don't shit me, girl, what's happened to you?' Until that moment everyone had been treating her with kid gloves, but this chatty and friendly nurse was different and made things seem normal.

She was the first person not to talk to her like she was fragile and about to break, and Linda felt an immediate connection with her. The nurse had a name tag, 'Glenda', on the collar of her uniform. While Linda gave her a summary of the last eleven hours of her life, Glenda took the teenager's blood pressure, watching her face closely while she detailed the main events. When Linda explained how the man had used superglue to stick her eyelids together, Glenda's eyes opened wide and she said loudly, 'Say what. He did what?' It was like a dam had been breached and Linda couldn't stop, and Glenda never stopped listening, encouraging her to talk about things.

'You're in Georgia now, girl,' she said. 'We take the law into our own hands here. We'll get a posse together and hunt him down for sure!'

15

RUNNING

WEDNESDAY 21 MARCH 1984

FLORIDA AND LOUISIANA

Wilder drove completely naked for the first hour. His right eye was puffy and stinging and wouldn't stop watering. She'd be able to tell the cops about his car, but the rego was false and that would delay any BOLO ('Be on the Lookout') alert. He took Interstate 97 south-west, crossed back into Florida and drove through the deserted oak-canopied streets of tiny Chattahoochee, high above the Apalachicola River. After a few kilometres on Interstate 10, he pulled over, climbed out into the drizzly rain and quickly got dressed.

By the time the sun started to rise, a few minutes after 6 a.m., he'd crossed yet another state line and had no intention of slowing down. He stopped off at Baton Rouge, the capital of Louisiana, and got a strong black coffee and some breakfast from a nondescript fast-food restaurant across from a large motel. After wolfing his food down, he washed his hands thoroughly in the bathroom and splashed water in his eye to soothe it. He then went back to his car, took a small screwdriver from his briefcase and sidled over to a Ford in a quiet corner of the lot, removed the plates and then put the Louisiana rego on his New Yorker. He got back behind the wheel and drove for another hour. As he crossed the famous 18-mile Atchafalaya Basin Bridge, Wilder was idly thinking the swampy river below would be the perfect dumping ground. Little chance of someone finding a dead body in the murky brown waters, among the leafy bald cypress, home to plenty of hungry alligators.

He eventually turned into a parking lot in a large shopping mall on the outskirts of Lafayette and approached a few girls, but was dog-tired, knew he didn't look his best and after half an hour gave it up.

DEEN STILL ROAD NEAR LAKE ALFRED
HAINES CITY, FL

Workmen carrying out power-line repairs made the grisly discovery of Theresa Ferguson's body, floating facedown in swampy green water, two days after she had been dumped by Wilder.

The autopsy would reveal she had been beaten ferociously with a tyre iron and suffered extensive bruising to her head and face, and lacerations to her left ear. Theresa's head injuries were so severe, a positive identification could only be made from dental records. Her feet were still bound with rope, and there was also rope attached to her right wrist and around her neck. There was no water in her lungs, which meant she had been dead when Wilder threw her, like a bag of trash, into the water. She was fully clothed in the brand-new outfit she had bought the day he took her. Her gold chain was still around her neck and her two rings, including boyfriend Dan's promise ring, were still on her fingers. Her purse and shoes were never found. Nearby, police also found duct tape and a plastic bag which had previously contained rope, and they were able to trace it back to a purchase from a store in Fort Lauderdale. It was further evidence of Wilder's organisation and meticulous planning. The only small comfort for her parents was the medical examiner's confirmation Theresa had not been sexually assaulted.

Police found the woman who had seen Theresa talking to the bearded man in the mall. She picked Wilder out of a photo line-up. Shortly after Theresa's body was identified, one of her friends got in touch with her stepfather, Don, and gave him one of Wilder's business cards. She told him that Wilder had photographed her two years previously after approaching her on the beach. Don would later write to the Sydney detective Geoff Shelley, who compiled the background reports for the FBI about Wilder's criminal and family history in Australia.

If you are curious as to why I write, it is not as a fellow law enforcement officer, it is because I had a bright, funny beautiful twenty-one-year-old daughter whom I loved with my whole heart. She was Wilder's first confirmed victim. Nothing will bring her back and my insides will live with this hurt until I die, but now there is a desperate need to know more about the man himself.

Meanwhile, the skeletal remains found in Canaveral Groves close to where Wilder was pulled out of the sand by the tow-truck driver were positively identified, from dental records, as pretty 25-year-old Nancy Kay Brown, from Rantoul, a small village in Champaign County, Illinois. She had disappeared on 6 June 1983, while on holiday in Cocoa Beach with her family. She had gone for a walk alone along the beach and never returned. Like Theresa Ferguson and Colleen Orsborn, she was dumped near water. Her skull had been crushed and severely damaged, her carcass picked clean by turkey buzzards. A later audit of Wilder's credit card receipts showed he had stayed at the Howard Johnson Motor Inn at Daytona Beach, for him a short seventy-minute drive from Cocoa Beach, on the day Nancy went missing. Wilder is the main suspect in Nancy Kay Brown's unsolved case.

THURSDAY 22 MARCH 1984
FBI MIAMI FIELD OFFICE
MIAMI, FL

FBI agent John Hanlon stopped by the medical examiner's office – as he did every morning on the way into the office – to check whether the bodies of Rosario Gonzalez or Beth Kenyon had turned up. He was, as always, both thankful and disappointed there was no sign of them. When he reached his desk, there was a mountain of correspondence waiting for him. He removed his jacket and carefully hung it over the visitor's chair opposite. While he cleaned his glasses with a soft cloth he kept in his shirt pocket, he sorted the paperwork stacked in neat piles on his desk into 'important' and 'not so important'.

The most interesting item that Thursday morning were two court-ordered psychological reports on Wilder, which had been prepared in 1977 for a court case in which he'd been accused of sexual battery and orally raping a sixteen-year-old girl. The girl was the daughter of a couple whom Wilder had been working for, building them a staircase in their Boca Raton home. Hanlon leaned back in his chair and, resting his feet on the partially pulled-out bottom drawer of his desk, read through the details of the case. Wilder, thirty years old at the time, had been watching and chatting to the schoolgirl for a week while he worked on the staircase.

One afternoon, the slim, pretty teenager, wearing shorts and a tight T-shirt, her long brown hair in a ponytail, sat down and started telling him about her plans to become a secretary after she graduated. Wilder pounced on the opportunity, told her his boss was looking for a secretary and offered to take her for an interview immediately. The excited teen agreed and happily got into Wilder's car, but they had only driven a couple of kilometres when Wilder claimed engine trouble and pulled over into a quiet, secluded spot. The girl immediately felt uncomfortable and told him she wanted to go home, but as she went to open the passenger door, Wilder flew into a rage, grabbed her arm and slapped her hard across the face.

'You are goddamn going to do what I want!' he said, pawing at her clothes. The teen desperately tried to push him away and babbled that she had an STD, hoping the lie would make him stop. Wilder hesitated a moment, stared at her intently, and told her if she gave him oral sex he wouldn't hurt her any more. After it was over Wilder dropped the girl near her home and drove away quickly. The distraught teenager immediately told her shocked parents what had happened. Wilder was arrested and charged three days later, and a judge ordered that he be assessed by a psychiatrist and a psychologist, ahead of his trial. Hanlon could see that the psychiatrist, Dr Edward Adelson, had interviewed Wilder on New Year's Day 1977.

Defendant states that he was fully aware of what he was doing and was conscious of his motives and actions at the time of the alleged offense. However, he adds, that he cannot understand why he did not restrain himself at the time and why he could not control his impulses to act as he did.

Defendant states that he knew he had committed an offence, realised he was 'in trouble' and wanted to get it over with.

Hanlon, who had already received a full copy of Wilder's criminal history in Australia and the US, recognised that he had lied to Adelson, by telling him: 'He was never arrested for, nor committed any prior sex offenses. He was arrested once in 1968 on a disorderly conduct charge – a misdemeanour.'

Wilder hadn't mentioned his Australian 1963 conviction for the gang rape offence, nor his 1969 arrest for the blackmail and rape of Jane the Sydney student nurse. Instead, Wilder had talked himself up and, in order to avoid jail, had stated his willingness to undergo treatment. Adelson's report continued:

He thinks of himself as generous and allows himself to be taken advantage of because of it. Defendant again reiterates his eagerness for treatment in view of this offense and wants to understand the basis for his recent behaviour, acknowledging he must have a 'problem'.

DISCUSSION AND RECOMMENDATIONS:
Defendant does not appear to be a mentally disordered sex offender. He is not insane and does not have a mental disorder. He has some underlying tension and anxiety and admits to having committed an offense of sexual battery. In my professional opinion, he is not dangerous to others because of a propensity for sex offenses and therefore does not satisfy the criteria of a Mentally Disordered Sex Offender as defined in Fla. Statute 917.13

Hanlon then picked up the second medical report, from psychologist Dr Geraldine Boozer, who spent three hours interviewing Wilder a couple of days after Dr Adelson. She had quickly deduced Wilder was a liar:

As an interview informant he was not altogether reliable; he would offer statements and then retract them, and at times he contradicted himself. He followed directions rapidly and readily, and appears to be of average or better intelligence. Overtly he was at ease.

Father was the boss and the disciplinarian. Defendant was closer to the mother who was warm, too easy and gave them whatever they wanted.

In view of what had taken place in the intervening years since the two evaluations, it was clear to Hanlon that it was Dr Boozer who had got the better handle on who Wilder truly was. He highlighted a number of sections in her report:

He has fantasised rape, with masturbation, to climax, for the past couple of years.

In free situations and when left to his own resources he is also self-assertive, at times passive and at other times aggressive. His reality ties are virtually non-existent and at best tenuous. He shows defective judgement and weak reality testing but has some hold on reality at present. He is tense, fearful, and apt to experience emotional upheavals which result in complete loss of intellectual controls.

At such times he may behave in a manner detrimental to the safety of himself or others.

Special problem areas are those concerning his heterosexual role in this society, and his ability to assume the responsibilities of a dominant, male adult. He has also problems concerning male authority figures, and his ability to identify with that figure . . . he is angry when 'pushed and frustrated' and he is 'ashamed of himself' and yet is ambivalent as he also says he likes himself and would not want to be someone else. He recognizes that he does 'not love others' and is hostile towards controlling persons.

While Adelson had recommended Wilder receive structured and supervised treatment, he had also advised the judge that he didn't believe he was dangerous or a 'mentally disordered sex offender'. Boozer, who hadn't seen Adelson's report, had a very different view.

Defendant does not appear to be brain damaged nor mentally retarded. He does appear to be legally competent, at this time. He is presently sane for purposes of trial. He is also a mentally disordered sex offender as per Florida Statutes. He experiences episodes of extreme emotional upheaval, he is basically psychotic and in need of treatment. When left to his own resources, and under stress, he disintegrates, i.e. regresses. He presents a facade, in an interview, that covers his underlying psychotic orientation. At this time, he is not safe except in a structured environment and should be in a resident program, geared to his needs.

Wilder had broken down when he was interviewed by Boozer, sobbing uncontrollably as he explained why he had raped the girl. 'I was feeling down in the dumps. I saw her and something came over me. I knew it was wrong, but I did it anyway.'

At the time of the offence Wilder had told his attorney, Nelson Bailey, who owned property near his own in Loxahatchee, to keep him from going to prison at all costs.

'I don't want to go to jail, I'm terrified of jail. I will plead guilty and get therapy, anything they want,' he told the lawyer.

Wilder pleaded not guilty and a jury, unaware of the two reports, deliberated for less than one hour before acquitting him of all charges. Wilder had exuded a relaxed confidence in the court-room, dressed in a tailored suit and silk tie, with a gold Rolex visible on his wrist and a friendly smile on his face.

John Hanlon, troubled by Dr Boozer's conclusions about Wilder's psychotic state of mind and his likely violent behaviour if he was challenged while under stress, dictated a caveat that he directed must be attached to every FBI communication issued about the fugitive: 'Subject is armed, extremely dangerous and has suicidal tendencies.'

Hanlon was under orders to stay in regular contact with both Miami and Metro-Dade homicide, so he put his first call of the day through to Nazario for an update, and the nuggety detective told him Wilder's probation officer was beginning the process of revok-ing his probation. Putting the phone down, Hanlon arranged to have both the medical reports he'd read that morning forwarded to the Behavioural Science Unit in Quantico, the bureau's train-ing and research centre in Virginia. The unit had only recently been established, at the behest of President Ronald Reagan, amid mounting concern over a surge in serial murder rates worldwide. As Radford University's Serial Killer Database would later confirm, America and Australia have produced more serial killers per head of population than any other country, so perhaps it was no surprise that Wilder, a product of both, was one of the worst.

The phone rang on Hanlon's desk. It was an FBI special agent based in Fort Pierce, around 200 kilometres north of Miami. He told Hanlon a local physician, Dr Roland Grober, had contacted him that morning about his nineteen-year-old daughter, who had been abducted in Tallahassee and later escaped in Bainbridge, Georgia.

Hanlon's pulse started to race. He stood up suddenly in front of his desk and began twirling the phone cord nervously around his left index finger. 'What's the description of the unsub [unknown subject]?' said Hanlon, his voice tight. As soon as the agent began listing the perp's features – well dressed, slight accent, tall with neat beard and moustache – Hanlon knew it was Wilder. The clincher came when the agent said the doctor had told him his daughter had seen what she thought was an Australian passport in the man's briefcase. Thanking the agent, Hanlon cut the connection and rang Nazario back.

'Grab your coat,' said Hanlon, 'we're flying to Georgia. I'll pick you up in thirty minutes. Bring that photo line-up with Wilder in it; we've had a breakthrough.'

BAINBRIDGE MEMORIAL HOSPITAL
BAINBRIDGE, GA

Hanlon had chosen the experienced Metro-Dade homicide detective to accompany him rather than any of the Miami detectives because he'd been impressed by Nazario's 'get up and go', enthusiasm and long experience. A car picked up the two men from the tarmac when they touched down at Decatur Airport, and a ten-minute drive later, they were walking through the main doors of the hospital. Linda Grober was sitting up in bed when they reached her room. She bore the signs of having undergone a severe bashing, with ugly-looking bruises discolouring her face, her eyes still raw from them being glued shut, and burns on her forearm, caused by the electric torture device. Both men had daughters a similar age to Linda, and were astounded by her resilience and strength, as she talked them through her ordeal in detail. Hanlon had been handed a copy of Jim Morris's incident report the moment they landed, so he had a basic idea of events ahead of the interview, and he didn't waste any time before asking Linda to look at a photo line-up to see if she could recognise the man who had abducted, raped and tortured her. The photo display had six suspects, all very similar with chubby, roundish faces and thinning hair, with full dark beards and droopy moustaches. Each photo was numbered, one through to six. Linda didn't hesitate, pointing immediately to number three at the far right on the top row.

It was Wilder.

While Nazario asked her more questions that would help them understand how Wilder operated and behaved when he drove and checked into motels, Hanlon made the call to Miami that would see the FBI take over responsibility for the manhunt. The US Attorney's office in Atlanta, Georgia, authorised the federal prosecution of Wilder for the kidnapping and rape of Linda, setting bail in his absence at $5 million. John Hanlon was now calling the shots as the special agent investigator in charge. His next call was to chase up a search warrant for Wilder's house in Boynton Beach, and his third call was to arrange for Nazario to be seconded to the FBI for the duration of the case.

WHITTAKER INVESTIGATIVE CONSULTANTS
MIAMI, FL

That day, Ken Whittaker Jr received the first of several calls over the next week from bureau agents wanting to debrief him further about Wilder and his knowledge of the serial killer's background.

'I helped them, of course I did,' said Ken, 'but I also told them, "Now you fucking want my help. It's a little late!"'

16

UNFINISHED BUSINESS

**UNSUB; TERRY DIANE WALDEN, 00:MM DALLAS FBI
FILE 7-2203**

THURSDAY 22 MARCH 1984
BEAUMONT, TX

Wilder had put another state between himself and the police, but he spent a frustrating and ultimately fruitless afternoon approaching female students on the campus of Lamar University, a ten-minute drive from downtown Beaumont, Texas. Until recently an oil-rich boom town on the west bank of the Neches River, 50 kilometres inland from the Gulf of Mexico, Beaumont was now struggling. The world energy crisis and collapse in the price of crude oil had hit hard, with petroleum companies shedding workers and closing rigs, the real estate market collapsing and a string of banks going under.

Money was tight, especially for students, and Wilder had been confident of success, but the new 'butterfly' he chose to join his collection wasn't impressed when he approached her. Terry Diane

Walden was a blonde and slim 24-year-old young mum with hazel eyes, which twinkled mischievously whenever she laughed. Terry was as American as apple pie, a shy nursing student, who was into fashion, made a lot of her own clothes and worked part time at St Elizabeth Hospital. She had married John Walden, a divorcee, six years ago. He had been a few years ahead of her at Forest Park High School. Four years ago, she had given birth to their daughter Mindy, and not long after that, Sabrina, John's nine-year-old daughter from his first marriage, had come to live with them.

That Thursday lunchtime she told John, a night-shift worker at the local Goodyear plant, all about a strange and unsettling encounter she'd had at the university campus. She described how a bearded man, in his late thirties, wearing a smart suit and carrying a camera and a briefcase, had stepped forward as she walked between classes and asked her if she was interested in a modelling career.

'He offered me a free photo shoot if I went with him right away,' she told her husband. 'I told him, "No way," and just carried on walking, but he just wouldn't take the hint. He started following me and said if I went with him to his car, he'd show me samples of his work. He was really pushy and said I could earn a lot of money doing nude modelling. In the end I called him a dirty pervert.' Perhaps unusually for someone so attractive, Terry hated having her photograph taken – she'd even struggled with her own wedding photos – and Wilder's offer hadn't interested her at all. Terry would have given Wilder an even bigger piece of her mind, but one of her friends had walked over at that moment and started chatting, and he had hurried away towards the car park.

———

Although he was seething, Wilder still wasn't ready to call his game off for the day, but he realised he would have to get off the campus in case the potty-mouthed bitch reported him to security. He left and drove fifteen minutes across town to the Parkdale Shopping Mall. He approached one young woman, using a stolen business card in the name of Lynn Ivory, claimed he was doing a photographic shoot for the mall and asked would she pose for him, because she was pretty enough to be a model. She turned him down and felt so uneasy about the conversation, she rang the mall to check his story. They told her there was no such photographic project underway, so she called Crime Stoppers.

BEST WESTERN GULF COAST INN
WINNIE, TX
While Hanlon and Nazario were flying in the FBI jet back to Miami, Wilder was checking into room 234 at the Gulf Coast Inn on Interstate 10 at Winnie, Texas, 40 kilometres from the shopping mall where he'd just lucked out.

FRIDAY 23 MARCH 1984
PALM BEACH COUNTY SHERIFF'S OFFICE
PALM BEACH, FL
Tom Neighbors sat in morning roll-call nursing a mug of steaming hot coffee. There were about twenty detectives in the briefing room, representing all the various units, from homicide to auto theft, to vice and missing persons. The latter was Tom's current deployment. His remit covered child and sexual abuse, runaways and abducted children, challenging and difficult work even for an experienced cop. The duty sergeant was standing at the podium talking through the major overnight incidents and developments. The daily BOLO list

had been copied and was handed round the room as the meeting got underway. Tom, sitting towards the back, had a cursory look at the tightly typed piece of paper, headed 'Hot Sheet', and almost dropped his coffee when he saw item number two. The colour drained from his face as he read it through carefully.

#2 AM.FCICI,NIAM4.
FBI MIAMI IS REQUESTING WE RELAY BOLO FOR STATEWIDE BROADCAST IN FLORIDA AND GEORGIA. REQUEST ALL AGENCIES BOLO REF KIDNAP SUSPECT. SUBJ VEH 1973 CHRYSLER, 4DR, WHI W/ BLU VINYL TOP, BEARING UNK FL TAG W/PALM BEACH CO DESIGNATION, VIN/CS41T3C360116. VEH POSSIBLY DRIVEN BY CHRISTOPHER BERNARD WILDER, W/M, DOB 031345, 5 FT 11 IN, 180 LBS, BRO HAIR, BLU EYES, FOR WHOM FEDERAL KIDNAP WARRANT ISSUED 032284. SUBJ SHOULD BE CONSIDERED ARMED AND EXTREMELY DANGEROUS. IF CONTACT IS MADE REQ YOU CALL FBI MIAMI, 305-XXX-XXXX, IMMEDIATELY.

Even though the sergeant was still addressing the room, Tom grabbed at the desk phone and hurriedly dialled his home number. There was a knot in the pit of his stomach, and it seemed to be growing as he counted the rings, whispering to himself, 'C'mon, Dana, pick up, please pick up.'

He was gripping the receiver so hard his knuckles were white, but on the fourth ring there was a click, and his wife was speaking. Tom let out a huge sigh, looked up at the ceiling and closed his eyes briefly. If he hadn't been in a room full of people, he might have cried at that moment. He swallowed hard and said to Dana, 'Chris Wilder, what's his middle initial?'

'B,' she replied, surprise in her voice. 'Why are you asking?'

'Know what the B stands for?' said Tom, fearing her answer.

'I think it's Bernard,' she told him.

The detective slipped into his working voice, talking slowly and clearly so there was no doubting the seriousness of what he was saying. 'The FBI is looking for him for abduction and murder. I know you have a lot of his stuff in the house; I want you to go right now and lock all the doors. Then go and get your gun, and if he comes to the door, don't open it. If he tries to come in, shoot him.'

'He's meant to be coming at ten o'clock to pick up his racing suit,' said Dana in a tight voice.

Tom was on the police radio to the nearest patrol car before he'd even hung up. Knowing Dana was safe, he rang one of his best buddies, who was the local FBI agent in the West Palm Beach field office. They had worked several cases together over the years.

'Jim, I'm looking at a BOLO. You're looking for Christopher Wilder?' he asked.

'Jesus, Tom, I've been up all night, the entire bureau has been up all night looking for this guy,' replied Jim Cavanaugh, a former Texas cop, who was now a bureau-trained hostage negotiator. 'The whole of the FBI has been mobilised,' he added.

'I know the guy,' broke in Tom.

'How do you know him?' said Jim, thinking Tom might have interviewed or arrested him previously.

'Well, he's been inside my house many times,' explained Tom, describing how Dana did all the monogramming for his racing suits and knew him very well as a customer.

'You need to come over here,' said Jim. 'We're going to have a meeting in about an hour, and I need you there.'

Before picking up his jacket and gun, Tom delayed leaving for five minutes while he ran Wilder's name through the department's records system, which covered everyone arrested and processed through the jail, including all the neighbouring counties. When Wilder's name popped up time and time again, even listing all his known aliases going back almost ten years, the detective was gobsmacked.

Like Ray Nazario, he was quickly seconded to the FBI for the duration of the investigation and Tom and Dana became, for the next few days, the bureau's primary intelligence source on Wilder.

LAMAR UNIVERSITY
BEAUMONT, TX

Yesterday had been a wash-out for Wilder, but instead of moving on, putting more kilometres on the clock and increasing the distance between him and the police, he cancelled his plane ticket back to Australia then headed back to Lamar University in Beaumont.

GINGER BUSH'S OFFICE
BOCA RATON, FL

Tom Neighbors immediately teamed up with Jim Cavanaugh, and a little later that morning they were knocking on Ginger Bush's consulting room door. The detective knew Ginger quite well from his role in missing persons, where he regularly dealt with kids who had run away after being victims of sexual abuse. They had worked together on several difficult cases and had built up a good working rapport. The meeting went awkwardly at first, when Ginger told Cavanaugh that she couldn't discuss confidential details about her patient with the FBI. The agent, who had been up all night and was in no mood for niceties, cut right across her.

'Well, listen here, doctor,' he replied, 'this patient of yours is a serial killer. He's on the run and murdering young women as we speak, so you might want to revisit that answer.'

'Ginger,' said Tom softly, 'I think you should consider co-operating here. These are very unusual circumstances and we really could do with your help to find Chris.'

The therapist looked at him and then over at Agent Cavanaugh, thought hard for a few moments, and then nodded. She took the two men quickly through her most recent contact with Wilder, and it was soon clear to them she knew his demons and darkest secrets better than just about anyone. Tom had the best rapport with her, so it was agreed he would return once the therapist had been able to review all her notes, and then work with her to build up a detailed report on his likely behaviour pattern.

LAMAR UNIVERSITY
BEAUMONT, TX

Terry Walden got up at 7 a.m. to prepare Sabrina for school, and organise breakfast and packed lunches for everyone. She told John she was going to do some shopping after her classes and would be back between 1 and 2 p.m. She then got in her car, drove Mindy to her day-care centre and headed off to campus. Witnesses later recalled seeing Terry at 11.30 a.m., walking through the university student centre, running late for her last class, with a pile of books in her arms.

This morning when he'd arrived, he'd recognised her burnt-orange 1981 Mercury Cougar XR7 straight away and had parked right next to it. Then it was just a question of waiting, and he'd always been a patient man.

WILDER'S HOUSE
BOYNTON BEACH, FL

FBI agents, Metro-Dade homicide detectives and forensic scientists executed search warrants at all of Wilder's properties, as well as on the Cadillac he was driving when Beth Kenyon disappeared, starting with his home in Boynton Beach. Traces of blood were found on the carpet in the den, on the living room wall, on a bedroom nightstand and on two knives in the kitchen. The repairman who had fixed the smashed sliding door the day after Beth Kenyon disappeared was found and interviewed, and he confirmed there was 'a hell of a lot of blood'.

A police source told Edna Buchanan, 'Something went on in the house, somebody or something got cut up bad in there.'

Wilder had claimed one of his dogs had cut its paw, but when agents later examined all three dogs none of them had suffered any kind of injury. However, Wilder's scrupulous insistence on supervising the blood clean-up and the type of chemical he'd insisted the cleaners use had done the trick. 'We can't even say for sure it was human or animal,' said Edna's contact, revealing blood tests had proved inconclusive.

Eighteen items were seized, including photographs of naked and near naked women, a seatbelt with silver-grey duct tape on one end, stacks of personal papers, three tubes of superglue and a number of air-conditioner filters, but forensic examiners were never able to directly tie any of them to any of Wilder's known or suspected victims.

After finishing up their interview with Ginger Bush, Neighbors and Cavanaugh drove over to Mission Hill Road to assist with the search of Wilder's house. It was Neighbors who would make one of the most important discoveries, and by accident. The children's cartoon TV show *Scooby-Doo* was popular at the time, and the teenage characters and their hero canine were always finding hidden chambers in haunted houses by knocking on the walls to discover the entrance. Neighbors jokingly began tapping the walls in one of the guest bedrooms and was surprised to hear a hollow thud. He tapped a couple more times, harder this time, and the whole wall sprung open. Inside was what agents later dubbed the 'torture chamber', a small room full of whips, chains, manacles and painful-looking sexual sadism devices. They would eventually track down and interview some of the models and escorts whom Wilder had paid to be photographed in the room. The girls, all teenagers, said as long as he paid them and they didn't get hurt, they didn't mind, as they knew there was a lucrative market for those kinds of sadomasochistic photographs.

As news spread locally about Wilder, it was discovered that the Boynton Beach Kmart had a package of photos that Wilder had dropped off to be developed. When they were printed, they were found to be pornographic images taken in Wilder's house of women and children in various stages of undress. In many, the young faces appeared trancelike, as if they were under the influence of narcotics.

The torture room discovery was important because it fitted with what Bush had told them about Wilder's obsession with dominating women sexually, physically and mentally. The therapist had given them a list of the five main fantasies that Wilder talked about obsessively.

1. Selling white girls into slavery.
2. Keeping a woman captive. (Wilder had mentioned *The Collector* movie and book a number of times, and several copies were found during the search.)
3. Twisting the nipples of his captive.
4. Sticking his fingers into her rectum.
5. Kicking and hitting her with powerful blows.

BEAUMONT, TX

At 5 p.m., the day-care centre called John Walden to say Terry hadn't arrived to pick up their daughter, Mindy. John checked the university and shopping mall for her car, but there was no sign of the Mercury Cougar. An hour later, he reported his wife missing. Police checked with hospitals and medical centres, and put out a call to all patrol cars to keep an eye out for her car.

17

CATCH ME IF YOU CAN

SATURDAY 24 MARCH 1984
SEBRING INTERNATIONAL RACEWAY
SEBRING, FL

It was the dead of night under a waning moon. A dozen heavily armed FBI agents, with local police backup, surrounded the sprawling competitors car park in the middle of the racetrack. Caravans, campers, motorhomes and brightly coloured tents covered almost every blade of available grass at the historic Sebring road circuit. The famous 12 Hours of Sebring sports-car endurance race was due to begin later that morning, and Wilder was scheduled to compete alongside his co-driver Van McDonald in car number fifty-one. The agents crept forward silently until they reached their target, a large Winnebago registered to the Wilder racing team. Confident they had the advantage of surprise, the signal was given and several agents began pounding loudly on the door and windows. McDonald explained Wilder wasn't racing at Sebring because he'd claimed, 'He had to go and sort something out back in Australia.'

McDonald, a maths and physics high school teacher, had been the chief instructor when Wilder attended a Friday night school for car-racing beginners. When McDonald's own co-driver said he was moving on, Wilder had offered to rent his car for the season, and they had ended up becoming drive partners along with DeFranceschi in long endurance events, each taking two-hour shifts at the wheel. McDonald and his wife had stayed at Wilder's home, he'd been to Thanksgiving dinner with their family, and they considered him to be a genuinely nice guy. McDonald's grandmother had even gone so far as to say Wilder was the nicest young gentleman she had met for many years. Van recalled many nights out with Wilder during the two years they had raced together. 'You always had elegant times when you went out with Chris Wilder,' he told an FBI agent. Now he listened in disbelief as the lead agent told him his racing buddy was wanted for murder, probably multiple murders. Everyone in the team when they were told the news about Wilder had the same reaction: 'Bullshit.' They continued with the race in the hope that Wilder would try to watch his car compete, but when the starting flag went down, Wilder was actually 2000 kilometres to the west in Dallas, Texas.

FBI MIAMI FIELD OFFICE
MIAMI, FL
John Hanlon had moved his workstation to the middle of the large open-plan FBI office. The previous night he'd dashed home to kiss his wife, hug his kids and pack enough clothes to last a few days. He was standing on the balls of his feet, hour after hour, as information and leads streamed in from other field offices, FBI forensic laboratories, Interpol, local law enforcement departments and agents across the US. If he wasn't reading the never-ending

stream of teletype messages from the bank of machines along the side wall, he was dictating new leads to be chased, based on incoming information. He also had to write regular reports for the director in Washington, who was keeping a watchful eye now that this was well on the way to becoming one of the biggest stories in the country. Wilder was moving about and covering ground so quickly that by the time the FBI was getting information on any telephone or credit card charges, he was long gone.

Edna Buchanan's large Saturday morning story in the *Miami Herald* contained almost as much information on the case as Hanlon knew himself. Beneath the headline 'Aussie Racer Sought in Kidnapping of Model', and accompanied by a photograph of Wilder, the article started:

> A wealthy Australian-born race car driver and amateur photographer – the suspect in the baffling disappearances of two Miami models – is now the target of a massive FBI manhunt in the kidnapping of a third model, federal agents said Friday.
>
> The suspect was identified as Christopher B Wilder, 39, a Boynton Beach electrical contractor and self-described modeling agent. He is on probation for a 1980 rape in Palm Beach and faces trial in Australia next month for another rape.

The article covered the abduction of Linda Grober from the Tallahassee shopping mall, although she wasn't mentioned by name, and said the FBI was 'looking at Wilder' for the murder of Theresa Ferguson, whose body had been found on Wednesday.

In addition, it carried quotes from the colourful and flamboyant attorney Barry Cohen, who said he was acting for Wilder. Cohen was a high-flying criminal defence lawyer based in

Tampa Bay with a penchant for wearing vests, braces and two-tone shoes. He was the go-to man if you were in serious trouble and had deep enough pockets to pay for the best legal representation. Cohen didn't have to reveal any information, but he told Edna Buchanan that Wilder:

> '. . . denies any responsibility whatever for the models' disappearances, and any criminal episodes here in Florida.
>
> The mere fact that he was involved in something previously doesn't mean he's responsible for something like this. He's certainly not a fugitive to my knowledge.'

Cohen said he was confident the parole violation against Wilder was also a mistake and would soon be dismissed. Hanlon ignored Cohen's comments. He was more concerned that, even though Wilder had cashed in his plane ticket back to Australia, he would still attempt to flee the country, so he sent out a message to all field offices directing them to parking lots at major airports to check for the Chrysler. The bureau was chasing scores of leads. All over the country, from New York to California, agents were tracking down and interviewing Beth Kenyon's friends and former boyfriends, Wilder's family, his ex-girlfriends and car racing associates, poring over his home telephone records and those from the motel rooms where he had stayed, travel agency bookings, old credit card statements and the personal papers seized from his home.

Wilder's probation officer was staggered by all the developments surrounding the polite and charming felon he had been responsible for monitoring. 'I never had the vaguest idea he would do anything like this,' he said. 'I'm not so sure there isn't someone else out there just like him, and no-one has any idea who he is.'

DALLAS, TX

By Saturday lunchtime, Wilder had clocked up 450 kilometres driving north-west, through miles and miles of national park forest. He took a toilet break in the small town of Crockett, named after the American folk hero from the Battle of the Alamo in the Texas war of independence, then headed off towards Dallas. It had turned into a beautiful day. Wilder wound his window down and leaned his left elbow out, letting in a blast of the warm wind with its strong scent of sweetgum and hickory. He cranked up the music and tried to relax.

Wilder eventually stopped at a shopping mall in Dallas, which was staging a media event to advertise the forthcoming Dallas Grand Prix coming to the city in early July. His name and photograph were all over the Florida newspapers and TV bulletins, but there had been little coverage so far in Texas. Terry Walden's body still hadn't been discovered. Wilder, wearing tan slacks, cowboy hat and boots, was coolly watching the early stages of the race on television at a motorsport event, surrounded by unsuspecting reporters. Tiffany Conley, a leggy promotions model working at the Dallas event, caught Wilder's eye. He asked her if she wanted to go on a date with him that evening when she finished work, but the model, although giving him her phone number, said she couldn't. Wilder tried to contact her twice afterwards, and days later, when she saw publicity about the case, she contacted the FBI and told agents about her encounter. Hanlon, frustrated at the lost opportunity, got agents to monitor her phone and the shopping mall in case Wilder returned. He never did.

DELRAY BEACH, FL

Two days after Linda Grober escaped from Wilder, Zeke Kimbrell still hadn't grasped the full nature of the crimes mounting up against his missing partner. It was Saturday afternoon when he noticed three black SUVs following him. When he parked in his driveway and went inside, the vehicles all pulled up and parked in a line across the street. Horrified, he watched from the front window as dark-suited men began taking up positions everywhere, climbing into neighbours' gardens and hanging out of trees. About forty minutes later, there was a loud knock on the door and a man's voice said, 'This is the FBI.'

'Come in, it's open,' Kimbrell shouted out. He was sitting at the dining room table where he could see the entrance.

Several agents, led by Hanlon, came through the doorway, guns drawn. 'Are you carrying a weapon and are there any in the house?' shouted one of the agents.

'No, and no,' replied Kimbrell calmly.

While one agent patted him down, the other agents started moving through the house.

'This is a federal warrant giving us the right to search your property,' said Hanlon, sitting opposite Kimbrell at the polished red cedarwood table. 'Where is Chris Wilder? And I would advise you to think very carefully before you give me some bullshit answer.'

'I don't know, all you guys and that prick of a private detective scared him so much, he just ran,' said Kimbrell.

For the next hour Hanlon grilled Kimbrell. 'If you're holding back information you could be charged as an accessory,' he told him.

Hanlon threatened that could mean a firing squad or a hanging, depending on the state he was tried in. Kimbrell protested his innocence, but Hanlon wasn't convinced and wanted him to take a lie detector test. They took him to a hotel in West Palm Beach and hooked him up for three hours. He passed.

Afterwards, each time he picked up the phone, Kimbrell knew his call was being monitored by the FBI. If he stepped outside, even to go to the shops for a newspaper, he looked for agents following him. He'd come clean about giving Wilder his credit and business cards and was instructed not to cancel them under any circumstances.

HOLIDAY INN SOUTH
OKLAHOMA CITY, OK

After Tiffany Conley turned down his dinner date offer, Wilder cut his losses, got back on the road and headed out of Dallas and north across the Great Plains, the flat, mostly treeless land broken up only by the giant billboards advertising everything from Coke to the local real-estate schmucks. Wilder ignored them and the tall grasses and shrubs, huge ranches and herds of cattle in the distance. He was hungry and wanted to get to Oklahoma City as quickly as possible.

He pulled into a Holiday Inn just before 9 p.m. He checked in using Kimbrell's credit card and recorded that he was driving a Ford with a (stolen) Louisiana licence plate. Before going to his room to catch up on the race at Sebring, he went to the hotel restaurant and ordered the largest New York strip steak they had, with pepper sauce. He ate quickly and dined alone, lost in thought. When he finished his meal, he left a good tip and headed upstairs.

<h1 style="text-align: center;">18</h1>

WRONG CRITERIA

UNSUB; SUZANNE W LOGAN, 00:MM FBI FILE

SUNDAY 25 MARCH 1984
HOLIDAY INN SOUTH
OKLAHOMA CITY, OK

Wilder had stayed up late, listening to coverage of Sebring and checking all the late-night news bulletins for any items about himself. He did the same in the morning, going to a nearby diner for breakfast and to read the newspapers. It was gone 10.30 a.m. when he checked out of the hotel. He was in a terrible mood. That should have been him crossing the finishing line at the racetrack – it was his team, his car, he was paying for it – but, once again, when anything good happened, it was taken away from him. He'd make someone pay for it today. He stopped at a Texaco service station, filled up Terry Walden's Cougar and set off for the Penn Square Mall.

PENN SQUARE MALL
OKLAHOMA CITY, OK

Suzanne Wendy Logan, a 21-year-old secretary at American Fidelity Insurance, was shopping when she disappeared from the centre sometime in the afternoon. The attractive English-born young woman, with shoulder-length brown curly hair, hazel eyes, double-pierced ears and long red painted fingernails, had only been married nine months. That morning she had driven her husband, Brian, to his work at the Save-A-Stop supermarket in the city, given him a quick hug and a kiss, and arranged to pick him up at the end of his shift. Halfway back to her home, she'd stopped off at the mall. Suzanne, wearing a light-coloured sweater, short-sleeved blouse and blue jeans, had a few things she wanted to do. She picked up a wristwatch she'd had on layby, bought herself a soft drink and then spent a while visiting several stores looking for a gift for her mother. She had an appointment later that afternoon to meet a friend about becoming a Tupperware dealer, but it wasn't until 4 p.m., so she was in no hurry.

Suzanne had always harboured the dream of a career as a model. Three years ago, after leaving high school, she had put together her own photographic portfolio and had attended the Tulsa Modeling School near where she lived with her ten-year-old brother and parents, Jack and Agnes Duchan. Not long afterwards she had met Brian, got married and moved to Oklahoma, but although her dream had been put on hold, it hadn't gone away, and the couple had recently been considering moving to Dallas, so she could pursue a career in fashion design.

I-35 INN

NEWTON, KS

Mid-afternoon, Wilder crossed another state line into Kansas and then drove another couple of hours north, past neat parcels of farmland on either side of the road, through Wichita to the small town of Newton. He checked into room 30 of the I-35 Inn using the name Larry Kimbrell, gave a false address in Riceland, Louisiana, and listed he was driving a Ford with the stolen Louisiana licence. He requested the very end room, which was nearest the car park. He put the hairbrush in the bathroom, sprayed the bedsheets with *Tatiana* by Diane von Furstenberg, connected the electric torture machine to the bedside socket, cut lengths of rope and duct tape and found an aerobics channel on the television. He then thoroughly washed his hands, calmly lay back on the bed and watched television.

As the sun went down, snowflakes falling lightly outside, Wilder sneaked outside and carefully opened the boot of his car. Suzanne was lying terrified, gagged and hogtied. He went through the same careful process that he had gone through with Linda Grober, zipping her into the blue sleeping bag and then smuggling her into his room. Suzanne then, just like Linda, endured hours and hours of physical and mental torture. The only difference between Suzanne's tragic story and Linda's was Suzanne didn't escape.

BRIAN AND SUZANNE LOGAN'S HOUSE
THE VILLAGE, OK

Brian Logan first started worrying when Suzanne didn't pick him up from work. He finally gave up waiting for her and went home, thinking she must have forgotten what they had arranged. When there was no sign of her at home, Brian really started to panic. He didn't waste any time, going straight to the police to report her missing.

The Oklahoma police department received an average of sixty missing person's reports every week, so Suzanne was only one in a very long list. Despite Brian and her parents calling several times a day to harass them about progress, the police, in truth, did little to search for Suzanne.

'Unless there's some kind of information that a crime has been committed, there's not much we can do,' Sergeant Don Helm told them at the time.

It would be three days before police found Suzanne's car at the mall where she'd left it.

'They gave us the impression that they weren't interested,' said Suzanne's father, Jack, a design engineer. 'They told us that she was a runaway, that nothing could be done, and she must have decided to leave her husband.'

Helm said later he'd discovered the couple had money troubles and added, 'There was enough indication that there was a serious domestic problem. It just seemed very, very improbable to me that, if an aggressive type of abduction had taken place on a Sunday afternoon at the mall, it just seemed to me there would have been some witnesses.'

With, in his opinion, no evidence of a crime, Helm argued he couldn't place Suzanne on the National Crime Information Center's database. She didn't meet the database's criteria, he said.

Later, Brian would tell the FBI that he was certain his wife would not have hesitated in going with a well-dressed, well-spoken man with expensive camera equipment, who was full of compliments and offering to make her a model.

MONDAY 26 MARCH 1984
IRRIGATION CANAL
BEAUMONT, TX

Three days after she'd vanished from the campus of Lamar University, Terry Walden's body was found at 8.30 a.m. by a council worker checking an irrigation canal. She was facedown in the water, wearing a pink jacket and jeans, the top two buttons undone. Her bra was found nearby. The autopsy revealed she'd been gagged with tape and tied up at the ankles and wrists with three different types of rope. Wilder had struck her violently behind the left ear, beaten her severely about the face and stabbed her three times in the left breast, puncturing her lungs and heart. All the blows had been inflicted while she was bound up and defenceless. There was sticky adhesive residue around her mouth from the duct tape, and one of the stab wounds was so violent it had gone clean through her body, while another had fractured two of her ribs. Wilder had then watched the young mum bleed to death before removing the ropes binding her and heaving her body into the quaggy canal water. The medical examiner could find no direct evidence that Terry had been tortured or sexually assaulted, but he couldn't rule it out either.

A major search involving scuba divers, a Texas Rangers spotter plane and officers on the ground turned up a strip of silver duct tape on the muddy bank, a set of shoe prints nearby and tyre tracks that led to a farm road that connected to the highway, but they could not find any trace of Terry's car. The case attracted huge local publicity, and a schoolgirl came forward days later to tell detectives how on the afternoon Terry went missing, she had seen a white Chrysler being driven down the dirt road. She described a bearded man driving and said a woman, wearing what looked like a red coat, was sitting in the front passenger seat with her head leaning against the window. Approximately an hour later, the girl said, the same car returned, driven at high speed this time, and the man was alone. It was thirteen days before Wilder's white Chrysler, by then on every police watch list in the country, was discovered by a patrol cop, in a car park up the street from the Barbizon Modeling agency in Beaumont, a fifteen-minute drive from where Terry was found. The licence plates had been removed. The car was examined at the FBI lab, and Theresa Ferguson's hair fibres were found on the passenger seat and traces of her blood in the boot.

MISS TEEN USA PAGEANT
MEMPHIS, TN

Margaret Gorman became the first Miss America in the inaugural pageant held in Atlantic City in 1921. Over the following decades the pageants would become a core part of US culture. They would be controversial for many reasons, mostly for being sexist and racist, but their popularity would never diminish. Many young American girls dreamed of being crowned Miss America, and a huge chunk of US female stars got their first taste of fame in a beauty pageant, including Oprah Winfrey, Halle Berry, Katy Perry and even the highly respected journalist Diane Sawyer.

But for sexual predators like Wilder, they were also the perfect place to find beautiful victims, and Memphis City police, security personnel, public relations staff and the FBI were taking no chances on the eve of the Miss Teen USA beauty contest. They had a crisis meeting to work out how to protect many of the country's most beautiful girls, if Wilder attempted to attend the event. It was decided to go ahead with the pageant, but all contestants would be housed in one location and escorted by chaperones at all times. No press or photography sessions would be allowed unless cleared in advance by the organisers or public relations officers who, along with the security guards, were all issued with photos of Wilder.

MILFORD LAKE

JUNCTION CITY, KS

One thousand kilometres north-west of Memphis, Wilder, who had been driving along tapping the steering wheel to the Eurythmics hit 'The First Cut', was disposing of his latest victim.

Milford Lake, a giant man-made lake in the Flint Hills west of Junction City, had over 250 kilometres of shoreline and was the fishing capital of Kansas.

Wilder pulled over, close to the lake next to a tallgrass prairie.

Suzanne was still breathing and bleeding heavily when he dragged her out of the car and along the rocky soil, dumping her under a cedar tree. He made no attempt to hide her body and at 1.50 p.m. she was found by a passing fisherman. The medical examiner estimated her time of death as between 11 a.m. and 1 p.m. Suzanne had been raped, brutishly beaten and stabbed several times with a 20-centimetre knife. Her wrists were wrapped with silver duct tape, and there were small cord ligature marks on her wrists and ankles. A short length of braided nylon cord, tied into slipknots, was found in the back pocket of her jeans. There was a 2.5-centimetre scar at the hairline in the centre of her forehead, and as well as the circular black bruising above her right eye, there was a small cut to her upper right eyelid, bruising to the bridge of her nose, deep bite marks on both breasts and more bruising to her legs and buttocks. There were also six or seven small puncture wounds in the centre of the spine above her buttocks, an example of the torture cuts Wilder liked to administer with the tip of a sharp knife.

Suzanne had died from a violent stab wound below the left shoulder blade, inflicted by a 3-centimetre-wide and probably double-edged knife that passed almost entirely through her body.

She was dressed, wearing her sweater, short-sleeved blouse and blue jeans, but no shoes or underwear.

A little over an hour after getting rid of Suzanne, Wilder was tucking into a steak and salad at the Conoco Travel Center restaurant in Junction City, chatting to the waitress like she was an old friend.

I-35 INN
NEWTON, KS

The cleaner entering room 30 of the I-35 Inn thought there must have been some mistake. The room she had been rostered to clean was immaculate and looked as if it hadn't been used. The bed was made, the drinking glasses were lined up perfectly next to the bathroom sink, and the towels all hung neatly on the racks. The only sign of occupation were Suzanne's long brown locks of hair in the wastebasket.

DENVER, CO

Eighteen hours after abducting Suzanne Logan in Oklahoma, Wilder was heading west, crossing the border into Colorado on his way to Denver, the state capital. It had been nine days since he'd left Boynton Beach for the final time and 3500 kilometres, seven states, one kidnapped student and three murdered girls later, neither the FBI nor local police were close to finding or catching him.

19

CATCH UP

**MAJOR CASE 57 00: MIAMI, SUB: CHRISTOPHER
WILDER, FBI NUMBER 5417 25 L2**

TUESDAY 27 MARCH 1984
FBI MIAMI FIELD OFFICE
MIAMI, FL

John Hanlon was sick of playing a losing game of catch-up with
Wilder. The FBI agent's every waking hour was being dominated
by the chase for a fugitive who was moving too fast. That morning's
Miami Herald hadn't helped his mood. Five days into the fugitive
hunt, the article as good as said the FBI had no idea whatsoever
where Wilder was.

FBI SEARCHES FOR RACER, TWO MODELS

Federal agents from California to Florida combed the country Monday in search of Christopher B. Wilder, the suspect
in the disappearances of two Miami models, the kidnap-rape
of a 19-year-old coed and the murder of another young

woman whose body was found dumped in a Polk County swamp. FBI spokesman Chris Mazzella was quoted saying the massive manhunt was intensifying by the day.

'This is a nationwide manhunt,' he said. 'We are checking every part of the country.'

Hanlon was receiving every police report of a young woman going missing in the southern states. A telex arrived with details of a female body discovered near a lake in Kansas. Hanlon had been keeping one piece of information about Wilder's modus operandi secret from the press in case of copycat killings. The identifying fact, which would tell them if she was a Wilder victim, was the silver-grey duct tape that Linda Grober had described and which had been found at the Theresa Ferguson and Terry Walden crime scenes and seized from Wilder's house. The formal identification of Suzanne Logan from dental records would take many more days, but immediately upon reading about the silver duct tape around the victim's wrists, Hanlon just knew Wilder had claimed another victim.

He couldn't set up roadblocks when he didn't know which state Wilder was in. As things stood, he wasn't even sure what car he was driving, never mind the licence number. Telex messages warning about Wilder with his description were going out regularly to every police department in the search area, which was widening every hour they failed to find him. While the media blitz on the story had produced leads and brought forward witnesses, Hanlon decided to switch his focus away from worrying what Wilder was doing and try to get ahead of him, by figuring out where he was going next. The race at Sebring had been the first attempt at the strategy but had proved fruitless. The Miss Teen USA pageant was under lock-down with everyone briefed about Wilder, and the Toyota Grand

Prix taking place in Long Beach, California, on the upcoming week-end would also be targeted by FBI agents, who would be undercover in the pit lane and photographers area.

AMERICAN FAMILY LODGE MOTEL
WHEAT RIDGE, CO

Wilder had left a motel in Denver early that morning. His prac-tised routine was never to check out at reception but simply to leave the key in the door. He found somewhere to have a scram-bled eggs breakfast and then drove half an hour east to a gun shop in Aurora, Colorado.

He took quite some time browsing before he picked out and test fired a Colt Trooper MK III Magnum revolver with a 15-centimetre stainless steel barrel. He paid for the six-round double-action weapon, used by many law enforcement agencies, with cash and stocked up with ammunition. Wilder asked the gun shop owner for the most powerful round and was very keen to take the .357 Magnum jacketed hollow-point bullets the owner recommended when he explained that they were engineered to deliver the most amount of damage possible.

When he'd paid and left the shop, Wilder climbed behind the wheel and cranked up the car's cassette player. He punched through several Eurythmics tracks until he found the one he was looking for, 'No Fear, No Hate, No Pain (No Broken Hearts)'. Driving along, singing loudly, he cradled the gun in his right hand.

It was 6.30 p.m. when he next surfaced, at the American Family Lodge Motel on the other side of Denver in Wheat Ridge, on the western side of the Great Plains close to the southern edge of the Rocky Mountains. Before he got out of the Cougar, he reached for his new gun, where he kept it, under the driver's seat, close to hand. He signed in as Mr Kimbrell and paid $24.54 for the room on his business partner's credit card.

WEDNESDAY 28 MARCH 1984
RED RIVER INN
RIFLE, CO

After a couple of nights in unmemorable motels on his route west through Kansas and Colorado, Wilder next drove 140 kilometres up to Colorado's biggest ski resort at Vail, 2500 metres above sea level in the middle of the White River National Forest. Although it was a chilly 4 degrees, the ski season would be over in less than four weeks and there wasn't much snow. Wilder didn't care; he had no plans to go skiing. He was just passing through. After stopping for a brief lunch, he was back in the car for the long stretch of Interstate 70 down the other side of the mountain. His route took him alongside the Colorado River, through the cattle ranches to Rifle. Wilder got out of the car and stretched his legs, looking out to the wide blue sky, sprinkled with clouds, the mountains in the distance a constant and impressive backdrop. He yawned heavily and strolled through the parking lot to the reception desk of yet another featureless motel. The clerk at the Red River Inn didn't even bother looking up as he booked Wilder in under the name of LK Kimbrell, Wilder once again charging the $23.82 to his old business partner's credit card.

20

FLASHDANCE

UNSUB; SHERYL L BONAVENTURA, 00:MM DENVER FBI FILE 7-1441

THURSDAY 29 MARCH 1984
MIAMI HERALD
MIAMI, FL

The latest *Miami Herald* report on the state of play in the search for Wilder didn't do a lot to reassure readers an arrest was on the horizon.

The fruitless manhunt for Wilder continued Wednesday amid conflicting reports. Chris Mazzella, Miami FBI spokesman, said the last confirmed sighting of Wilder was when he allegedly fled the Glen Oaks Motel in Bainbridge, Ga., on March 20, leaving an abducted coed screaming for help and pounding the walls, barricaded in the bathroom.

The FBI says Wilder was reportedly driving a 1973 Chrysler New Yorker.

But Miami police spokesman Michael Stewart said Wilder was last seen in Boynton Beach Friday in a silver 1983 Cadillac Eldorado.

'I don't know what they're talking about,' Mazzella said.

GINGER BUSH'S OFFICE
BOCA RATON, FL

Palm Beach detective Tom Neighbors had a second meeting with Ginger Bush. He was on his own this time, and the therapist was as good as her word, providing a lot of information and background material about Wilder that would help the bureau better understand how he operated. Back at the Fort Lauderdale FBI field office, Neighbors helped Special Agent Jim Cavanaugh type up a seven-page report, which was forwarded immediately to John Hanlon in Miami.

In an effort to project what actions Wilder will take at this point, Bush suggested that he will continue his activities and attempt to pick up various women at shopping centers and beaches primarily, utilizing the ruse of being a photographer.

His forms of assault will be in all probability more frenzied and violent, due to the pressure he is under from the investigation to locate him and media coverage. Wilder will become more and more aggressive due to the fact that he can not maintain the pattern he has set for himself over the past several years in connection with his picking up of women.

She expressed her opinion that Wilder's actions will be 'unpredictable' in the sense that his movements and possible destinations will be random rather than of a structured means. There exists the possibility that Wilder will return to this area, in as much as his cars and dogs have become of great importance to him, but she advised that her initial opinion would be that he would flee the area, shaving his beard and moustache, and possibly obtaining a form of disguise (hair piece).

MESA MALL

GRAND JUNCTION CITY, CO

He was on the road early for the spectacular drive down the western slope of the Rocky Mountains. A couple of hours after setting out, Wilder arrived in Grand Junction, the biggest town in western Colorado, and treated himself to a good breakfast. Back in Denver, as well as buying the gun, he had done some clothes shopping and visited a couple of modelling agencies, where he had picked up some new props for his act.

———

Sheryl Lynn Bonaventura, an eighteen-year-old blue-eyed, blonde aspiring model, had a job at the leather goods store at the mall, but she wasn't working that day so was casually dressed in a white sweatshirt with a 'Cherokee' logo, faded blue Levi jeans, rust-coloured cowboy boots with silver-toe caps, gold rings and gold bracelets. Sheryl had gone to the mall to pick up some last-minute toiletries for a ski trip she was taking with her best friend, Kristal Cesario.

One of Sheryl's friends later recalled cycling past the mall and seeing Sheryl sitting in her bright yellow Mazda RX-7, outside Mervyn's department store, talking to a man fitting Wilder's description. The friend said she saw the man, bending down, talking to Sheryl through the open driver's window.

———

By 3.30 p.m., when Sheryl hadn't arrived, Kristal became worried and called Sheryl's parents, James and Sandra. James, who like Wilder's father had served many years in the US Navy, took a drive over to the mall and discovered his daughter's Mazda parked where she had left it, outside the store. The sunroof was open and her favourite sunglasses were lying on the dashboard. He knew immediately something was very wrong.

Sheryl's family had moved to Grand Junction four years earlier, when she was in ninth grade. Not long after she had started dating Terry, whom she met at high school. He encouraged her modelling ambitions and Sheryl had done several professional shoots. Terry kept one of the photographs in his dorm room at college, which showed Sheryl in a leotard with leg warmers and headband, sitting with her hands on her knees, just like Jennifer Beals in the hit movie *Flashdance*, which had been released the previous year. Wilder had been obsessed with the film, according to Kimbrell, and had seen it at least seven times.

Kristal said later that she had no doubts Sheryl would have been very excited at being approached by a photographer and asked to take part in a shoot. 'We were always dreaming of someone coming up and saying, "You're found. You're *Vogue* material," she said, adding, 'I would have done it.'

Witnesses reported seeing Sheryl with a bearded man a few hours later at a diner in the historic mining town of Silverton, 200 kilometres away. The table waitress who served them described to FBI agents who swooped on the sleepy backwater how Sheryl seemed nervous and talked a lot in a singsong, childlike voice. The host realised afterwards when being questioned by agents that the teenager had made a point of giving her full name and that they were headed for Las Vegas. Although, at the time, she had thought the encounter a little awkward, she hadn't picked up on the warning signals and never for one moment guessed the smiling and well-dressed man with the teen was cradling a .357 revolver under the table with the barrel trained on Sheryl.

When Wilder was paying the bill with cash, Sheryl chatted to the diner owner and said her grandfather, Nick Bonaventura, had once worked in the town as a baker, making donuts. The owner recalled how the tall man, in cowboy boots, with blue eyes and a neatly clipped moustache, stood right beside her, smiling, as Sheryl bubbled over with nervous energy and enthusiasm. He even bought a sack of donuts to take with them when they left.

Eighty kilometres further along Route 550, past Haviland Lake and the San Juan National Forest, Wilder turned the Cougar into the Thunderbird Lodge at Durango in La Plata County, Colorado. He signed into the motel as Mr and Mrs WL Kimbrell, from Riceland, Louisiana, but, when later quizzed by police, no witnesses could recall seeing his 'wife'.

FRIDAY 30 MARCH 1984
MIAMI HERALD
MIAMI, FL
The *Miami Herald* ran Edna Buchanan's interview with Zeke Kimbrell.

'Turn yourself in and quit running. It's useless,' he appealed to his fugitive friend. 'Please. Go to the nearest police station and face this thing; try to get it out in the open. And if you do know anything about those missing girls, please tell the police and their parents where they are.'

Kimbrell, like a lot of people who thought they knew Wilder, was still having difficulty reconciling the man he'd worked alongside for eight years with the cold-blooded serial killer who was now being revealed. 'He was always a happy-go-lucky, easy-going guy. Nothing bothered him. He was always smiling, laughing, joking around,' said Kimbrell, clearly bewildered.

'This guy would stop in the middle of the road if a turtle was crossing the street. I've seen him get out in traffic and dodge cars to carry the turtle to the side of the road where it would be safe. He sends money to funds like Save the Whales and Save the Seals. He has three big, shaggy, hairy dogs.'

Edna asked Kimbrell if the man he knew was capable of the crimes he was wanted for.

'Right now, I don't know. I pray to God he'll turn himself in. I pray to God every night that those missing girls are alive,' he told her.

FOUR CORNERS MONUMENT
TEEC NOS POS, AZ

Sheryl made it through the night with Wilder. The next morning, they left the motel at 9 a.m. and ninety minutes later stopped at the Four Corners Monument, a visitor attraction where the states of Arizona, Colorado, New Mexico and Utah come together, the only point in the country shared by four states. It was a hot day, with just dust and scrub as far as the eye could see, but Sheryl was glad to get out of the car and stretch her legs. Wilder told her that if she tried to raise the alarm or escape, he would shoot her. He reinforced the point by taking the gun from under the driver's seat, showing her the fully loaded chamber and describing what the hollow-nosed bullets did to a human body on impact. He removed one and pressed the cold metal against her cheek threateningly, telling her to act naturally with him and look like she was enjoying herself.

Wilder, camera in hand, then forced her to mingle with the tourists as he took photographs and gave her instructions on what poses to strike. He was intoxicated with the total domination he now exerted over Sheryl, parading her in front of the unwitting tourists, who had no idea the nervous-looking young woman smiling for the camera was a terrified kidnap victim.

Afterwards, Wilder drove another 300 kilometres, then checked them both into the Page Boy Motel on the north Arizona border. Sheryl sustained a second night of torture and brutal sexual assaults.

SATURDAY 31 MARCH 1984
UTAH–ARIZONA BORDER
US ROUTE 89

When Sheryl's missing person's report landed on John Hanlon's desk, his heart sank. He knew immediately Wilder had struck again. Sheryl's friend, who had seen Sheryl speaking to a bearded man at her car, picked out Wilder's photograph, as did a girl he had approached in the mall earlier that afternoon. There was further confirmation when agents interviewed staff at the Page Boy Motel, and a maid remembered seeing Wilder with a young girl, whom she picked out as Sheryl when shown photographs by investigators.

The bureau was able to follow Wilder's progress through Colorado from the use of Kimbrell's Visa card, with which he paid for accommodation over successive nights in Denver, Wheat Ridge and Rifle, but it took twenty-four to forty-eight hours for the transaction details to be made available by the card issuer, and Wilder covered ground so quickly, by the time agents scurried out to a motel, he was long gone.

Meanwhile, Wilder had woken up at dawn on that Saturday and decided he was tired of Sheryl. It was time to kill her. Shortly after leaving the Page Boy Motel, on a lonely stretch of road on Route 89, he stopped the car, tied her up, put duct tape over her eyes and mouth and shoved her in the boot of the Cougar. He then drove for 120 kilometres through the desert, pulling off the road at a remote beauty spot not far from Kanab in Utah, just north of the border with Arizona. The small town on the north rim of the Grand Canyon, founded in 1870 by ten Mormon families, had been dubbed 'Little Hollywood' due to its long history as the filming location for many famous movies, including *Stagecoach*, *The Lone Ranger* and *Planet of the Apes*.

Wilder stabbed Sheryl several times, and shot her in the chest with the gun he'd purchased four days earlier. He dumped her in the scrub at the foot of a small tree.

21

HIDING IN PLAIN SIGHT

**UNSUB; MICHELLE KORFMAN, 00:MM LAS VEGAS FBI
FILE 7-683**

SATURDAY 31 MARCH 1984
SAWTELL, NSW, AUSTRALIA

Wilder's father, Coley, picked up the ringing phone at the family home in Australia. It was Edna Buchanan calling long distance from the *Miami Herald*, wanting to know if his son intended to return to Sydney for his trial in three days' time. Coley gave the persuasive reporter the only public comment he would make about his son during the entire manhunt. 'We really don't know if he'll be in Sydney on Tuesday, I can't speculate,' he said. 'We really don't know how much trouble he is in. We've heard from some pretty reliable sources that it may not be as bad as the newspapers are painting it.'

AMBASSADOR MOTEL
LAS VEGAS, NV

After disposing of Sheryl Bonaventura's body, Wilder drove 320 kilometres through the desert to Las Vegas and checked into the Ambassador Motel, paying $38.52 for the room with Kimbrell's Visa. As usual, he supplied false details about the make, model and licence plate of his stolen car.

SUNDAY 1 APRIL 1984
THE *GRAND JUNCTION DAILY SENTINEL*
GRAND JUNCTION, CO

The front page of the *Grand Junction Daily Sentinel* featured a photograph of Sheryl, who was still missing, her body not yet discovered. Her father, James, was quoted: 'You can't imagine what an awful feeling it is not to be able to do anything but sit here and wait. We're coping the best we can. Everyone has been just great, especially the police, who started looking into it instantly.'

The story described a man posing as a photographer who had been seen talking to Sheryl but did not mention he had been identified as Wilder.

AMBASSADOR MOTEL
LAS VEGAS, NV

Wilder checked out of the Ambassador Motel at 10 a.m., stepping out into the bright, glaring sun. He walked over to his car, which was parked under a few listless palm trees. Usually, Wilder was obsessive about leaving his motel and hotel rooms immaculately neat and tidy, but this time cleaners found a number of abandoned items, including a tan bra, tan panties, nylons, black strapless slip, blow-up doll and a dildo. That evening, he relocated to another cheap motel on the Vegas strip, taking an end room with a car park space directly outside.

Meanwhile, Edna Buchanan had been investigating Wilder's criminal history and business affairs. The *Miami Herald* carried her story:

Christopher Wilder is a rich man. Palm Beach property records show he owns $338148 in real estate, including 10 acres of land in Loxahatchee, a lot in Wellington, homes in Lake Worth suburbs. He owns the building at 314 NE Third St., Boynton Beach. It houses his Sawtel Construction Corp., and Sawtel Electrical Corp., which he founded two years ago with a partner. The two firms employ 70 persons.

Wilder lives in high style, or did, until St Patrick's Day when he packed a suitcase, checked his dogs into a kennel and fled.

The story revealed courthouse records showed Wilder had been building a property portfolio through complex real estate deals since the late 1970s, when he'd first arrived from Australia. He also had eight traffic violations against his name, mostly for speeding, and in 1979 the Internal Revenue Service had taken out a claim on his property for an unpaid federal tax bill for $22000. It was withdrawn the following year after he settled the debt.

Wilder's next-door neighbour Maria Izzo had also spoken to Edna, telling her, 'I can't believe he's done these things.' She described seeing his muscled physique in the garden and said that he had a 'sense of class and style' and liked to wear sleek leather jackets when he went out for the evening. 'He's got probably everything a girl can dream about in a man,' she told the reporter.

SEVENTEEN BEAUTY PAGEANT
MEADOWS MALL
LAS VEGAS, NV

It should have been one of the most heavily policed public events in the country, but the fugitive at the centre of a nationwide FBI-led manhunt casually strolled into a beauty pageant hosted by teen magazine *Seventeen,* at the Meadows shopping mall, 6 kilometres west of downtown Las Vegas.

Although Wilder must have known that there was a high chance organisers and security staff at the well-publicised competition would have been supplied with his photograph, he made absolutely no effort to disguise himself. He sat right next to the stage in the designated photographers area, unmissable in white slacks and brown jacket over a plaid shirt, a chunky gold watch on his wrist, watching the dress rehearsal intently and humming along to the Eurythmics song 'Sweet Dreams (Are Made of This)'. He wasn't carrying his Pentax, but he did use one of his stolen business cards to gain access to the stage area. A photograph capturing Wilder, relaxed with his legs crossed and with his hands in his lap leering at one of the young contestants in a white miniskirt, was discovered later and handed to the FBI.

During the competition, he approached and chatted to eight contestants with an invitation to photograph them for a free model portfolio. Several expressed an interest, but they were not keen on leaving the competition early, so Wilder made arrangements to meet them afterwards, outside the Caesars Palace Hotel.

The eighth girl he approached was seventeen-year-old Michelle Korfman, a blue-eyed Boulder City High School student taking part in her very first beauty pageant. Taller than most of Wilder's victims, at over 175 centimetres, with long dark curly hair, Michelle was quite shy and hadn't shown much of an interest in modelling before, but she had taken this competition seriously and asked her wealthy father, who had managed a casino in Las Vegas before moving the family to nearby Boulder City five years earlier, for money so she could submit professional photographs with her entry. It was a smart move because, of the hundreds of girls who applied, Michelle was one of only fifteen invited to compete in the finals.

An accomplished piano player and member of the school volley-ball team, Michelle, popular with her peers, also excelled at her hobby of photography and had recently become interested in politics, tell-ing her mother she planned on becoming president by the time she was thirty-five. Michelle had driven to the event that morning in her 1982 chocolate brown Chevrolet Camaro, a gift from her father for achieving consistently high grades and staying out of trouble at high school. The car had the personalised number plate 'TOMISH' ('To Michelle') inside a black frame with the tag 'Daddy's Girl'. Michelle was wearing white boots, blue jeans and a light-coloured blouse.

The pageant was finishing up when Wilder introduced him-self with one of his stolen business cards and told Michelle she had a big future in modelling if she wanted to pursue it. He told her he was looking for a blue-eyed model for a big magazine assignment he was doing, and she didn't hesitate to accept his invitation to pose for him. A number of witnesses, including two of her fellow con-testants, saw Michelle leaving the mall with Wilder at 4.15 p.m.

Sunset in Las Vegas was less than half an hour later, at 4.39 p.m., and the only other sighting was later by a former California highway patrolman, who reported seeing Wilder at the wheel of Michelle's car, on the California side of the state border with Nevada, 70 kilometres away.

GOLD KEY MOTEL
LAS VEGAS, NV
It was never clear what Wilder was doing heading away from Las Vegas with Michelle's vehicle, but later that evening he was back on the Las Vegas Strip, checking into the three-storey, eighty-room

Gold Key Motel, which advertised 'luxury at no extra cost', with a large heated swimming pool and coffee shop attached. It was directly opposite the Flame Steakhouse restaurant, where Wilder dined alone. He sat near the window with a view of the motel and his car, the Mercury Cougar, parked outside his room. If Michelle was still alive, and there is every possibility she was, she was lying, hogtied and blindfolded, in the boot while the busy Vegas nightlife passed by, and Wilder, the self-styled conductor of events, sat and watched.

KORFMAN HOUSE
BOULDER CITY, NV

When his daughter hadn't returned from the beauty pageant in time for dinner, Tony Korfman and his wife, Linda, started to worry. They rang around all of Michelle's friends and her boyfriend, but no-one had even known she was entering the beauty competition, never mind having heard from her. It was shortly before midnight that Tony rang the police to report her missing. The family was well known and respected in the city, as Tony was the manager of the Gold Strike Inn & Casino, and detectives were quickly assigned to the case, conducting several searches of the house over the following days, focusing on Michelle's bedroom in particular. They didn't find anything to suggest she had been thinking about running away from home. They were stumped as to why her Camaro hadn't been found at the shopping mall where the pageant had been hosted.

MONDAY 2 APRIL 1984
GOLD KEY MOTEL
LAS VEGAS, NV

A porter waved a cheery good morning to the guest emerging from the motel's very end room, whom he'd noticed checking in the night

before. He saw the well-dressed man, who he noticed had shaved his
moustache overnight, walk to the drugstore next door.

J EDGAR HOOVER BUILDING
935 PENNSYLVANIA AVENUE
WASHINGTON, DC

An urgent telex message from the director of the FBI, William H
Webster, went out to all bureau field offices. The four-page directive
outlined that 'Christopher Bernard Wilder, FBI number 541 725
L2, is a suspect or a prime suspect in multiple abduction/murder/
kidnapping matters.' The director reiterated what the Behavioural
Science Unit had already told John Hanlon: based on all the information sent to them, their opinion was that Wilder was going to
kill again.

GOLD KEY MOTEL
LAS VEGAS, NV

At the very moment the FBI directive was being disseminated and
processed in field offices, Michelle Korfman, following a long night
of torture and appalling sexual violence in the Gold Key Motel
room, was now bound, gagged and immobile in the boot of the
Cougar. Her chances of survival beyond the day were bleak in
the extreme.

TUESDAY 3 APRIL 1984
CAESARS PALACE HOTEL
LAS VEGAS, NV

Two days after she'd vanished, Michelle Korfman's car finally surfaced in the rear parking lot of the Caesars Palace Hotel, hidden
in a similar way to how Beth Kenyon's had been. The vehicle was

locked and the boot was empty. Police found a dried flower, similar to the ones presented at the pageant, sitting on the dashboard. Wilder had clearly returned Michelle's car to the car park after abducting her, leaving the flower to deliberately taunt his pursuers.

The story ran on the front page of all the local newspapers and led all the evening news bulletins. Police officers flooded the Meadows Mall to interview shoppers, and eventually a witness was found, who remembered seeing a very pretty girl, who looked like Michelle, with a bearded man in white slacks and a brown jacket, leaving the dressing room area at the Broadway department store on Sunday afternoon. When she was shown the FBI photo line-up of suspects, days later, she didn't hesitate in pointing to Wilder's picture. The bureau was doing an efficient and clinical job in tying Wilder to every missing or murdered girl, building a strong prosecution case against him in each instance, but it was still nowhere near arresting him.

PROUD PARROT MOTEL
LOMITA, CA

Two days and 500 kilometres after abducting Michelle Korfman from the beauty pageant, Wilder drove through the heavy traffic of South Los Angeles and checked into the Proud Parrot Motel in Lomita. He registered as Larry K Kimbrell and gave a false home address in New Mexico. He paid for the $35-a-night single room with Kimbrell's credit card and stopped at a drink dispenser on his way to his room. A member of staff who heard banging and went to investigate found him in a temper, angrily vandalising the machine, hitting it with his fists and swearing because it had failed to eject the brand of soda water he wanted. Wilder's eyes were red raw and bloodshot, and he looked as if he hadn't slept for days.

———

In the weeks following her disappearance, Michelle's boyfriend moved in with her distraught parents, and they all worked together, organising search parties in the desert and scouring by plane the sparsely populated border area between Nevada and California. 'We will keep searching,' said her mother, Linda. 'We search in the desert, we search in the mountains, in the water. We'll never stop looking for Michelle.' Tony Korfman spent more than $100000 on the search and printed 25000 posters, which were sent to shopping malls across the country. He offered a substantial reward and flew a film crew to Florida to record an appeal from Wilder's brother Stephen, who had arrived from Australia.

Michelle's badly decomposed body wasn't discovered until 11 May, forty days after she'd disappeared. Two cyclists discovered it in the Angeles National Forest, off the stretch of road between Las Vegas and Lomita. It lay unclaimed in the county morgue for another month, listed as Jane Doe #39, before finally being positively identified from dental records on 15 June. A broken-hearted Tony, speaking two days later on what was Father's Day, said, 'I think the worst image I probably have to deal with is the last five minutes of her life. I know in my mind she was yelling for me, and that was the time I couldn't be there.'

The medical examiner ruled Michelle's cause of death as asphyxiation due to her face being forced into the ground, with dirt and soil blocking her larynx and trachea so she couldn't breathe. Wilder had used his bare hands to kill her. There was no indication of knife or gunshot wounds, but the examiner believed she had been the victim of blunt-force trauma.

DANGEROUS PROFILE

TUESDAY 3 APRIL 1984

GINGER BUSH'S OFFICE

BOCA RATON, FL

Palm Beach detective Tom Neighbors had returned several times to talk with Ginger Bush now that the therapist was being fully co-operative, and he worked with her and FBI agent Joseph Del Campo to develop a psychological profile concerning Wilder's 'current and future modus operandi'.

Wilder looks for full bosomed, lightly clothed, sensuous look-ing, young (fifteen – twenty-three) naive, white females. Wilder is extremely intrigued by female breasts which apparently had its roots in the voyeurism of his mother (who was well en-dowed) during his adolescent years. Wilder avoids women who drink and are sophisticated, strong willed, and aggressive. He needs to dominate and therefore women in this category would not be appealing to him.

Wilder preys on impressionable highly motivated women

who are looking for something – namely that 'big break into modelling'. Wilder seeks women who are not well dressed, believing well dressed women are more sophisticated and less apt to believe his line.

Wilder had recently told Bush that he prefers to wear the baseball/racing driver type hat as he feels he is more attractive to women that way.

Bush believes Wilder is completely out of control and is a high suicidal risk, especially if faced with an apprehension situation. Wilder's rationale is that he cannot/must not get caught. Bush revealed that Wilder has a tremendous self-hatred, is completely remorseful of the acts that he has done, but at the same time is resentful of women.

FBI MIAMI FIELD OFFICE
MIAMI, FL

While Hanlon now had a comprehensive profile of Wilder, it hadn't yet brought him any closer to tracking him down. Wilder met the FBI's criteria of a serial killer, having murdered a minimum of three to four victims with a 'cooling off' period in between. Wilder had known Rosario Gonzalez and Beth Kenyon, had chosen them specifically, planned their deaths carefully and hidden their bodies so they wouldn't be found. However, all his other victims – Colleen Orsborn, Theresa Ferguson, Linda Grober, Suzanne Logan, Terry Walden, Sheryl Lynn Bonaventura and Michelle Korfman – were unconnected and had been chosen randomly. Wilder didn't identify with or feel sympathy towards any of them. As far as he was concerned, *he* was the victim, who had been dominated, controlled and ultimately rejected by women his whole life, and now this was his time to call the shots and to decide who would live or die.

Wilder was what the bureau's psych experts called a process-focused serial killer, meaning he got enjoyment from torture and the slow death of his victims. His motive was power, to control women and dominate them, as he had when he'd choked Linda Grober in the boot of the car, releasing his grip just short of strangling her and later threatening to take her back to the 'brink of death' if she didn't obey him. He became obsessed with enslaving young women. The inconsistent discipline from Wilder's parents when he was growing up was considered significant: his father, when he was around, was a nasty, alcoholic bully who took a belt to him, while his mother was too soft, the combination leading him to hate authority figures and manipulate women. The lack of a strong bond with his parents and siblings, and the constant relocating, led to Wilder becoming isolated. He filled the void with increasingly violent fantasies of domination. Addicted to and spurred on by these sexual fantasies, Wilder became classic serial killer material, a charming and intelligent white male in his thirties who was highly mobile and prepared to drive huge distances to satisfy his cravings. Dr Gary Moran, a professor of psychology at Florida International University, later described Wilder as a narcissistic sexual psychopath with impulse disorders. 'A person like that has a very good insight into his motivation,' said Moran. 'He knows what causes his disorder, but the problem is he can't control it. The man simply can't hold back. He probably sits there and sweats for half an hour. It builds up and he goes overboard.

'The world is full of people who are borderline narcissistic psychopaths,' continued Moran. 'Go to any singles bar in Miami and you'll find a whole damn room full of these people.'

John Hanlon wasn't big on trying to get inside Wilder's head. It didn't really interest him, and he didn't think it was the key to finding him. As far as he was concerned, Wilder was a predator who didn't deserve to draw breath.

WEDNESDAY 4 APRIL 1984
THE *MANLY DAILY*
SYDNEY, AUSTRALIA

Wilder was now an international fugitive and making front-page headlines around the world. His failure to appear in Manly Court on Sydney's northern beaches, the previous day, on charges of kidnapping and raping two fifteen-year-old schoolgirls, saw another warrant issued for his arrest. The *Manly Daily* dedicated the whole of its front page to the story, under the headline 'WANTED – Kidnap, rape suspect jumps $400000 bail'.

23

FINDING A KEEPER

UNSUB; TINA M RISICO, 00:MM LOS ANGELES FBI
FILE 7-2430

WEDNESDAY 4 APRIL 1984
THE *GRAND JUNCTION DAILY SENTINEL*
GRAND JUNCTION, CO

The headline in the *Daily Sentinel* newspaper in Colorado read 'Sex Offender Linked to Grand Junction Case'. The accompanying story reported Wilder was the chief suspect in Sheryl Bonaventura's disappearance as well as the abduction murders of six other women, and that he was a past sex offender who had been freed on a bond. Sheryl's mother, Sandra, was furious when she read that. 'I hope his lawyer never sleeps another night in his life,' she said. 'Just because Wilder has money, he's out.'

DEL AMO FASHION CENTER
TORRANCE, LOS ANGELES, CA

Sixteen-year-old Tina Marie Risico arrived at the Del Amo Fashion Center determined to find a summer job. She'd rung her boyfriend,

Billy Wattles, earlier that morning to say she was catching the bus to the mammoth mall after her morning lessons at Shery High School, 4 kilometres away. At 165 centimetres tall, with shoulder-length blonde hair and pale blue-grey eyes, Tina certainly stood out in her pink pants, pink heeled shoes, green sweater and red purse. As she arrived at the Hickory Farm gourmet food store to fill out an application form, a man standing just outside the front door smiled at her and said, 'Hi.' He was well dressed in a check shirt, slacks, cowboy boots and a brown leather jacket. Tina smiled, said 'Hi' back to him and went inside. Twenty minutes or so later she'd lodged her application, had a successful preliminary interview and was leaving the store when she heard a man's voice behind her: 'Miss, wait a minute, I want to check something.' It was the same man who had greeted her earlier. He asked if she could wait a few minutes while he went and looked over her application. Tina assumed he was one of the store management team and stood patiently waiting for him to return.

When he came back, he asked if he could talk to her about something while they walked, and as they strolled through the mall, he told Tina that he was the manager of a local modelling school and thought she would make a very good model, if she was interested. He briefly showed her a business card and assured her she could earn a lot of money. Tina could scarcely believe what she was hearing. She had a pretty face but had never imagined herself pursuing a career in modelling, as she wasn't very tall and, at 61 kilograms, didn't have a particularly trim figure. The man must have read her thoughts.

'I'll send you to the John Powers Modeling School to help you lose some weight. First, though, I want to drive you just around to take some photographs, this afternoon, if possible, and then talk to your mother about what we can do to launch your career.'

They had reached the exit to the shopping centre, and the man reached into his jacket and pulled out a brand-new $100 bill, which he put into Tina's hands.

'You're now officially being paid as a model,' he told her, 'and there is a lot more where that came from, if you do what I tell you.'

'I've never heard of the John Powers Modeling School,' Tina said.

'I'll show you where it is on the way to Huntington Beach, where I can take some photographs of you.'

Tina eagerly agreed – she'd noticed the expensive gold watch and rings he wore – and didn't hesitate getting into the rust-coloured Mercury Cougar when he stepped forward and opened the passenger door for her. His new approach of flattering them into the car was tiresome and harder work, but anyone watching the girl get into the Cougar of her own accord wouldn't have given them a second glance.

HUNTINGTON BEACH, CA

Wilder drove 6 kilometres to the South Bay shopping centre in Redondo Beach to show Tina the modelling school he'd mentioned, but he didn't bother stopping. Instead, he turned south and followed the highway for thirty minutes until he reached the northern end of Southern California's beach culture capital Huntington Beach, well away from the busy pier area opposite Main Street. The most popular surfing beach in the state, Huntington was known for its year-round ocean swells. Wilder had caught a few waves there himself in the past. He found a parking bay and walked with Tina down to the sand, carrying his camera and a woman's white jacket he brought from the car. Once on the beach he handed her the jacket and told her to put it on, but to take off her sweater and bra first. Tina went and got changed in a public toilet, and then slipped off her heels and posed for him on the beach in her bare feet.

After shooting a roll of film, Wilder said he needed more photos in a mountain setting, and when the excited schoolgirl didn't object, they walked quickly back to the car. Wilder drove east through Irvine and up into Trabuco Canyon in the foothills of the Santa Ana Mountains. During the journey, he repeatedly told Tina that it was important she did exactly what he told her if she wanted to be a successful model, get her photograph on the cover of magazines and earn lots of money.

He saw what he was looking for and pulled off the narrow canyon road onto a dirt trail. After about 200 metres, when he was sure they couldn't be seen by passing cars, he pulled up, cut the engine and turned to face the girl.

'I want you to take a really good look at that mountain up ahead,' he told her, indicating out the front windscreen. As she peered out at Trabuco Peak, towering 1406 metres above them, he reached under his seat. He watched her turn her gaze back to him, and saw the jolt of confusion and terror spread across her face as she found herself staring into the barrel of a gun.

'I've killed before, and I won't hesitate to kill you if you don't obey me,' he told her. 'Your modelling days are over, bitch. Now open your mouth.'

He forced the gun barrel halfway into her mouth, cocked the hammer with his thumb, and showed her his finger resting alongside the trigger.

'Stay absolutely still or I will kill you right here,' he told her, his eyes blazing with excitement as he curled his index finger around the trigger. After a few seconds he yanked the gun from her mouth, leaned forward and pulled a large black hunting knife with a serrated edge from inside his right cowboy boot. He placed the tip of the 20-centimetre blade under the girl's chin and, applying just the right amount of pressure, ran it slowly down her throat, between her breasts and down to her stomach. He didn't draw blood, but the knife left an ugly red line on her skin. The girl didn't flinch or utter a single word.

'You are going to do exactly what I say, and you will do it immediately. Nod if you understand.'

She nodded once, barely moving her head, her eyes wide and filled with fear and uncertainty.

'If you disobey me, I will not hesitate to kill you, and I will leave your body here to be picked clean by the wildlife. Say "Yes, sir" if you understand.'

'Yes, sir.'

'Good. Get undressed, your pussy is mine now.'

24

RULES OF THE GAME

Tina Risico's life to date had been anything but easy. She hadn't been born to a rich daddy or parents who doted on her, her upbringing had been difficult and about as far away from a fashion catwalk or a photography studio as it was possible to get. Her mother, Carol Sokolowski, had been an unmarried sixteen-year-old when she gave birth to Tina in Inglewood in south-western Los Angeles County. She wed the baby's father, Jasper Joe Risico, soon afterwards, but he abandoned his bride and his newborn daughter after only a few months. Left to raise a baby on welfare and handouts, Carol fell in with a motorcycle gang and led what she described as a 'hardcore life'.

When Tina was nine, Carol moved them to Mendocino County in northern California where they lived in a basic trailer, on the edge of town. Her ex never paid child support, and Tina grew up in a state of constant hunger, with no regular mealtimes and often no food at all, sometimes for days on end. While it was only 3 kilometres for Carol to pick up her welfare cheque, it was a 90-kilometre round drive to get it cashed, and while she had the use of an old car, she rarely had the money for petrol. Tina missed a lot of schooling and struggled when she did make it to the classroom. Things didn't improve even when her mother remarried briefly.

When her stepfather died, they returned back south and moved in with Tina's grandmother Genevieve, who lived in a small house that was part of a sprawling low-income housing complex in Torrance, 30 kilometres from downtown Los Angeles. Tina was almost thirteen and beginning puberty, and the house was not a happy place. It was the home every neighbour went out of their way to avoid, and Tina never had sleepovers or school friends over to play.

Wilder pushed his car seat as far back as it would go and pulled his trousers and briefs down around his ankles. Tina had known suffering before, and she had found a way to survive it; she could do it again, she told herself.

'Are you a virgin?'

Tina shook her head.

He instructed her to climb over onto his side and straddle him. 'Look like you're enjoying it and I won't hurt you,' he said.

Tina did what she was told. Afterwards, he told her to get back into the passenger seat.

Wilder cleaned himself quickly and then, zipping up his trousers, he got out of the car and went to the boot to retrieve his briefcase. He carried it around to the passenger side and placed it on the roof of the car, opened it up and took out a roll of silver duct tape and two lengths of rope. He ordered Tina, who was still naked, to get out of the car and stand in front of him.

'I'm going to tell you the rules of my game,' he told her, 'and if you follow them, you will live. If you do anything stupid, try to escape or don't please me then I sell you into a sex slave ring or kill you, like all the others, is that understood?'

'Yes, sir,' she responded, her head filled with only one question she didn't dare ask: 'How many others?'

'You will act natural at all times, you will smile, you won't cry, and you will carry on a normal conversation with me when I want you to,' he added.

'When I fuck you, you will be passionate and act like you are enjoying it. You can be aggressive when we do it, but you can't resist me in any way.'

'Yes, sir.'

He told her to get dressed, then tied her wrists together with the rope, covering the knots with tape. He made her sit in the car with her legs dangling outside while he repeated with her ankles what he'd done with her wrists. Finally, he motioned for her to put her legs back inside, ripped off two pieces of tape and pressed them firmly over her eyes, and slammed the door shut.

Before they set off, Wilder put the briefcase back in the boot and placed a pair of dark sunglasses on Tina's nose to hide the tape covering her eyes. She was in complete darkness, but she could hear him pulling on his driving gloves and starting the engine. He did a quick three-point turn and rejoined the canyon road heading back the way they had come. After a period of silence that Tina guessed was twenty minutes or so, he asked her if she was hungry. 'Yes, sir,' she told him. She hadn't bothered with breakfast that morning before leaving for school and now she was ravenous. She also felt light-headed and hoped some food might make her feel better.

She heard the indicator light and could sense the car slowing, then turning to the right and coming to an idling stop. The air con, which she'd noticed was always on maximum, making the car uncomfortably cool, was still blowing, but he must have opened a window, because her nose was assailed by the pungent smell of fried food, carried on a stale and tepid breeze. When a tinny far-off sounding voice said, 'Welcome to McDonald's, how can I help?' she realised they were at a drive-through, and for a split second she thought about screaming. He hadn't taped her mouth, that would have looked suspicious, but she didn't entertain the slightest doubt this man had killed before and would take her life without a second thought if she pissed him off. He placed something soft in her lap to cover the tape and rope binding her wrists, and Tina guessed it was the jacket he'd given her to wear at the beach earlier.

He ordered two large meal deals with Coke and was insistent that all the diced onions be removed from both burgers, telling Tina that he didn't want to taste onion on her breath when they French kissed and she gave him a blow job later. While they waited for the order, he told her they would eat while they drove. Tina, enveloped in total blackness with no idea what direction they were travelling in, felt nauseated attempting to eat in a moving vehicle. She couldn't stomach the idea of the burger, so she munched on a few fries and took a big glug of the Coke he placed in her hand. It crossed her mind he might have drugged it with something, but she was so thirsty she took the chance. When the car speeded up and settled into a rhythm, she knew they were on a highway, and that's when the music started. Wilder put on the Eurythmics album *Touch*, and, fast-forwarding through till he found the track he was looking for, 'No Fear, No Hate, No Pain (No Broken Hearts)', he sang along as he drove.

WEDNESDAY 4 APRIL 1984
EL DORADO MOTEL
EL CENTRO, CA

Wilder drove Tina more than 300 kilometres, firstly south on Interstate 5 to San Diego, then west on the I-8 through the desert and into the rural town of El Centro, just 20 kilometres shy of the Mexican border, in Southern California's Imperial Valley. Going from the stark Sonoran Desert to a valley filled with thousands of acres of picture-postcard, neat agriculture fields, Wilder had the air conditioner on full blast the whole way. It was a burning sun in a cloudless blue sky, and the temperature was north of 30 degrees.

On arrival ast the El Dorado Motel he followed his usual routine, putting a blindfolded Tina into a sleeping bag and carrying her into a room, which he had prepared by spraying it with air freshener and the bed with perfume. He then spent hours torturing and abusing her. He forced her to dance naked while he masturbated and watched her, then ordered her to give him oral sex. To enforce his regime of 'bondage and discipline' brainwashing, he made frequent use of his electric shock device, taping one wire around her toe and jamming the 'live' one against her neck, breasts, shoulders and even inside her ears. At one stage, the teenager was sitting on his lap when he did it, and when she flinched and stifled a cry of pain, Wilder became enraged and shocked her repeatedly until she almost passed out. Relaxing on the bed afterwards, with Tina bound, gagged and naked alongside him, Wilder started talking. He claimed he had come to San Diego to pick up a cocaine shipment from a contact of his called Pedro, who was across the border and also ran a sex-slave ring.

'If you don't keep me happy, I'll let you join the other bitches. Pedro likes to punish the girls by burning their skin with cigarettes.'

2 5

A CHANGE OF PLAN

THURSDAY 5 APRIL 1984

TORRANCE, CA

Tina's mother, Carol, reported her daughter missing to the Los Angeles police department in Torrance, telling them the teen hadn't returned home from school the previous day or been in touch overnight. It's doubtful police would have made it a top priority case at that stage, anyway, but her mum didn't help matters when she told officers that she suspected Tina was probably just 'upset over boyfriend problems and wanted to live with her father'.

EL DORADO MOTEL

EL CENTRO, CA

Three hundred and sixty kilometres away, Tina was naked, cold, exhausted and petrified, but she was still alive, the horrors of the previous hours of captivity in that tawdry room still raw in her mind. She had found it impossible to sleep, the dreadful flashbacks to the abuse she'd suffered jolting her awake every time she was on the verge of slipping into unconsciousness. For hours, she had lain staring at the ceiling, not daring to move a muscle, convinced if she did anything to wake him, he would demand more painful sex or, worse still, punish her with the 'wires'. It was all she could do not to choke on her own sick, the scent of the perfume he'd sprayed mixing with his body odour.

After waking, Wilder immediately turned on the TV to watch the morning news bulletins. They all featured a story about a girl missing from Las Vegas, showed Wilder's photograph and said he was also wanted for questioning about the disappearances of several other women. Tina heard it all and had no doubts about her fate; she was either going to be killed or sent across the border to join the sex-slave ring he ran with his partner.

After checking all her binds and telling her he would kill her if she did anything stupid, he left for ten minutes. She didn't move at all, fearful he was testing her and waiting behind the door for her to try and escape. When he got back with the newspaper, he read a story out loud while he sat next to her on the bed. It said he was being sought over the disappearance of six women and that the FBI manhunt for him was now focused on the West Coast following teenage model Michelle Korfman's disappearance from a Las Vegas shopping mall last Sunday. Her car had been found on Tuesday, but according to FBI special agent Dan Kelsay, the bureau had no information on her whereabouts. Wilder took the tape off Tina's eyes and turned the newspaper so she could see the photograph of him next to the story.

When he'd finished reading, he told Tina there had been a change in his plans. His cocaine shipment had fallen through because someone had been killed in Mexico, and the drugs pick-up, scheduled for Los Angeles, was now cancelled, meaning he wasn't going to be taking her back home.

SALTON SEA, CA

He was keen to get a move on now his photo was all over the TV and in the newspapers. He'd abandoned any thoughts of crossing into Mexico, certain all border guards would have been issued with his photograph and a description. He headed north, and after an hour or so they reached the Salton Sea, a massive saltwater lake, the largest in California at over 50 kilometres long and almost 25 kilometres wide. Wilder stopped the car in a secluded clearing overlooking the mammoth blue void, took a pair of scissors from his briefcase and, on the side of the road, ordered Tina to kneel down while he hacked away at her hair until it was much shorter. He was feeling the stress of being a hunted fugitive, he needed a distraction, to do something to convince himself he was still running the show and in control of things. He told Tina her long hair had irritated him last night by getting in the way when he wanted to watch her face as he fucked her.

A while later he stopped at a takeaway restaurant to buy some food, tucking the gun into his jacket and the knife inside his boot.

'I'll be watching you the whole time. If you move or do anything to raise the alarm, I'll come straight back and kill you.'

Tina was still tied up with the jacket over her lap, but he hadn't put tape over her eyes, so she could see him watching her while he waited for the food. She sat rigid with fear until he returned and drove them to a nearby rest stop where they ate in the car overlooking the lake.

When they'd finished it was 1 p.m., and Wilder carried on driving until turning into a blue and white L-shaped motel on the side of the lake. He took a room at the very end on the second floor, untied Tina and walked her up the stairs with the gun, hidden inside his jacket, pressed against the small of her back.

Inside, once he'd retied her, washed his hands and gone through the ritual of preparing the room while she stood in silence, he pushed her onto the bed and sexually assaulted her again. He then gave her numerous electric shocks with the torture device. Punishment, he claimed, for the poor oral sex. He taped over her mouth and eyes and made her dance for him, warning that she better make it sexy or he would start again.

At five o'clock he stopped and switched to the early evening TV news. Tina couldn't see it, but she listened to the story of his escape from Florida and noticed it had been moved up the bulletin. 'I'm not going to take you back to Los Angeles,' he said. 'We are going to New York instead.'

———————

The TV story had spooked Wilder. He knew he would feel better out on the highway, so after studying the road map carefully, he packed up, untied the girl and led her back down to the car at gunpoint. She was so easy, like leading a lamb to slaughter. He didn't even bother re-fixing the rope or duct tape, once they were back in the car. He knew instinctively she wouldn't try anything. She was too beaten down. He was in control.

Tina wondered why he hadn't bothered to tie her up. It had been a shock when he'd ripped the tape off her eyes, and she realised he'd removed his beard. His face and body were very tanned, but his neck and chin now looked red and sore from razor burn. She was determined not to give him a reason to tie her up again. The worst feeling was when she was blind, with the tape across her eyes, just sitting in the darkness, waiting, waiting to be stabbed, like those other girls in the news story.

MOTEL 6

PRESCOTT, AZ

Four hours later Wilder entered the car park of Motel 6 in Prescott, Arizona, having stopped to fill up with petrol just before crossing the state line. He loved to watch old western movies and may have chosen Prescott because of its links to legendary gunslinging lawman Wyatt Earp, who survived the famous Gunfight at the OK Corral.

With hundreds of modern-day lawmen on his tail, Wilder spent the night threatening Tina with his gun and knife, raping her and torturing her over and over with the electric shock punishment.

———

Meanwhile, earlier that same evening, Wilder's original getaway car, the Chrysler New Yorker, was found by an alert police patrolman in Beaumont, Texas. There was still no sign of Terry Walden's stolen Mercury Cougar.

26

MOST WANTED

FRIDAY 6 APRIL 1984
J EDGAR HOOVER BUILDING
935 PENNSYLVANIA AVENUE
WASHINGTON, DC

The search was going nowhere, and John Hanlon needed a circuit breaker to get back on Wilder's trail. Five days after Wilder had taken Michelle Korfman from the mall in Las Vegas, the FBI had little or no idea where he'd gone next.

That morning a media statement was sent out early, inviting the major networks and print journalists to attend an unusual news conference, held by FBI assistant director Oliver 'Buck' Revell. When the curious reporters were all seated, the screen behind Revell lit up with images of Wilder – both bearded and clean shaven, with and without a moustache – and the assistant director announced the Australian-born racing driver had been added to the list of the FBI's Ten Most Wanted Fugitives.

A poster, headed 'Wanted by the FBI', was also shown, containing the four photographs of Wilder underneath a list of six aliases he had used since fleeing Florida. Seventy thousand copies of the poster were printed and rushed out to post offices and government buildings, concentrated west of the Mississippi River, where the bureau now had over 500 agents dedicated to the manhunt.

'We don't normally do this,' said Revell, looking over his shoulder at the photo display, 'but [Wilder] represents significant danger. He's extremely active, very dangerous, and this approach may lead to his apprehension.'

The poster, which would feature on TV news broadcasts for days, stated Wilder 'usually wears trimmed beard and mustache, may be clean shaven, well spoken and presents a neat appearance, habitual fingernail biter'.

Underneath his criminal conviction for sexual battery was a warning:

CAUTION
WILDER IS BEING SOUGHT ON FEDERAL CHARGES RESULTING FROM THE KIDNAPPING, RAPE AND TORTURE OF A YOUNG FEMALE VICTIM.
CONSIDER WILDER ARMED, EXTREMELY DANGEROUS WITH SUICIDAL TENDENCIES.

Shortly after the FBI press conference ended in Washington, and John Hanlon was bracing himself to receive an avalanche of leads, the bureau held another in Oklahoma with local police to reveal that forensic experts had identified the body found near Milford Lake in Kansas as Suzanne Logan, who had vanished from the city ten days previously.

It meant detectives were able to inform Brian Logan that they had been wrong, and his wife of nine months hadn't run away from domestic problems at home. She had been abducted, tortured and murdered by one of the most dangerous men in the US.

'She had been beaten and abused prior to her death,' revealed Albert Buskey, chief investigator with the Geary County sheriff's office. 'She had a black eye and bruises on her chest' in addition to several deep stab wounds.

Oklahoma FBI chief Anthony Daniels said they had placed Wilder in the city at the time Suzanne went missing, and silver duct tape and cord marks found on her wrists and ankles were similar to those found on other Wilder victims, also found lying near water.

'When he's done with them he just dumps them like trash,' added Buskey.

Suzanne's dream of a modelling career, along with her trusting nature, had sealed her fate. The crucial piece of evidence confirming beyond any doubt she was one of Wilder's victims came a few weeks later, when police in New York found her wallet and the five rings she had been wearing when she disappeared hidden in the seat springs of a car Wilder was driving.

The District Court in Geary County, Kansas, charged Wilder in his absence with Suzanne's first-degree murder, felony murder, aggravated kidnapping and rape. The warrant listed bail at $2 million should he be apprehended.

MOTEL 6
PRESCOTT, AZ

At the exact moment he was being unveiled at FBI headquarters as one of America's Most Wanted, fulfilling the boastful prophecy he'd made to his racing buddies just a few weeks earlier, Wilder was chasing the white line in the Cougar, only now he was sitting in the passenger seat. It was Tina behind the wheel. There was a three-hour time difference to the nation's capital, and the sun had barely risen when Wilder handed the car keys to the shocked teenager in the motel room and told her she was driving. He'd studied the road map and was keen to get as far away as possible from California. The FBI were convinced he was going west, that's where they were concentrating the search, so he was going to go east all the way to the Big Apple. His other advantage, which caused him to smile, was the realisation that no-one was yet looking for Tina, so a woman driving would not attract any attention from highway patrol cops issued with a BOLO for him. He hoped with his newly shaved face and tan-coloured baseball cap, it would be enough of a disguise.

LAKE BUENA VISTA
ORLANDO, FL

Twenty-two days after schoolgirl Colleen Orsborn had played hooky and gone missing from Daytona Beach, a local fisherman stumbled across the badly decomposed body of a young woman protruding from a shallow grave at a remote wooded spot overlooking a lake, near Bali Boulevard in Lake Buena Vista, not far from Walt Disney World.

The medical examiner who did the autopsy estimated her age at fourteen to eighteen years old, height 160–163 centimetres and weight range 45–50 kilograms. He recorded she had brown eyes and light brown hair, wore a size 7–8 shoe and had no scars, fractures, other abnormalities or identifying marks, apart from very faint pink nail polish on her fingernails and two toenails. He said her ears weren't pierced and, while she did have cavities, it appeared that she had never received dental care. He tagged her as a Jane Doe and sent her to the morgue. The medical examiner, who would later be discharged following the discovery of multiple errors in other cases, ruled that the

Jane Doe was *not* Colleen Orsborn. He claimed the Jane Doe was Hispanic and did not, like Colleen, have a previously fractured arm. He was wrong in both instances. It wasn't until 2010, as part of a review of unsolved cases using newly developed DNA technology, that Orange County medical examiner Dr Jan Garavaglia was able to match Jane Doe's mitochondrial DNA sample – the type inherited from the maternal side – with DNA from Colleen's sisters.

Colleen had been lying in the morgue, as a Jane Doe, unclaimed, for twenty-six years. Her mother, who never stopped searching for her, who never stopped grieving and who agonised every single day over what had happened to her beautiful daughter, had already died by the time the discovery was made.

INTERSTATE 40
NORTHERN ARIZONA

When they'd left the motel early that morning, before throwing the keys to Tina, Wilder had placed his fully loaded revolver under the passenger seat and packed an extra box of the hollow-point bullets in the glove compartment. Tina drove along a newly constructed highway – a replacement for the historic US Route 66, which had been immortalised by Chuck Berry and the Rolling Stones, among others – through the interminable desert, crossing the Petrified Forest National Park on their relentless journey east. Whenever she glanced down, she could see the black handle of the long-bladed knife poking out of the top of Wilder's cowboy boot as he tapped his feet to the music. They passed a number of police highway-patrol vehicles, and whenever they spotted one, they both became extra vigilant and tense. He would lean across and check the speed-ometer, tell her to stay calm and drive a little bit slower, but she could tell by the tightness in his voice that he was edgy. She didn't want to die in the crossfire of his shootout with the cops, and she had no doubt he would fire first if he felt himself cornered.

When it was time to look for somewhere to stay, Wilder took over behind the wheel. They drove into Amarillo in the Texas Panhandle, passing long rows of clapboard ranch-style houses. The sun had already set by the time Wilder finally turned into a characterless highway motel. They had been on the road, apart from a couple of stops for petrol and to buy takeaway food, for well over fourteen hours, travelling more than 1100 kilometres.

Wilder threatened Tina again before leaving her in the car to go and register. He paid cash and kept his eyes lowered under his baseball cap as he filled out the guest form, but the clerk didn't give him a second glance.

ABC *WORLD NEWS TONIGHT*
WEST 66TH STREET STUDIOS
NEW YORK, NY

The expanding search for Wilder was the fifth item on the ABC's *World News Tonight*, anchor Peter Jennings telling the nation: 'Last night we reported that the FBI had added the name of Christopher Wilder to its Ten Most Wanted list for a series of seven kidnappings and murders across the country. Today, the FBI said Wilder is now a suspect in an eighth killing, this one in Oklahoma.'

AMARILLO MOTEL
AMARILLO, TX

Wilder was anxious to see the various TV news reports about his new status as the 385th fugitive in FBI history to be included on its Ten Most Wanted list, and the coverage seemed to energise him, which was the worst possible news for Tina, who was utterly exhausted.

Her eyes were raw from driving so long, her bones felt weary and she felt filthy, having been wearing the same clothes for three days. Wilder always made her shower before they had sex, and last night she had tried washing and rinsing out her underwear in the sink, but that morning they'd hit the road before her underwear had dried properly, so she'd been forced to put them on damp.

Wilder used the bathroom first, making sure to take the knife and gun with him, and after he washed his hands with a new tablet of soap and neatly refolded the hand towel, she watched him go to his briefcase and bring out the perfume bottle. Her heart suddenly felt like it had been pierced with a stake, as the fine mist of scent he sprayed over the mattress meant only one thing: he was going to force himself on her again.

Wilder was aware she was watching him as he pulled out the electric-wire machine she hated most of all, even more than the awful things he said and did to her during sex. While he was no longer tying her up, the torture sessions had not stopped.

Tina couldn't take the punishment any more. She was a tough girl, but the electric shocks were too much. She wanted to live, to get out of that horrible room and back to her boyfriend Billy, to feel the sand between her toes again, and go and watch a movie with a bucket of popcorn.

KIMBRELL'S HOUSE
DELRAY BEACH, FL
Zeke Kimbrell had just fallen asleep when the phone jangled on the bedside table next to his head. He was still groggy when he lifted the receiver and held it to his ear, unsure how long he'd been asleep and what the time was.

'Hello,' he said tentatively, stifling a yawn.

There was silence.

'Hello,' he repeated.

Silence.

Kimbrell's brain clicked into gear. This wasn't the first such call he'd had recently, though most of the others had been at work.

'Chris, is this you?'

No-one replied, there was just a crackly silence, but Kimbrell thought he could make out someone exhaling slowly. It creeped him out.

'If that's you, talk to me, Chris, or just grunt or something,' he said after a moment or two.

The FBI agents had told him that if the phone rang but no-one spoke, it was more than likely Wilder. They explained their theory that hearing his business partner's voice was important for Wilder; it helped keep him in touch with reality. They told Kimbrell his calls in and out would all be monitored, and he should try and keep his friend on the line for as long as possible. He was sometimes getting two calls a day like this one, then there might be several days before the next one.

SATURDAY 7 APRIL 1984
MIAMI FBI FIELD OFFICE
MIAMI, FL

John Hanlon put that morning's *Miami Herald* down on his desk, the front-page headline screaming back at him, 'FBI gets TV view of Wilder: suspect in rapes made dating tape'.

Part two of the strategy to flush Wilder out of hiding was going better than expected. While there had been a good public response to the bureau's decision to put him on its Ten Most Wanted list, Hanlon reckoned this development was even more likely to bring a result. Edna Buchanan's story revealed the manager of a Miami videotape dating service had contacted the FBI yesterday with a copy of Wilder's introduction video, recorded three years ago. Hanlon had supported the immediate release of the tape, confident no-one viewing it could fail to recognise Wilder if they came into contact with him. The article said:

> Christopher Wilder, one of America's most wanted fugitives, told all about himself on TV Friday. Relaxed and smiling occasionally, the elusive rape suspect, lisping slightly, described his needs and the type of woman he is seeking. [. . .] 'I want to date. I want to meet and enjoy the company of a number of women,' said Wilder, sought in the disappearance of seven young women since Feb. 26.
>
> 'I have a need,' he said, 'to meet and socialize on a more wider basis than I have been doing . . .'

The TV networks were running edited extracts from the matchmaking video in all their bulletins. Hanlon believed the tape completely exposed Wilder for what he really was, a slimy lounge lizard who was a lethal danger to all women. The Australian-born bachelor, sitting in his Boynton Beach home, boasted about his luxury trappings. 'I have quite a few playthings at home,' he said. 'I like sports cars . . . I keep a couple of what you would call "fantasy cars" at home.'

Wilder said his objective in signing up was to meet the right person, 'Somebody with depth. Somebody that might have some background. Somebody that I can feel comfortable with.'

What he wanted in a woman, most of all, he said, 'was sincerity and a long-term – but not at right this very moment jumping into a marriage – relationship'.

When he'd first watched the tape, Hanlon had been struck by Wilder's ego. Anticipating the interview he would have with Wilder following his capture, Hanlon had fewer doubts than ever that he would have the upper hand. 'I think he will love to talk about what he's done and save his skin for another day,' Hanlon told Ray Nazario.

FBI spokesman Chris Mazzella said the dating tape told the bureau a lot about Wilder's personality, adding, 'the interview shows no hint of the criminal mind. I think he is an actor. To be able to elude a massive manhunt the way he has . . . There are only two ways to do that. You have to be pretty tricky and pretty coy'.

The tape was released nationwide, 'so young girls can know what he looks like and what he sounds like', special agent Dennis Erich explained to reporters, adding by way of a warning, 'and God forbid, if he approaches you, don't go near the guy'.

The FBI pursuit of Wilder was now the biggest manhunt ever undertaken by the bureau, bigger than the search for James Earl Ray, the killer of civil rights leader Martin Luther King Jr, almost exactly sixteen years earlier. John Hanlon had been a young agent at the time, involved on the periphery of that investigation, but he was now the man responsible for marshalling the might of the world's most powerful law-enforcement agency to apprehend another ruthless murderer.

Hanlon had pursued Wilder, whom he suspected had taken and probably killed a sixteen-year-old schoolgirl missing from a shopping mall in Los Angeles earlier in the week, through Nevada, California and into New Mexico over the previous seventy-two hours, managing even less sleep than his nemesis.

All the charge and credit cards Kimbrell had given Wilder when he fled were on a watch list. The agent had a large road map of the country next to his desk, and every time he received a hit from a card transaction or a witness sighting, he marked it with a push pin. The only downside was it took the card issuer around forty-eight hours to process and pass on the information to the bureau. Looking over all the brightly coloured pins peppering the map now, showing a snaking trail from Florida west to California and then to the south of the state, Hanlon took a gulp of his third lukewarm coffee of the day and tried to discern a pattern. Since taking Tina on Wednesday, Wilder had driven over 1500 kilometres. Hanlon had no idea whether she was still alive or where Wilder was heading to.

SUNDAY 8 APRIL 1984
INTERSTATE 40
TEXAS, OKLAHOMA, ARKANSAS

Wilder was at least one step ahead of his pursuers again. They were mobilising resources to look for him in LA, but Wilder had been through the city, abducted a new girl and left Southern California days ago.

Serial killers who morph into spree killers don't normally stop the slaughter in the middle of their rampage. Wilder had killed or attempted to kill at least nine women in six weeks, the last six victims in the space of just three weeks, yet four days after her abduction, Tina was still alive.

The weekend was a seemingly endless road trip across middle America for the teenager, punctuated with constant threats, torture games and frequent vicious sexual assaults at the hands of a man more than twice her age. She was bruised and battered; her breasts, particularly, were very tender, black and blue all over, and with a chunk of flesh missing from one of her nipples where he had sunk his teeth in. She remained convinced that sooner or later Wilder would kill her like all the others whose photographs she had seen on television, but she was a savvy girl, as well as a brave one, and she wasn't giving up while she could still draw breath. She asked Wilder if she could do more of the driving and was surprised when he agreed, for while he was no longer tying or taping her up, he never went long without reminding her about the knife and the gun he kept within reach. Taking over at the wheel forced her to take her mind off things and made the interminable hours on the highway a bit more bearable.

Tina did almost all the daylight driving as they made their way across western Texas and into Oklahoma. Interstate 40 sliced through Oklahoma City, mirroring the course of the river, and they passed within a few hundred metres of the Save-A-Stop supermarket where Suzanne Logan had dropped her husband off for work two weekends ago. Tina was still at the wheel when they crossed the state line into Arkansas and remained there when, an hour later, they reached the pretty town of Fayetteville, with its wide streets and large comfortable homes, surrounded by giant oak and gum trees. Wilder directed her into an underground parking garage. He took the car keys, the gun and the knife and then, grabbing a screwdriver from his briefcase, stole the licence plates from a nearby silver Cadillac and transferred them to the Cougar. He threw the old plates into a garbage bin, and after stopping at yet another drive-through to buy hamburgers, they were on their way again.

Tina had pretty much figured out there were two sides to Wilder. There was the softly spoken charmer, who seemed most relaxed when he was in the car playing music and chatting, and then there was the dark and troubled monster who transformed without warning into a cold and cruel sadist, unable to get sexually aroused without inflicting terrible pain. It seemed every day the television and the newspapers had another story about him, with details about another young victim. Tina had a lot of time to think, especially at night while he snored and she only napped, naked next to him, terrified he would kill her in her sleep. Not knowing whether each day was going to be her last concentrated her mind, and she realised that Billy meant more to her than anyone. She steeled herself to endure whatever it took for the chance to see him again.

Wilder constantly told her to act naturally around him, to look comfortable and talk to him like she was enjoying herself. If it meant one less electric-shock session, she was going to do everything she could to obey. So she began telling her rapist and abductor her life story. She left out mention of her parents, or Billy, as she thought that was too much of a risk, but she filled the hours while they racked up the kilometres describing her childhood and all the funny things that had happened to her, particularly at school. The kind of normal, everyday things that the sadist next to her had never experienced. His school years had been largely unhappy times of isolation, seldom staying long enough in any one place to make friends.

After Wilder had stolen the licence plates in Arkansas, and they were back on the highway heading further east, he suddenly announced he wasn't going to take her to New York, he was going to send her home instead, once he found a suitable new female driver who satisfied him. Tina didn't believe him; he'd made the same empty promise before.

MONDAY 9 APRIL 1984
HIGHWAY MOTEL
GARY, IN

Four thousand kilometres across eight states in six days, and Tina was still alive. It was late in the evening when Wilder chose a motel on the outskirts of Gary, a grimy and struggling industrial metropolis 40 kilometres from downtown Chicago, to stop for the night.

Tina was still wearing the same underwear she'd had on when she was abducted; she hadn't eaten anything but hamburgers, pizza and chocolate; and she had been tortured, raped, threatened and humiliated at least once, sometimes several times a day, but she was still alive. The courageous teenager was also slowly becoming a victim of Stockholm syndrome.

The syndrome was first recognised and named after a 1973 bank robbery in Stockholm when four hostages developed a psychological alliance with their captors as a subconscious survival strategy during captivity. Psychiatrist Dr Frank Ochberg, working with the US National Task Force on Terrorism and Disorder, studied the phenomenon and came up with a generally accepted definition.

Initially, he said, a captive experienced a sudden, terrible event that left them convinced they were going to die. They were then subjected to brainwashing and a type of infantilisation – they were not allowed to eat, speak or go to the toilet, et cetera, without permission. After a while, any small act of kindness, such as being given water or having their shackles loosened, prompted them to feel a primitive and powerful positive feeling towards their captor, leaving them in denial that this was the person who had endangered them in the first place. In their mind, their abductor became the person who was going to let them live, and they started to develop a bond and feelings of trust or affection, even sympathy, for their jailer.

The most famous example of the syndrome is the kidnapping of Patty Hearst, the nineteen-year-old granddaughter and heiress of American publishing magnate William Randolph Hearst, by a US terrorist group known as the Symbionese Liberation Army in 1974. Hearst, abducted in a violent shootout during which a machine gun was fired, was locked in a closet blindfolded with her hands tied for weeks and repeatedly threatened with death. She said later she was also raped. Her captors let her out only for meals when, still blindfolded, she was allowed to join in their political discussions. Eventually, she was given a choice, join them or be killed. She said she lied to save her life and the blindfold was removed. For the next eighteen months, until her arrest, Hearst was involved in a number of crimes with the SLA, including a bank robbery when two men were shot and two failed attempts to kill policemen. She was tried over her role in the robbery and, convicted by a jury, received a seven-year jail term. President Carter later commuted her sentence to the twenty-two months she had already served, and, on his last day in office in 2001, President Clinton granted her a pardon.

The FBI has amassed evidence that roughly 8 per cent of abduction victims show evidence of Stockholm syndrome. It seems Tina was one of them.

27

LITTLE MA MA

I hate beyond hate.

— John Fowles, *The Collector*

UNSUB; DAWNETTE S WILT, 00:MM INDIANAPOLIS FBI FILE 7-1924

TUESDAY 10 APRIL 1984
LOS ANGELES FBI FIELD OFFICE
LOS ANGELES, CA

The flipside for the FBI in putting Wilder on its Ten Most Wanted list was the enormous public scrutiny and pressure that came with it. The might of the bureau was now pitted against a lone deranged individual, and the public expectation was that agents would be kicking a door down or swooping on a car to make a dramatic arrest very quickly. As the days ticked by and that didn't happen, despite hundreds of leads and tip-offs across the nation, the media began to ask more questions and press for regular briefings about the case.

Now that the frontline of the hunt had switched to the west coast, the bureau called a press conference at its LA headquarters to confirm that Wilder, described as a suspect in the abduction or murder of at least eight women, was in California.

Special Agent John Hoos told reporters Wilder had been seen in Las Vegas on 2 April, and then stayed in the Proud Parrot Motel in Lomita, a short drive from LA airport, almost a week ago, checking out on 4 April. 'Through various means of investigation, it has been confirmed as a positive identification of Wilder,' said Hoos. Revealing that agents were scrambling to pick up the trail, he announced, 'We've placed him in Southern California now; he's right in our own backyard.'

Asked when he expected the FBI to make an arrest, his response, 'It's a big piece of real estate out here to cover,' hinted at the bureau's mounting frustration.

Hoos revealed they believed Wilder to be driving a 1981 burnt-orange Mercury Cougar.

Later that day in Los Angeles, Torrance police lieutenant Robert Armstrong told reporters a sixteen-year-old high school student had gone missing the same day as Wilder checked out from the Proud Parrot Motel. 'As soon as I saw the flyer with her picture, I got a terrible sinking feeling,' said Armstrong. 'I hope I'm wrong,' he added.

FBI MIAMI FIELD OFFICE
MIAMI, FL
Back at the FBI's Miami office, where John Hanlon was still co-ordinating the nationwide search, another press conference was held to reveal Wilder was now wanted for questioning about the 3 March disappearance of college student Virginia Scott, from Grand Ridge in the north of the state. While Wilder wasn't an of-ficial suspect, said an FBI spokesman, he was a person of interest

because Virginia had gone missing between the disappearances of Rosario Gonzalez and Beth Kenyon, and lived less than an hour's drive from Tallahassee, where Wilder had abducted Linda Grober on 20 March. Hanlon, watching the conference from the back of the room, shared the frustration of his fellow agent Hoos in Los Angeles. For weeks now he had been leaving nothing to chance, sending agents to interview every new name that came up, chasing down every aspect of Wilder's history, hoping for a break. So far it hadn't worked.

TWENTY-SECOND AVENUE
SAWTELL, NSW, AUSTRALIA
Edited copy of teletype message from the US legal attaché in Canberra:

TO ALL FBI FIELD OFFICES PRIORITY
MODNAP. KIDNAPING. OO MIAMI
SUBJECT'S PARENTS COLEY AND JUNE WILDER INTERVIEWED AT THEIR RESIDENCE TWENTY-SECOND AVENUE SAWTELL, NEW SOUTH WALES (NSW) BY LEGAT ON APRIL 10, 1984. FOLLOWING INFORMATION OF LEAD VALUE EXTRACTED FROM EXTENSIVE INTERVIEW:

PARENTS ADVISE SUBJECT DROPPED OUT OF HIGH SCHOOL BETWEEN EIGHTH AND NINTH GRADES AND BEGAN A FOUR YEAR CARPENTRY APPRENTICESHIP.

OWING TO BREAK-UP OF HIS MARRIAGE WITH CHRISTINE XXXXXX, SUBJECT MOVED TO FLORIDA AND BEGAN WORKING IN CONSTRUCTION THERE.

MOTHER ALSO ADVISED SUBJECT HAD MEN-
TIONED ROMANTIC ATTACHMENTS TO A NUMBER
OF GIRLS IN ADDITION TO VIKI ~~XXXXX~~ OF CON-
NECTICUT.

CANBERRA CONTINUING INQUIRIES WITH
AUSTRALIAN AUTHORITIES. SUBJECT SHOULD BE
CONSIDERED ARMED AND EXTREMELY DANGER-
OUS: SUICIDAL TENDENCIES.

SOUTHLAKE MALL
MERRILLVILLE, IN

Half a world away from his parents, weeping their way through
the interview with the US legal attaché, and 3306 kilometres east
from the FBI's Los Angeles press conference, Wilder made Tina
drive to Indiana's largest shopping mall in Merrillville. He told her
they were going hunting for a girl to take over as his driver, so Tina
could then go home. Before they got out of the Cougar, Wilder
threatened to shoot her in front of everyone if she attempted to flee
or to alert security. Wilder gave her a pair of blue jeans to wear from
a bundle of women's clothes he kept in the boot of the car. She
still wore her pink high-heeled shoes and the diamond studs in her
double-pierced ears. Her long fingernails were still painted pink,
although the varnish was chipped and flaking.

The pair, who onlookers would assume were father and daughter, strolled around for quite some time while Wilder 'cased' the
busy mall. The night before he'd run out of *Tatiana*, his favourite
perfume, and they tried a number of stores before he found a bottle
to buy. He took his time choosing a target, but finally he settled on
a slender brown-haired girl, whom he'd watched walk into several
shops with 'Hiring Now' cards in the window.

SUSIE'S CASUALS CLOTHING STORE
SOUTHLAKE MALL
MERRILLVILLE, IN

Sixteen-year-old Dawnette Wilt had spent the late afternoon traipsing from store to store in search of a part-time job. She desperately needed money but hadn't yet found the courage to tell anybody why. She had recently returned to live with her mum, Cheryl, and her twelve-year-old brother in Dyer, 20 kilometres away, for her junior year at Lake Central High School. Her parents were divorced and she'd spent her sophomore year at another school in Mooresville, three hours away, where her father lived.

Dawnette had settled back into Lake Central quickly, joining the cheerleading squad and playing in the school band. Her mum, an assistant manager at Rosalee's dress shop at the mall, loaned Dawnette her red and white Chevrolet Malibu so she could drive over after school and go job hunting. Cheryl had also bought her a new outfit so she would look smart, and when they met up after Cheryl's shift finished at 5 p.m., she gave her daughter a good-luck hug and told her not to be late home for dinner.

Dawnette, skinny with warm eyes and long dark hair, had filled out several applications already and was running out of enthusiasm by the time she left the Susie's Casuals fashion store. A girl approached her and said she could get a job with her boss, who was one of the managers, if she was interested. She said her name was 'Tina Marie Wilder' and that he was keen to talk to her if she was into modelling and having her photograph appear in magazines. The clothes the girl was wearing looked a bit tarty, thought Dawnette, but Tina had given her a friendly smile when she introduced herself, and so Dawnette agreed to follow her back to the store.

Before they reached the entrance, a well-dressed man appeared, and Tina introduced him as her manager. Dawnette's first reaction was that he looked like a slightly overweight male model, tall and well dressed with a gold chain around his neck, an expensive-looking gold watch on his wrist and a diamond ring on his pinkie finger. His voice sounded smooth and confident as he told her she was very attractive and had lots of potential to be a successful model. Dawnette blushed and felt butterflies in her stomach as the man explained that he would like to employ her as a model in the mall at weekends, and that the pay would be very good indeed.

He asked how old she was, and when she told him, he said that was okay but she would need to sign some extra paperwork he kept in his car. Tina, who hadn't said very much at all while they had been talking, accompanied them out to the parking lot. The man chatted casually the whole way and explained to Dawnette, who was getting more excited about the opportunity with every passing minute, that he needed her contact details so he could ring her mother and get her approval as well.

When they reached the car park, he led the way to a Mercury Cougar, which was in a quiet spot away from the mall entrance. Dawnette, who'd been listening but not really watching as they talked and walked, now turned to look at the man, and found herself staring at a gun.

SOUTHLAKE MALL CAR PARK
MERRILLVILLE, IN

'Get in, baby, this is real. I'm not afraid to kill you,' the man said. 'Isn't that right?' he added, nodding towards Tina, who stood immobile on his right.

'Yes,' she replied nervously, looking over at Dawnette briefly, 'I know he's done it before.'

Dawnette saw a blankness in Tina's eyes and wondered why she hadn't noticed it earlier.

Wilder opened the car door with his left hand and motioned with the gun in his right for the girl to get into the back seat. She did as she was told. He handed the keys to Tina and told her to drive. While she walked around the vehicle, he got into the front passenger seat and, twisting around to threaten her with the weapon, instructed the new girl to lay down flat. He'd scouted the perfect place earlier and gave directions to Tina on how to find it again. When they reached the secluded area in nearby parkland, Wilder worked quickly, opening his briefcase, taking out rope and duct tape and cross-tying the girl's hands and feet together, then taping over her eyes. He didn't put the cloth gag in her mouth and tape it at this stage; instead, he jammed the barrel of the revolver into her mouth until she gagged, repeating that if she didn't cooperate, he would kill her like the others. He took her bag and purse, removed all her identification and possessions, including two pairs of earrings, a gold chain with a heart and her diamond ring.

'I want you to be my fuck for as long as I want,' he said, making her lie down on her left side so that her head was nearest to him. She was only small, under 50 kilograms and less than 162 centimetres, and easily fitted on the seat. He then had to give Tina, who was trembling as much as the girl, directions back to the mall. For the rest of the short journey back, he kept the gun in the girl's mouth while he told her what he was going to do to her that night and how much worse it would be if she didn't obey him. Whenever she answered him, he told her, she had to say 'Yes, sir' or 'Yes, dear.' He made her nod to make sure she understood that was important. She did.

When they reached the car park, he made the girl sit up while he uncovered one of her eyes. He forcefully ripped the piece of tape off and, as she blinked several times to adjust to the sudden light, told her to direct them to her car. When they found the red and white Malibu, Wilder turned to Tina and told her to follow them in the girl's car.

'Remember, I'm a racing driver and much faster,' he said, just in case she had any ideas about trying to escape. 'If you try and get away, I will easily catch you up and shoot you, so don't be a fucking idiot and die today. Who are you, bitch?'

'Yours, sir,' Tina answered, lowering her eyes as he put the keys he'd taken from the girl's purse into her hand.

He watched her carefully as she got into the Malibu and backed slowly out of the space. He didn't replace the tape over the girl's eye, just covered her with a beach towel and a coat and, checking in the rear-view mirror that Tina was still following, told her not to move.

'What's your name?' he asked over his shoulder.

'Dawnette,' said a timid voice from the back of the car.

He fired another question. 'Have you ever had sex?'

There was a silence before she said, 'Yes.'

'How old were you the first time?' he fired back, his urgency and eagerness to know the answer palpable. This time the silence was longer, and when she started to cry, he became impatient. 'Well, what's the fucking answer?' he said aggressively. 'You belong to me now, bitch, and if you don't do as I say, it won't go well for you, do you understand?'

'I'm nine, almost ten weeks pregnant,' was all she managed to say between stifled sobs, a tear rolling down her cheek onto the maroon velour seat, seeping into the fabric and creating a tiny wet patch.

'If you are lying, I will kill you,' said Wilder. 'There is a slave ring in Mexico that pays well for American sluts like you, pregnant ones especially. Or I will put you to work in New York turning tricks for my friends, who will shoot you full of coke.'

Dawnette pressed her face into the seat cushion and sobbed.

CALUMET CITY, IL

After 15 kilometres, Wilder turned west on Interstate 94, and twenty-five minutes after leaving the shopping mall, he crossed the state line into Illinois. Dawnette had stopped crying and composed herself enough to steal a look out of the window. She saw two signs flash by. The first said 'Welcome to Calumet City' and the second pointed to the Dolton Hotel. Wilder turned into a nearby car park and rolled down his window. When Tina pulled up alongside a few seconds later, he pointed to where he wanted her to leave Dawnette's car.

———

He'd thought everything through very carefully. Removing the girl's car from the mall and dumping it in the opposite direction to where they were going was, he believed, a masterstroke that would flummox the local police.

Tina parked the girl's car and got into the driver's seat of the Cougar. Wilder had replaced the tape over the Dawnette's eyes, and when Tina was settled behind the wheel, he casually mentioned what Dawnette had said about being pregnant. Tina's body tensed but, fearing it was another one of his tests, she didn't react or say anything.

'She's my little Ma Ma,' chortled Wilder. Holding the blade up to her face, he drew the tip of the knife slowly across her cheek, tracing a path to the middle of her chin.

'Lick the blade, little Ma Ma,' he commanded. Dawnette, disorientated and cowed, did as she was told. The steel felt hard, slippery and extremely sharp, and she said a silent prayer as he held the serrated blade across her tongue, panic-stricken he was going to cut it in two.

'I am your master now. If you resist, I will kill you like the others.'

'I know he will,' said Tina, her voice breaking the oppressive spell Wilder had created inside the car. 'Sir,' she continued, 'should I stay on the 90? How far do you want me to go?'

It was the first time she'd spoken, and the question distracted Wilder from his cruel game. There seemed to be confusion about whether they were heading for Florida or New York. Dawnette heard both locations mentioned, but they eventually seemed to agree on a plan and an awkward silence descended on the car. Every once in a while, he would suddenly reach back and push her down hard on the seat. After the first couple of times, she cottoned on that they were going through the highway toll booths.

CONVENIENCE STORE
WAUSEON, OH

Three and a half hours after setting off from Calumet City, Wilder directed Tina to turn off the highway and stop at a convenience store. Wilder took the gun, knife and car keys, issued a chilling threat about what would happen if either of them moved and left them in the car while he went inside. Dawnette, tied up and blind-folded on the back seat, thought about Tina, who sat silently in the driver's seat. Dawnette struggled to understand what part Tina was playing; she didn't know if Tina could be trusted. Everything the man had asked Tina to do, she'd done like an obedient slave, but she hadn't joined in the bullying or abuse. Dawnette didn't under-stand, if she was a victim like her, why she hadn't fled earlier in Dawnette's car. If she'd been Tina, she would have driven as fast and as far as she could until she found a police station or a patrol car. Then she heard the door open. The man was back.

'Little Ma Ma and her baby will need their energy if they're going to last the night,' he said, ripping the tape off just one of Dawnette's eyes and giving her a carton of milk and a chocolate bar.

'Eat it now or I'll force it down your throat.'

BEST WESTERN DEL MAR
WAUSEON, OH

Ten minutes later, Wilder booked into the Best Western Del Mar, a standard one-storey budget motel off Interstate 90. Repeating his threat to kill them if they tried anything, he left the two girls alone in the car while he went to reception, paid in cash for an overnight stay and signed in under the name CJ Bain.

This time, while he was gone Tina talked quickly in hushed tones to Dawnette. She didn't say much, just letting her know that his name was Chris, that she had been taken from a mall in Los Angeles about a week earlier, and that her hair used to be much longer until Wilder had cut it himself, because he liked it short. Dawnette listened but had trouble processing, or even compre-hending, any of what Tina told her. She was overwhelmed and stressed that if she made one mistake, it would cost her life. She vowed, though, that if an opportunity came along, like the one Tina had been given earlier, she wouldn't hesitate to grab it and try to escape.

When Wilder returned, he told Tina to park outside room 18, which was opposite the motel's small drained and closed-off swimming pool. After unpacking his bags and briefcase, spraying the room with lilac air freshener and turning on the TV, he carried Dawnette inside and threw her onto the bed. She was still tied up but he removed the tape from her other eye.

He disabled the lock on the bathroom, washed his hands thoroughly and then ordered Dawnette to take a bath. He made Tina lie on one of the two double beds and watch television while he went through the ritual of untying Dawnette's wrists and ankles, then removing her clothes and carefully folding them. When she was naked, he pushed her into the bathtub and told her to get washed but not to get her hair wet. When she was finished and had dried herself Wilder led her back into the bedroom.

'Go take a shower,' he told Tina. 'I want to play with little Ma Ma.'

Tired and numb, Tina did as she was told. As she started undressing, she saw him push Dawnette down on the bed and start spraying her with a new perfume bottle.

Wilder took out the revolver, cocked the hammer and forced the muzzle into Dawnette's mouth. 'You're my little Mummy,' he whined in a high-pitched, childlike voice.

Tina turned away.

Wilder picked up a bullet and held it up in front of Dawnette's face, telling her in detail how a hollow-nosed bullet would explode inside her. 'That's what will happen if you don't do everything I say,' he said, smiling down at her.

He got undressed and raped her. At some point, Dawnette realised that Tina was back in the room, watching TV on the other bed. Wilder was barking commands at Dawnette.

'Oral.'

'Mount me.'

If she was too slow or didn't look like she was enjoying herself, he lost his temper and started hitting her in the stomach.

'I'll hurt the baby,' he shouted at her.

Dawnette did her best to deflect the blows, begging him to stop, but the more she resisted, the harder he struck her. Finally, as tears ran down her red-raw cheeks where his coarse stubble had rubbed against her skin, he tied her wrists and ankles once more and left her exhausted on the bedraggled bedclothes. As she drifted off to sleep, she saw Wilder move to the other bed where Tina lay naked on top of the threadbare sheets.

WEDNESDAY 11 APRIL 1984
BEST WESTERN DEL MAR
WAUSEON, OH

Early the next morning, before the sun had risen, Wilder was back in Dawnette's bed and sexually assaulting her yet again. When he'd finished, telling her angrily she still wasn't showing him enough passion, he said he was going to teach her a lesson.

'Go take a shower,' he ordered Tina.

She dutifully got up, and Dawnette could hear the water running as Wilder tied a wire to her right little toe.

'Don't move,' he told Dawnette, pushing a second wire deep into her vagina.

'Please, don't forget I'm pregnant,' Dawnette begged him.

Wilder ignored her, carefully cut more strips of silver duct tape and rammed them onto her mouth.

A moment before he flicked the switch, he said, 'It will only last a minute. If you make one single sound, you'll regret it.'

Dawnette had never experienced pain like it before. She couldn't scream because of the tape, but it was impossible not to moan.

It infuriated Wilder.

He flicked the switch twice more.

Dawnette felt her warm urine trickle down her legs.

Wilder lost his temper completely.

Grabbing the revolver, he pushed it into her breast and began twisting the barrel down hard into the flesh. The pain was excruciating. Dawnette tried to stop herself moaning by biting down on the inside of her cheek. She felt herself losing consciousness.

Wilder leaned down and whispered in her ear. 'Time to get showered and dressed. Slut.'

Dawnette walked into the bathroom as Tina walked out. The two girls, who had barely said a word to each other since their worlds had collided, passed each other in heavy silence. She wondered how many other girls there'd been. The television was still playing loudly in the background and, as she dragged on her clothes, watching him carefully pack his bag and briefcase, the news headlines came on. Dawnette looked up as a black and white photograph filled the screen. She recognised it instantly and turned towards Wilder, who had also stopped to watch.

'They're looking for me,' he told her, an arrogant half smile on his thin lips. He sat down alongside Tina, who was perched on the end of the double bed nearest to the door, and watched the rest of the bulletin.

When it had finished, Dawnette realised her chances of staying alive were non-existent. There had been no mention of Tina, which was odd. She wanted to know what had happened to the pretty girl, Michelle, but didn't dare ask.

'You're driving again,' he told Tina. Dawnette felt a strange pang of jealousy.

———————

Wilder had plans, and he didn't want the new girl to get in the way; he didn't trust her yet, sensing she wasn't fully broken in. He'd given her some of his clothes, a blue T-shirt and denim jacket, to replace the blouse he'd ripped when he first undressed her. He knew she was going to spend a lot of time tied up today and it would get cold in the back of the car. He took three blue tablets from a small pill bottle he kept in his briefcase.

'What about the baby?' Dawnette pleaded.

Wilder took out the knife.

Dawnette swallowed the pills and started crying. 'My mum doesn't even know I'm pregnant yet.'

Wilder slapped her across the cheek. 'Shut the fuck up, bitch.'

He threw her into the back of the car and covered her with some clothes from the jumble he kept in the boot.

28

NATURAL ATTRACTION

WEDNESDAY 11 APRIL 1984
TORRANCE, CA

The FBI and Torrance police told the media they believed Tina Marie Risico was Wilder's latest victim. Officer Ronald Traber, standing alongside Special Agent John Hoos, informed reporters Tina had been seen with a man who looked like Wilder shortly before she vanished. 'We consider her a "critical missing", because if it is Wilder she was with, then she is in serious trouble,' Traber said.

The owner of the Hickory Farms store where Tina had her job interview was questioned later that day and told agents that a man he noticed following the teenager out of the store could have been Wilder.

Tina's divorced parents put their differences aside to attend the press conference together. Her mother, Carol, said, 'If this guy does have her, so help me God, he better not cross my path. I'm not excluding the possibility she could have been captivated by his charm. I hope she didn't become that stupid.'

Tina's father, Joe Risico, described his daughter as 'the average sixteen-year-old; she has fantasies of being a model just like any other girl'.

The bureau announced that the disappearance of Virginia Scott was no longer being linked to Wilder – she had been found. Meanwhile, Democratic assemblyman Richard Robinson spent $4000 from his campaign funds to buy a full-page ad in Wednesday's *Sacramento Bee* with a modified version of the FBI's 'Wilder Wanted' poster. Michelle Korfman, who had gone missing from the Las Vegas beauty pageant on 1 April, was his wife's cousin. The ad generated dozens of 'look-alike' sightings that kept police busy for days, but none of them checked out.

MIAMI, FL

John Hanlon sent an FBI agent to interview Wilder's brother Stephen, freshly arrived from Australia at the request of their father, Coley, to see if a direct appeal from a family member might persuade his eldest son to give himself up and end the rampage bringing shame to the family. The bureau's Behavioural Science Unit at Quantico discussed the possibility of backing such an appeal, but warned it would only work if the relationship between the two brothers was amicable and positive.

The agent who did the interview phoned in immediately to inform Hanlon that according to Steve Wilder, 'There is a good deal of jealousy and animosity between the two brothers.'

The advice from the BSU was clear: 'If the relationship was one as described by Steve Wilder, the publicity given to Steve and Wilder's ill feelings toward him might provoke Wilder to commit more crimes as a means of drawing more attention to himself.'

RAINBOW BRIDGE

NIAGARA FALLS, NY

After five solid hours on the highway along Interstate 90, from one end of vast Lake Erie to the other, Wilder told Tina to follow the signs to Niagara Falls. Erie, fed by the Detroit River at one end and draining into the Niagara River and Niagara Falls at the other, sits on the international boundary between the US and Canada. Dawnette had slept most of the way and was still groggy when Wilder found a quiet spot to stop the car, tightened all her bindings, put more tape across her mouth and eyes, and covered her again with the clothes. He told her he was leaving a tape recorder on the front seat, and if he found out when he got back that she had made even the slightest noise, he would kill her immediately.

Dawnette lay, slipping in and out of consciousness, for almost an hour, while Wilder and Tina abandoned her to visit one of the world's most spectacular natural attractions. No-one looked at them twice as they mingled with the other tourists. At one point, Wilder gave Tina his camera, removed his baseball cap and posed for a photograph with the waterfalls as the backdrop.

Six days earlier, he'd been within 20 kilometres of the Mexican border, and now Wilder was less than 200 metres from Canadian soil, standing with Tina on Rainbow Bridge, watching foot passengers push through the metal turnstile to begin the process of crossing over into Ontario. How tempting it must have been to tag along behind a large group of tourists and make his escape across the border, but – wrongly, as it turned out – he believed the chances of him being stopped were too high. He had been issued with a new US passport less than a year previously, on 9 June 1983, but when the FBI requested a copy in order to supply details to every port of departure, the State Department couldn't comply – there was a backlog of more than a million passports waiting to be micro-filmed and logged. There is every chance, then, that Wilder and his passport would have passed through unnoticed in the melee of tourists crossing back and forth. The FBI, frustrated by the admin-istrative backlog, was reduced to making a formal request to be notified immediately if Wilder applied for a replacement.

EXIT 45 MOTEL
VICTOR, NY

By the time Wilder and Tina returned to the Cougar, Dawnette was awake, cold, hungry and distraught at being left alone in the black-ness. Wilder took the tape off one of her eyes but kept her bound and gagged while he took over at the wheel. They continued east on Interstate 90 for another ninety minutes until they hit the small town of Victor, in the north-west corner of Ontario County, and he pulled into the rundown Exit 45 Motel. Craning her neck on the back seat, Dawnette could just about make out the faded and peeling white and blue painted pillars. There was a double billboard outside, facing the highway, but she couldn't make out what it said. Tina, sitting in the passenger seat in silence, noted the mostly empty restaurant at the very front of the building. It was still late afternoon when Wilder registered as Mr and Mrs LK Kimbrell, paying once again with Zeke's Visa card. He drove the car to the end of the block and backed it up almost to the door. He carried all the bags and his briefcase inside and went through his usual ritual.

Dawnette's legs were so cramped and sore from being tied together for endless hours that she staggered forward and had to grab hold of the door frame as she stumbled into the room. She thought momentarily about screaming, causing a scene or making a run for it to the reception area, but despite having slept a large portion of the day, she was physically drained. She was also certain he would shoot her in the back without a second thought.

Once inside the room, the full horrors of the previous night were replayed, while Tina lay on the second bed watching television. Wilder raped Dawnette several times, stopping regularly to give her lengthy electric shocks, which he claimed were punishment for her poor performance. When he was finished, he reached into his briefcase and took out a little bag of white powder.

'Cocaine, stick out your tongue,' he told Dawnette.

She hesitated, and he punched her in the stomach. When she got her breath back, he ordered her again to stick out her tongue. This time, she obeyed instantly. He covered the inside of her lips and the tip of her tongue with a generous dusting of powder.

'Swallow, bitch. It will help you relax. You'll be a much better fuck,' he barked at her. 'Now put your tongue into my mouth,' he added, facing her so that his sour breath washed over her. Wilder bit down hard and clamped her tongue between his teeth. He made her repeat this several times until her tongue was so sore and swollen, she could barely manage to say, 'Yes, dear,' when he asked if she had enjoyed fucking him. There was no way she would be able to scream for help now.

'Let that be a lesson. You are not acting naturally and pleasing me. Who do you belong to, little Ma Ma?'

'You, sir,' she choked out.

He took the wire from her toe, ripped the tape off her eyes and gave her a pair of scissors. 'Go and cut your hair.'

He watched her for a while, but soon became impatient, grabbed the scissors off her and hacked away at her thick curls. Then he ordered her back to the bed and trimmed her pubic hair. If she flinched, he jabbed her with the live wire until her skin singed. Then he forced both girls to drink several glasses of water, because they wouldn't be eating that night, told them to get on the bed together, and then told 'little Ma Ma' to follow his instructions and make love to Tina. Both teenagers looked each other in the eye, embarrassed. Dawnette could see the extent of Tina's injuries. Her body was covered in ugly brown scars from the electric shock treatment, but it was her breasts that had borne the brunt of Wilder's inhumanity. Every possible colour of bruising was evident, from black through to bluish-green circles caused by the revolver muzzle being twisted deep into the breast tissue. Dawnette gasped in silence when she saw the number of bite marks, including one that seemed to have removed some of Tina's flesh.

ABC *WORLD NEWS TONIGHT*
WEST 66TH STREET
NEW YORK, NY

Anchor Peter Jennings reported the latest on the hunt for Wilder in segment ten of *World News Tonight*, broadcast from the network's New York studios.

'Some word today about a manhunt that's become familiar to a lot of people across the country,' said Jennings. 'The federal authorities now say that Christopher Wilder, already wanted for at least two and as many as eight murders coast to coast, was seen in Torrance, California, the same day that a young girl disappeared. Authorities fear the girl may be Wilder's ninth victim.'

THURSDAY 12 APRIL 1984
THE TIMES
GARY, IN

A story in Dawnette's local newspaper back home in Indiana, *The Times*, reflected how much Wilder was confounding authorities.

The brief article was next to the obituaries under the headline 'Teen girl missing', but it made no mention of Wilder. The authorities still hadn't linked Dawnette's disappearance to the fugitive.

'DYER – Police have issued an appeal for information on the whereabouts of a sixteen-year-old girl last seen Tuesday night.

'Dawnette Sue Wilt, a student at Lake Central High School, was last seen at 7 p.m. Tuesday at Southlake Mall, Lake County Police Spokesman Michael Higgins said today.'

EXIT 45 MOTEL

VICTOR, NY

In the early hours of the morning, Wilder woke up Dawnette and forced her to watch while he blindfolded and then raped Tina. Afterwards, he took a length of thin plastic rope from his briefcase, tied it around Dawnette's breasts and laughed as he explained how he wanted to see his 'Mummy's baby milk'. He pulled the rope tighter and tighter until her breasts turned blue, then raped her, stopping only when she was on the brink of unconsciousness.

29

GOOD VS EVIL

THURSDAY 12 APRIL 1984
EXIT 45 MOTEL
VICTOR, NY

Wilder decided to take his first shower since his abduction of Dawnette. Wary of leaving the girls alone, he jammed a chair under the handle of the main door and made a point of showing them the fully loaded gun he was taking into the bathroom with him. He shaved, then quickly got under the shower. As he was getting dressed, Dawnette suddenly let out a gasp and turned to Tina.

'It's your mum.'

David Hartman, the host of ABC's *Good Morning America*, was talking through the show's major exclusive on the FBI manhunt for Christopher Wilder. Showing photographs of the fugitive and his latest missing victim, Tina Risico, he said they had both last been seen in Los Angeles on 4 April. Then he introduced the studio's special guest, Tina's mum, Carol. He invited her to make a very personal mother's appeal to Tina's abductor. Looking directly into the camera, her voice trembling, Carol asked Wilder to spare her daughter's life. Dawnette and Tina, sitting on the two motel-room beds, and Wilder, who stood in the bathroom doorway, were captivated as they watched Carol beg him to show mercy to her daughter. Wilder was visibly agitated. Tina was crying quietly.

'That's it, you're going home!'

He ordered the girls to get dressed while he packed his suitcase and briefcase, a little more haphazardly than was his normal routine. This was unplanned and uncharted territory for him, and he was freaked and well out of his comfort zone. He liked order and control, to have a plan to follow, and now he felt enormous pressure. It was the kind of pressure psychologist Dr Geraldine Boozer had warned the court about years earlier, the kind of pressure she said made Wilder psychotic and in urgent need of treatment. Left to his own resources, she predicted, he would disintegrate and regress even further.

WELKER ROAD

BARRINGTON, NY

Before they left the motel shortly after 8 a.m., Wilder forced a pro-testing Dawnette, at gunpoint, to swallow two more of the blue sleeping tablets. He wore the same brown corduroy trousers and pale grey close-knit wool cardigan as yesterday, but he'd put on a fresh polo shirt featuring horizontal red, white and blue stripes, with 'Australia' printed on the left breast. He was still wearing his favourite pointy-toed Wagner boots.

They headed east on Interstate 90, and thanks to the pills, Dawnette soon fell asleep. She woke up to hear Wilder telling Tina to pull over by the side of the road. She could tell they were in a woodland area, off the beaten track. Despite her grogginess, Dawnette knew she was in trouble. Wilder got out, walked around to the boot and came back with the briefcase and gun.

'Get out of the car,' he ordered Dawnette.

He took the car keys out of the ignition and, pushing her in the back with the gun, told Dawnette to 'start walking'.

Tina also got out of the Cougar, but Wilder looked back over his shoulder and shook his head. 'Turn around or you will end up like those girls from Miami,' he told Tina.

Dawnette was shortening her steps and trying to move as slowly as possible.

'I will let you go if you obey me and don't try to escape,' Wilder said.

'Please don't do this, please don't do this,' Dawnette cried.

'Kneel down, bitch,' he shouted, shoving her in the shoulder with the barrel of the gun. She dropped to the damp ground, and Wilder put down the briefcase with his left hand while pointing the gun at her with his right.

He was in the woods with Dawnette around half an hour, torturing and abusing her. When he was finished and she lay on the ground sobbing, her clothes ripped, Wilder ordered her to kneel again and started tying her hands and feet behind her back. Dawnette, knowing she was about to die, said a silent prayer and asked Wilder for one final wish.

'Please, Chris,' she begged him, using his name for the first time, 'at least make it quick and use the gun so we don't suffer. Not the knife, please.'

Wilder gave a snort of derision as he ripped off three pieces of duct tape, pressing them firmly over her mouth one by one, smiling and shaking his head slowly as he did it.

He lowered his head so it was beside hers and whispered in her ear, 'Do as you're told and hold your breath. Nod when you can't hold it any longer.'

She held her breath a moment and then gave a quick nod. There was still some air left in her lungs; she'd kept a bit in reserve, not knowing what he had planned.

Wilder grabbed her nose and pinched her nostrils together tightly so that her eyes began to water. Summoning up every last ounce of energy and determination she could find, she began to struggle, wriggling and twisting from side to side. His grip on her was vice like, but pain had lost all relevance to her. She was going to go out fighting. A couple of times, she broke free just long enough to draw a short breath before he grabbed her again.

The desperate grapple went on for a while before Wilder gave up, threw her down to the ground, pulled out his hunting knife and stabbed her twice in the back. Then, turning her around to face him, he delivered another thrust of the knife into her chest. She began crying hysterically and he watched her intently as blood started pumping from her wounds. She tried to turn onto her side in an attempt to protect her unborn child, pleading between sobs for him to stop and help her. Wilder ignored her completely, closed his briefcase, stood up and walked away.

Dawnette shouted, with all the venom she could muster, 'I hate you, I hope you die . . .'

Wilder broke his stride. He bent down, grabbed a handful of large dead leaves and used them to clean the blood dripping from his hunting knife. After drawing the blade across them two or three times, he dropped the leaves and pushed the knife into its normal position in his right boot. He still didn't turn around, just tilted his head to the side and told her, 'Shut up and die, bitch.'

———

Tina sat in the Cougar, not daring to move. She had wound down the car window and strained to listen, but she didn't hear a gunshot or any screams. When she finally saw Wilder walking back hurriedly to the car, she looked behind him, but there was no sign of Dawnette. When he got a bit nearer, she could see he was shaky. He wasn't carrying the gun in his hands, and she couldn't see any bloodstains on his clothes. He put the briefcase on the back seat, handed her the car keys and told her to get them the hell out of there.

The spot Wilder chose to kill Dawnette was a long way after turning off Interstate 90, around 50 kilometres on Route 14A, which passed through Yates County in New York's Finger Lakes Region. It was a sparsely populated area of rolling farmland dissected by numerous creeks and waterways. Twenty minutes further along, at the southern tip of Seneca Lake, was Watkins Glen International, the legendary home of the United States Grand Prix and the mecca of American road racing. Wilder had always wanted to race there.

CAMPBELL JUNIOR HIGH SCHOOL
DAYTONA BEACH, FL

Twenty-eight days after Colleen Orsborn played hooky to go to the beach, there was an announcement at her high school about her disappearance. Her fellow student Angela Graham came forward and described her strange encounter with the bearded man in mirrored sunglasses at the basketball court on that fateful day. The next day an FBI agent and Daytona Beach detective showed the schoolgirl a photographic line-up of suspects. Angela didn't hesitate, pointing straight to the picture of Wilder and giving them a description of the car he had been driving, which was very similar to a Chrysler New Yorker. John Hanlon and the FBI had placed Colleen on a list of suspected Wilder victims days earlier, based on credit card charges that put him in the general area on the day she went missing. Now they had an eyewitness who placed him only a couple of hundred metres from Colleen's home and the boardwalk where she was headed.

30

GUARDIAN ANGEL

THURSDAY 12 APRIL 1984
WELKER ROAD
BARRINGTON, NY

Dawnette was tough. Having lived through forty hours of terror, she wasn't about to lie back and die in a scrubby grass field far away from home. She told herself over and over, like she was repeating a mantra, that she was 'not going to let him win, not going to let him win'. Light-headed and woozy, 'I am a survivor,' she said out loud, forcing herself to sit up slowly. Bleeding heavily, she told herself she couldn't give up. In her frantic struggle with Wilder, the rope around her wrists had loosened enough that after a few tugs, she managed to free her hands. She immediately pressed her fingers against her wounds and could feel the warm stickiness of her blood as she used her fingers like a compression bandage.

She knew moving would make the blood loss worse, but she had no choice. Taking a couple of long deep breaths to try and calm her throbbing pulse, she took her hands away from her chest, reached down and untied the bindings on her feet. The ground seemed to move beneath her as she attempted to get up. Closing her eyes and forcing herself to focus, she managed a bent-over crouch, clutching at her chest again. She noticed her bra and shirt, which Wilder had ripped off her, lying in the grass nearby, and she shuffled over and picked them up, wrapping them around her chest, above and below the stab wounds, twisting them as tightly as possible to slow down the blood loss. She'd lost one shoe in the struggle and put her bare foot down first. While she lurched forward, she didn't fall. She took another dozen steps and stopped to catch her breath and check her makeshift bandages. Her bra was turning crimson, but it seemed to be stemming the blood loss. She stumbled forwards, but when she was almost back to the road, she heard a car engine. Wilder. He must have come back. Dawnette looked around anxiously, trying to find a hiding place in the small woodland forest of oak, hickory and towering red maples.

———

Wilder was panicking. Three times he'd stabbed her with the serrated knife, twice in the back and then in the chest, and that should have been more than enough, but she'd startled him when she had shouted at him as he walked away; he didn't like that at all. He should have gone back and finished her off straight away. Stupid. It had been fifteen minutes. Surely she would have bled out by now. But he had to make sure. He couldn't take any chances.

He left Tina in the car again and ordered her to wait. He was confident she would. She hadn't said a single word; it was as if she had shrunk herself into the car seat.

He found the blood, so he knew he was in the right place, but he couldn't see Dawnette anywhere. He twisted around, his movements jerky and confused, trying and failing to pick up her trail. He panicked and careened back to the car. Tina could see he was highly agitated. He flung open the driver's door and pushed her across into the passenger seat.

'She's gone, she's gone, the fucking bitch has gone,' he mumbled angrily, fumbling for the car keys in his trouser pocket. His hands were shaking so much he couldn't get them out, and he kept looking in the rear-view mirror, then out the front windscreen, his eyes darting everywhere, as if expecting to see a ghost.

'We've got to find another car,' he said, more to himself than to Tina, as he finally freed the keys, jammed them into the ignition and pulled away in a squeal of tyres.

———

Dawnette had heard his cowboy boots crunching through the leaves and fallen tree branches. She had been squatting behind a fallen oak trunk, holding her breath and praying.

The moment she heard the car take off, she stood up delicately and resumed her slow, limping walk towards the road. She was still scared, uncertain Wilder had really left. She knew how cunning he was and how much he liked to play mind games. He could simply be waiting for her to appear out of the woods and then run her down, but she had no choice. She needed to get help urgently. Welker Road was little more than a dirt road servicing a few local farms; it was not a shortcut to anywhere and saw very little passing traffic. When it did, it was usually because the driver was lost. Fortunately for Dawnette, tractor mechanic Charles Laursen picked that very day to go off-course on his way to a repair job. The Vietnam vet had just realised his mistake when he reached the crest of a small hill and saw a bedraggled young girl staggering along the roadway towards him. The 41-year-old hit the brakes and sprang out of his truck, catching the distressed teen in his arms.

'I've been stabbed,' she mumbled, barely conscious.

Laursen lifted the girl gently onto the back seat of his car. Covered in blood, with ripped clothes tied around her chest, she was rambling, crying the man who had done it had left her to die, then come back looking for her.

Laursen wasn't taking any chances. He covered her with his big jacket. 'Stay down,' he told her, as he headed off towards the nearest hospital.

SOLDIERS AND SAILORS MEMORIAL HOSPITAL
PENN YAN, NY

Laursen did the fifteen-minute journey in a frantic ten minutes, squealing to a halt directly outside the emergency trauma unit in the bay reserved for ambulances. He was honking his horn before he even stopped, and two paramedics taking a quick break nearby stubbed out their cigarettes and ran to help.

'It was pure luck I found her,' Charles told the sheriff deputies, who arrived ten minutes later. There were two Martin farms on Welker Road, and if he hadn't gone to the wrong one, he never would have spotted her.

LAW ENFORCEMENT TRAINING CONFERENCE
BATAVIA, NY

Ron Spike, chief deputy sheriff of Yates County, had been groomed to carry a badge and a gun from almost the moment he was born. His father, George, had been sheriff for twenty-three years until his retirement three years earlier, and Spike had lived in the Penn Yan sheriff's residence, which was attached to the county jail, most of his life. The young officer, who'd only got married eighteen months earlier, was a good investigator, calm and confident with a cheeky sense of humour. He was already a decorated officer after saving a homeowner's life in a house fire.

That morning Spike and his partner Dale Mitchell were attending a conference on outlaw motorcycle gangs in Batavia, a 125-kilometre drive west on Interstate 90. They'd arrived a little early before the training started, and Ron got them both a strong coffee and picked up a copy of USA Today. On the second page, under the heading 'News Makers', he found himself engrossed reading about a wealthy playboy racing driver who was a wanted fugitive for the suspected murder and abduction of a string of beautiful women. It was the first time he'd heard the name Christopher Wilder, details of his crimes or of the federal manhunt for him.

The focus of the FBI search had remained in Southern California where the last sighting of Wilder had been confirmed. While the bureau's field offices nationwide had been copied in on the teletype updates about the case, the 'Wanted' flyer posters featuring Wilder's photograph had so far been distributed only west of the Mississippi River. No law enforcement agency in New York State had received one.

During a break in training, the conference organiser received a message for Spike from the Penn Yan sheriff's office. Immediately on being handed the note, Spike excused himself and went outside to a find a payphone and call in. 'You'd better get back here quick, a young girl was left to die by the side of the road in Barrington and was taken to Soldiers and Sailors Hospital with stab wounds,' the deputy said frantically.

Spike hung up, grabbed the issue of *USA Today*, ripping out the article about Wilder, waved his partner over and, minutes later, was behind the wheel of his cruiser, tearing down the highway, siren and lights flashing. Spike had a hunch. He pulled the creased clipping out of his jacket pocket and handed it to his partner.

'Read this,' he told him, 'I think that's who we're looking for!'

They made the usual ninety-minute journey in not much more than an hour.

SOLDIERS AND SAILORS MEMORIAL HOSPITAL
PENN YAN, NY

Yates County sheriff Jan Scofield got to the hospital and took control on the ground until Spike arrived. Officers were sent with Laursen back out to Welker Road to find, search and secure the crime scene, while three were stationed at the hospital to stand guard over Dawnette, who was being treated and examined by doctors for multiple injuries. Despite suffering from severe trauma, blood loss and serious internal injuries, she had been able to tell the first-responder officers she had been kidnapped from a shopping mall in Indiana by a man called Chris, and a young girl who had called herself Tina Marie Wilder. Sheriff Scofield alerted the FBI in Buffalo.

WELKER ROAD CRIME SCENE
BARRINGTON, NY

Meanwhile, back at Welker Road the evidence was starting to mount up, including the bloodied pile of leaves Wilder had used to clean the knife, the discarded rope Dawnette had managed to untie from her wrists and ankles, her shoe that had come off during the struggle to stop him smothering her, and a plaster cast of her abductor's boot print with a pointed toe and distinctive heel. Officers also made inquiries at the farms in the area and found a couple of workers who recalled seeing a Mercury Cougar parked on the side of the road with a young girl sitting inside. They had thought it was odd because the second time they saw the car, it was parked on the other side of the road, facing in the opposite direction, and this time there was a man who seemed to be trying to hide from them as they drove past.

FBI FIELD OFFICE
BUFFALO, NY

Urgent FBI teletype messages were sent to police departments across Pennsylvania, New York, New Jersey and Maryland, warning them Wilder was now a suspect in the kidnapping and attempted murder of a sixteen-year-old girl and could be heading south to Florida along Interstate 95. Troopers in upstate New York were put on 'maximum alert' and ordered to set up roadblocks and check every motel along a 40-kilometre stretch of Route 9 between Schenectady and Saratoga Springs.

KENYON FAMILY'S HOUSE
LOCKPORT, NY

As soon as word came through that Wilder could be in New York State, John Hanlon had agents contact the sheriff of Niagara County to provide protection for Beth Kenyon's family.

3 1

ALL THAT GLITTERS

I mean I never feel I feel what I ought to feel.
— John Fowles, *The Collector*

UNSUB; BETH S DODGE, 00:MM BUFFALO FBI FILE 7-662

THURSDAY 12 APRIL 1984
EASTVIEW MALL
VICTOR, NY

Single mum Beth Dodge was beginning a new chapter in her life after recently divorcing her husband. The couple had stayed good friends, and they carefully juggled the care of their four-year-old daughter, Stephanie. Beth had kept the family home, a renovated ranch-style house in Phelps, Buffalo. The pretty, slender 33-year-old was a systems analyst for the Mobil Chemical Co. in Pittsford, a thirty-minute drive away along Interstate 90, and every morning she dropped Stephanie off with a babysitter on her way into work.

In most ways, Beth was an average, everyday American mum. There was just one anomaly, one indulgence: her love of flash cars. Her 1982 two-door metallic gold Pontiac Firebird was a real head-turner, with gold hubcaps and a black eagle logo emblazoned on the bonnet. Unfortunately for Beth, it was just the type of car that a racing-driver psychopath on a killing spree would notice.

A few of Beth's work colleagues saw her leave for lunch at 12.55 p.m. that day. She gave them a quick wave as she zipped away in the Firebird. A few minutes later she turned into the Eastview shopping mall, where she was meeting friends for lunch.

———————

Meanwhile, after fleeing Welker Road, Wilder had only one thought on his mind: to find another car before the alarm was raised and Terry Walden's stolen Cougar became the hottest car in New York State. He knew if Dawnette had survived and got help, the quiet back-water would be quickly sealed off and swarming with cops and FBI agents. He swapped seats with Tina and made her drive while he studied the map and barked out directions. They headed to the shopping mall closest to the motel where they had stayed the previous night in Victor, which was only 70 kilometres away. Keeping to the back roads as much as possible, it took them well over an hour. Wilder parked the Cougar in a quiet part of the car park with a view of the entrance.

He'd hardly spoken to Tina since Dawnette had vanished, but now he turned and told her he was going to let her go home. Tina sensed this time he really meant it. He expected to die soon, he told her, and he didn't want her to get hurt or be around to see it. Tina sat with her hands in her lap, looking out of the front windscreen, not saying a word.

Wilder was watching dozens of cars enter the mall car park without interest when he saw a glittery gold high-performance Firebird Trans Am, the pop-up headlights recessed in its sleek bodywork. It appeared to be driven by an attractive brunette. He started up the Cougar and tailed the Firebird through the car park until it pulled into an empty spot. Wilder eased into the space directly behind and told Tina to get into the driver's seat and follow the Firebird.

Beth Dodge, wearing a lavender business suit, nylon stockings and blue shoes, stepped out of the Firebird. Wilder walked straight up to her and pointed the gun at her head.

'Get back in the car and climb into the passenger seat,' he barked out. 'I have killed before, and I will shoot you if you don't obey me.'

Beth, petrified, did as she was told. Wilder climbed into the car after her and slipped behind the wheel. He kept the gun trained on her and told her to crouch down as low as she could in the passenger floor area.

Tina, in the Cougar behind, watched it all. She noticed a man working on a green car in a nearby alleyway looking directly at the Firebird. He stood rooted to the spot as if he couldn't quite believe what he had just seen.

When Wilder drove away, holding the steering wheel in one hand and the gun in the other, Tina followed directly behind. The two-car convoy drove carefully, obeying all road rules and speed restrictions, for almost half an hour before Wilder found what he was looking for on a quiet stretch of Cork Road, roughly 8 kilometres from the mall. It was a paved road with occasional traffic in both directions, but with an area, behind a large mound of dirt and gravel, that couldn't be seen by passing cars. Wilder had parked off the side of the road and when Tina pulled up behind him, he told her to hand over the keys to the Cougar and wait. He walked to the passenger side of the Firebird and opened the door, motioning with the gun for Beth to get out.

Tina wound down the driver's window as far as it would go.

Once he was out of sight Wilder didn't waste any time, telling Beth to kneel down and then shooting her, once, in the back. Beth wasn't tortured, tied up or raped, Wilder didn't care about her at all, he simply wanted to have her car. She was killed instantly where she fell, facedown in the dirt, the .357 jacketed Magnum bullet piercing her heart and exiting through her breast.

Tina jumped when she heard a loud 'boom' and straight away assumed it was a gunshot. Wilder came quickly back, looking hyper, and threw her the keys to the Cougar. 'Follow me into town,' he barked at her.

GRAVEL PIT AT CORK ROAD
VICTOR, NY

Less than fifteen minutes later, two Sears delivery men, stopping for a roadside smoke and lunch break, found Beth Dodge's body. They were never able to explain why, but the men decided to complete their delivery *before* reporting the discovery, so police weren't alerted until an hour after Beth had been killed.

MCGHAN'S NEARLY FAMOUS PUB
VICTOR, NY

Meanwhile, Wilder was searching the sleepy town for somewhere to dump Terry Walden's stolen Mercury Cougar. On Victor's main street he stopped outside a rundown petrol station and hurriedly transferred all his bags to the Firebird. He told Tina to park the Cougar outside a local tavern called McGhan's Nearly Famous Pub, then removed the licence plates and released the air from the front right tyre until it was flat.

KENYON FAMILY'S HOUSE
LOCKPORT, NY

The FBI still had no clear idea where Wilder was, so three sheriff's deputies armed with shotguns were stationed inside the Kenyon house, in case he came looking for Beth's family. Bill and Dolores were still in Pompano Beach searching for their daughter, but Beth's brothers William and Tim were put on alert at the grocery stores the family owned in the area. Bill Kenyon, a veteran of the Korean War, believed Wilder was headed to the house because he had Beth's New York driver's licence, with the address on it, and a key to the front door, which she'd carried in her purse.

TINA RISICO'S HOUSE
TORRANCE, CA

Dawnette's statement that Wilder had been with a girl calling herself Tina Marie Wilder had filtered out to the media. Tina's mother, Carol, was besieged by newspaper and TV reporters on the telephone and at her front door claiming her daughter had become Wilder's accomplice, brainwashed like Patty Hearst.

'She is doing whatever she has to do to survive,' Carol told them. 'Tina has a strong desire to stay alive.'

SOLDIERS AND SAILORS MEMORIAL HOSPITAL
PENN YAN, NY

FBI agents from the Buffalo field office arrived at the hospital in Penn Yan with a copy of Wilder's 'Wanted' poster and a big-city attitude. They headed straight for Dawnette's room only to find their way barred by two Yates County sheriff's officers. The agents were in a hurry to show the teenager the poster and see if she could identify Wilder as her abductor, but Spike, who had arrived from Batavia, refused to let them past. There was an ugly stand-off, as the agents flourished a copy of a federal warrant issued in Georgia for the arrest of Wilder over the kidnap and rape of Linda Grober, only for Spike to counter with, 'And I have an attempted murder in my town, another Wilder victim who has survived.'

The stocky, level-headed chief deputy sheriff argued any positive identification from the poster would be inadmissible in a New York court if a trial ensued, because the only photograph on it was of Wilder. He asked them to give him ten minutes to prepare a proper photographic line-up that would hold up as evidence to put before a jury. The Yates County sheriff's office was only a few hundred metres from the hospital, and Spike was able to dash over and quickly assemble a nine-suspect array of photos. When he went in to Dawnette's room with the lead FBI agent and showed her the montage of faces, the two men held their breath. The courageous teen moved her eyes across the three rows of suspects and pointed straight to Wilder's photo, telling them, 'That's him, that's the man who kidnapped and tried to kill me.'

The FBI agent did a quick interview with Dawnette before she was wheeled into the operating theatre and sent a memo to the director that was forwarded to every bureau office in the country. The frontline of the fugitive search switched from Southern California in the west right across the country to the upper eastern states, particularly New York, New Hampshire and Pennsylvania. The memo read:

Dawnette stated she was able to talk to Tina Wilder occasionally and understands Tina was kidnapped about one week prior in California. At that time she had long hair. Subject cut her hair off real short. Victim indicated subject appeared to like Tina better than her, allowed her to drive the automobile and gave her more freedom.

FBI FIELD OFFICE
BUFFALO, NY

Evidence of the chaos and confusion surrounding the dramatically escalating events was apparent at a hectic afternoon news conference hosted by FBI special agent Philip D Smith in Buffalo. He described the latest reports of Wilder's possible flight across the country to New York State as 'solid enough so we're concerned. It's a very good chance this could be Christopher Wilder'.

He revealed the kidnapped girl, whom he didn't name, had been able to describe how she'd been abducted by a man and a young woman at gunpoint in Lake County, Indiana, earlier in the week.

'The description she gave matched Wilder's to a T,' said fellow agent Michael Kogut, adding she'd also been able to tell them the pair were driving a Mercury Cougar, sporting light-coloured out-of-state licence plates, with a clothing rack in the back.

Smith then told reporters that it didn't look like Wilder had any connection with a woman's body found in Victor earlier that afternoon.

PHELPS POLICE DEPARTMENT
PHELPS, NY

It was the babysitter who raised the alarm at 6 p.m. when Beth didn't arrive to pick up Stephanie. She tried contacting her at work, without success, then rang her ex-husband William. When he got worried and contacted police, it didn't take long for officers to match his description of Beth to the unidentified body found earlier near Victor.

MCGHAN'S NEARLY FAMOUS PUB
VICTOR, NY

The Mercury Cougar that Wilder had dumped outside the bar on Victor's main street was found at 10.30 p.m. by a sharp-eyed patrolman who recognised it from the statewide BOLO description. Inside, he could see a man's wristwatch hanging from the indicator stick. Had Wilder left it behind by accident, or was it some kind of subtle message to his pursuers? The footwells of the car were filled with debris and fast-food packaging, and there were bloodstains visible in the boot. A mobile FBI lab was dispatched immediately to begin a forensic examination.

32

WRITE THE BOOK, KID

THURSDAY 12 APRIL 1984

INTERSTATE 90

NEAR WESTMORELAND, NY

Wilder had engineered enough time to escape from Victor before the noose tightened. He'd removed all identification from the businesswoman before he'd shot her, hoping it would take a while before the cops realised he was driving her car. Now he was going to put Tina on a plane back to California. That way, especially if he put her on an overnight flight, she would be well out of the way, and out of the clutches of the FBI and the cops, while he made a dash for Canada. The car was a good one, with a powerful engine, one that would give him a fighting chance against the cops if he got into a chase. The gun was still safely nestled under the driver's seat in case he was cornered.

Wilder pulled into the next rest area they reached, at mile marker 250 on the eastbound side of Interstate 90 about 11 kilometres outside of Westmoreland, and grabbed his camera, several stolen licence plates, newspapers, paper towels, a pair of his shoes,

Dawnette's bag and identification papers, then dumped them all in a green metal garbage bin.

INTERSTATE 90
NEAR ALBANY, NY

Several hours after leaving Victor, just twenty minutes shy of Albany, Wilder tuned in to the radio news. The top item was the discovery of an unnamed teenage girl from Indiana, found alive after being stabbed and left for dead, by a suspect believed to be the wanted fugitive Christopher Wilder. Wilder switched off the radio and told Tina he was taking her to Boston airport instead of New York, so she could fly home. Tina's heart leaped in her throat, but she didn't say anything, terrified she might change his mind. On the drive to the airport, Wilder became expansive, unburdening himself as if he was in a therapy session with Ginger Bush.

ABC *WORLD NEWS TONIGHT*
WEST 66TH STREET STUDIOS
NEW YORK, NY

ABC news anchor Peter Jennings was broadcasting the latest, some of the details incorrect. 'The FBI says that two young women were found today in upstate New York,' Jennings told the nation. 'One girl alive and the other dead, and both appear to have been victims of Christopher Bernard Wilder. He is the man wanted in connection with a string of kidnappings and murders of young women nationwide. The FBI believes the dead woman is Tina Risico of Torrance, California, who disappeared last week. The other girl is believed to be from Indiana.'

LOGAN INTERNATIONAL AIRPORT
BOSTON, MA

After more than six tense and draining hours on the road, expecting a roadblock on the ground or a chopper in the sky, Wilder parked the Firebird in Boston's Logan International Airport. It was almost 9 p.m. when he escorted Tina inside the terminal, walking unchallenged past an army of security officers and patrolling police. Wilder had the revolver tucked into his pocket as he strode up to the Delta Air Lines ticketing desk. The cut-off time for the non-stop service to LA had passed, so the only other option was the red-eye, which entailed three separate flights with two stopovers in Atlanta, Georgia and Fort Worth, Texas. Wilder bought a one-way ticket with Kimbrell's Visa card in the name of Tina Kimbrell. Wilder handed her all the money in his wallet, several hundred dollars.

'Kiss me on the cheek,' Wilder said, looking at her.

She did as she was told.

'I'm probably going to Canada. Say hi to the law, they'll get a kick out of this. I'll enjoy watching it on TV.'

There was an awkward moment's silence, then he said, 'All you gotta do, kid, is write a book.'

They were his final words as he walked away and never looked back. As she watched him disappear, she dared to hope that maybe, just maybe, she was going to survive this, she was going to live, she was going home. She didn't think about calling the police or raising the alarm, she just wanted to get back with her family, as quickly as possible. She headed back inside the terminal, bought herself some French fries and sat down at a table. She started to laugh, the laughter became hysterical, then she started to cry. At 2.10 a.m., Tina got on the plane.

33

TIME TO THINK

FRIDAY 13 APRIL 1984
LOS ANGELES INTERNATIONAL AIRPORT (LAX), CA
Delta flight 933 touched down a few minutes late into LAX. Tina had slept most of the way on her third connecting flight, moving to an empty row of seats near the back to stretch out. In the terminal she tentatively followed the signs for the exit, still wearing her pink heels and the unwashed clothes Wilder had given her days ago. She walked straight past several banks of payphones but didn't stop to make a call. She hadn't said anything to any of the flight crews, and as she snaked her way through the crowds of passengers, pulling and pushing suitcases and trolleys, she kept her head down and ignored everyone, including the police and security officers patrolling the airport. Her photograph had been running on almost every news bulletin and in every newspaper for a week, particularly in Los Angeles, but not one person recognised the shabby-looking teenager walking among them, carrying no luggage or purse.

It was a sunny 24 degrees in Los Angeles, and Tina had to

squint as she stepped out of the terminal. She joined the queue at the cab rank, and for a moment felt like everything had been just a bad nightmare. When she reached the front of the queue and her taxi pulled up, she hesitated. Her mind was a complete blank and she had no idea what to do. She hadn't cried since her episode in Boston airport, and now she felt weird, like she didn't care about anything. She decided to go shopping.

She told the cab driver to head to Hermosa Beach, which was about twenty minutes away. It was her favourite beach and place to chill in LA. As they got nearer, Tina directed the cabbie to a women's fashion and lingerie store called The Tushery and asked him to wait for her outside, showing the roll of banknotes in her pocket to reassure him she could afford it. Stepping outside, she paused on the sidewalk and looked up at the sky. For days, she had spent almost the entire time in a car or a motel room, being tortured or raped, in fear for her life every waking minute. She took a moment to fill her lungs with the fresh, salty sea air. She was worried about her boyfriend Billy and her family. She knew her life was about to be hurled into a media storm, that the police and FBI would be grilling her, asking a million questions. She needed time alone, time to get prepared.

Tina had been freaked out by her mum's straight-to-camera nationwide TV appeal twenty-four hours earlier. That morning's newspapers were full of stories about her and Wilder, many of them reporting that the FBI thought she had become his collaborator.

'Federal authorities are now wondering whether a sixteen-year-old California girl kidnapped by Christopher Bernard Wilder has become his accomplice,' reported the Associated Press.

THE TUSHERY
HERMOSA BEACH, CA

Tina walked into the plush store, to a blast of cool air conditioning. It was a store she had often looked in but had never had the cash needed to step inside. She asked the assistant whether she could look at 'teddies' and lacy one-piece undergarments. The shop assistant thought the new customer looked familiar and was trying to place her when Tina announced, straight out, 'I'm the girl who's missing after being kidnapped. He gave me some money and put me on a plane in Boston last night.'

In the fitting room, Tina continued chatting away while she tried on different items.

'I don't want to call home yet,' she explained. 'I want to think about it. I'm really confused. I needed to do some shopping and have some time alone, because I figure I won't be alone much for a while.'

Amy Clement, the senior sales clerk, listened incredulously as Tina described how Wilder had forced her to drive across the country after intimidating her with a knife, a gun and other weapons, including an 'electronic instrument' that she could see had left extensive bruises on her chest. Tina bought six garments for $104.50 and paid for them with cash. When she was leaving the store, just before noon, Amy called the police to report what had happened, but by the time officers responded, they could find no sign of Tina. Amy described to them how the teenager had been 'very nonchalant – no emotion at all – like she was in a state of shock'.

Tina had taken a taxi to another store nearby, where she spent a further $200 on clothes, earrings, a swimming costume and a photo frame. The manager told police later that Tina had revealed who she was immediately and explained away her odd behaviour by saying, 'I just need peace and quiet.' The manager had told her it was Friday the thirteenth, and there was a lot of bad luck around, but Tina had replied, 'I'm lucky to be alive today.'

TORRANCE POLICE DEPARTMENT
TORRANCE, CA

Tina climbed back into the taxi with her arms full of shopping bags, but she still didn't go home to her grandmother's house, or to the police station. Instead, she headed over to her boyfriend Billy's place. There she showered and changed clothes. Since the tip-off from the lingerie store, every available cop had been carrying out a grid search around Hermosa Beach looking for her, but an hour later Tina walked into Torrance police headquarters, with Billy at her side, and turned herself in.

'He was going to kill me unless I cooperated,' she announced to everyone who would listen.

Police captain Jim Popp spent several hours interviewing and debriefing the teenager with detectives, FBI agents, doctors and a psychiatrist. He told a news conference, 'my personal opinion is that she was acting under a great deal of duress and coercion. The man killed ten, and she did what he wanted her to do; she did not have an opportunity to escape'.

Tina told them all that, in terms of Wilder's other victims, she was only aware of the two women he picked up while she was with him. She knew Dawnette's name, she said, but not the woman Wilder kidnapped at gunpoint and drove away in her gold Firebird. Tina said he had never mentioned any other abducted girls to her, apart from those he claimed to have sold into sexual slavery in Mexico, which the FBI found no evidence to support.

She said she'd protested when Wilder told her to approach Dawnette in the mall and bring her over to him, but he'd threatened to shoot her if she didn't, so, fearful for her own life, she had followed his orders. Later, when he told her to follow him and drive Dawnette's car, she did it, she said, because she had seen news reports describing him as a race-car driver, and he told her he would catch up and kill her if she attempted to flee. She denied ever assisting Wilder to tie up or threaten Dawnette or Beth Dodge and said she wasn't present when he stabbed Dawnette or shot Beth.

The FBI agent who interviewed Tina ended his written report to the director:

> Risico provided the above narrative matter-of-factly with no emotion other than apparent relief at having been spared. She could offer no suggestion or explanation for Wilder letting her go other than, 'He began to appreciate me as a person rather than just another female body.'
>
> It appears Risico was candid and honest in her statement and was genuinely intimidated by Wilder and did constantly fear for her life. If she had refused to obey him or attempted to escape, she truly believes she would have been killed.

During a break in the interviews, Tina's parents arrived at Torrance police station. 'It was a tearful reunion, with hugs and kisses, very touching. They were ecstatic,' said Sergeant Rollo Green, describing the moment to reporters.

Following her interview, an FBI agent took Tina to the Rape Treatment Center at Santa Monica Hospital with her mother, where after a medical examination, she received psychological counselling from Dr Roland Summit, before being transferred to Torrance Memorial Medical Center for the night.

'There is no indication that Tina Risico was anything but a fearful, terrified victim,' Dr Summit, a specialist in child abuse cases, told reporters. 'Ten days ago she was a free citizen,' he said. 'A moment later, she was under the influence of a man who represented himself as a friend and helper, and she moved willingly into a world that offered some promise.

'That promising world changed to terror when a weapon was produced and, from that point on, she was impressed repeatedly with the fact that her life stood in the balance.' Tina was 'subjected to sexual humiliation and brainwashing. The pattern follows explicitly one in which terror and obedience are instilled in the victim,' he added.

Asked why he thought Wilder had spared Tina's life, the doctor said, 'She did not meet his need to murder and destroy. I believe there was a kind of humanness, a kind of gentleness, a kind of need in this young woman that somehow did not provoke the kind of rage Wilder experienced with other people.'

34

FRIDAY THE
THIRTEENTH

*All I had to do was kill myself, then the others could think
what they liked.*

— John Fowles, *The Collector*

FRIDAY 13 APRIL 1984

ROUTE 128

WENHAM, MA

Nineteen-year-old Carol Hilbert, from Billerica, Massachusetts, had
broken down on her way to work. She was standing by her stalled
car, with the bonnet open, on the side of Route 128 in Wenham,
around forty minutes north of Boston. She had unsuccessfully tried
to start the engine so many times, her battery was flat. Cold and
late, she didn't think twice when a kind and charming motorist in
a gold-coloured sports car pulled up alongside and offered her a lift
to a nearby garage. Carol knew the area well and began to give him
directions, but she quickly noticed he wasn't following them and
was actually heading away from town. She glanced sideways at her
good Samaritan and started panicking. She'd followed the TV news
reports and seen the warning in the newspaper asking people in the

Boston area to be on the lookout for a rampaging serial killer. Now, the colour draining from her face, she realised she was sitting right beside him. Wilder was slowing down as they approached a stop sign and hadn't noticed his passenger had recognised him. Carol yanked the door handle as hard as she could and threw herself out, tumbling onto the hard shoulder and rolling over before coming to a stop. She jumped up immediately, and despite the cuts and grazes on her knees and elbows, she ran towards the first house she saw, hurdled the steps up to a small porch and pounded frantically on the front door until someone opened it. Only then did she look over her shoulder and see the Pontiac picking up speed and disappearing down the road.

WHITE MOUNTAIN ATTRACTIONS TOURIST OFFICE
EXIT 32, ROUTE 112
NORTH WOODSTOCK, NH

Wilder had put his foot to the floor after the girl had taken him completely by surprise by throwing herself from the car. He'd been so startled he hadn't even considered going after her; he'd just got onto the highway and not stopped again until he'd covered over 200 kilometres. When he reached North Woodstock on the edge of the White Mountain National Forest, he needed to stretch his legs and use a bathroom. He was stressing, needing to wash his hands and wanting a shave.

He parked outside the local tourist office and went inside, passing a sign that pointed to the restroom. David Downing was on duty behind the counter when Wilder re-emerged, wringing his hands to dry them, and asked him three quick questions: how did he get to Route 3? How far was Colebrook? How far was the Canadian border? Downing handed the well-dressed, well-tanned motorist a copy of the Innkeeper's Map of New England and traced the route for him. He noticed the man's accent, which he wrongly assumed was from England, and the chunky gold necklace and pendant around his neck. He gave him directions to Route 3, explaining that it was a ninety-minute drive to Colebrook, and the Canadian border crossing at Canaan was only 15 kilometres further on. Wilder thanked him politely, and Downing watched him walk out and get into a gold-coloured sports car parked outside.

Soon after leaving North Woodstock, Wilder drove through the Franconia Notch State Park. For a man in a hurry, the winding 12-kilometre stretch of highway between the Kinsman and Franconia mountain ranges, which had only one lane, must have been frustratingly slow. The road wound through unlogged old forests, with colossal hardwoods like yellow birch, beech and sugar maple, and the occasional softwood species, such as red spruce. He emerged on the other side and drove through several sleepy towns until he reached Colebrook. The Firebird was dangerously low on petrol.

MAIN STREET
COLEBROOK, NH

State troopers Leo 'Chuck' Jellison, Wayne Fortier and Howard Webber had just finished lunch at the Speedy Chef restaurant with Colebrook police chief Wayne Cross. Fortier had recently been transferred to the town and Jellison had organised the get-together to introduce his new partner around. After settling the bill, Jellison drove Cross and Webber to Colebrook police station and dropped them off. Jellison and Fortier were in plainclothes in an unmarked patrol car. As they came to a stop sign, Jellison picked up the police radio to log them on with dispatch. Before they moved off again, Fortier pointed to a gold Pontiac Firebird parked at the bowsers in the Getty service station on their left. It was similar to the vehicle they'd been alerted about earlier, same make, model and gold hubcaps, and there was no licence plate on the front. Jellison had printed out the teletype advisory message when their shift started, and it was tucked into the sun visor above his head. The two officers could see a tall white male standing between the petrol pumps and the car, wearing brown trousers, a light tan jacket over a blue shirt and a baseball cap. He was looking directly at them, a cautious look on his face, and continued staring at them as he walked inside the service station.

The manager of the service station thought the driver of the Firebird looked stressed when he walked in to pay for the fuel.

'What papers do I need to get into Canada?'

'A US driver's licence will probably do it,' he said, looking out of the window as a station wagon pulled onto the forecourt.

'What about insurance papers, with a name and address on?' asked the man, who was becoming increasingly agitated.

'I don't really know,' the manager replied, shrugging his shoulders.

'That's the son of a bitch we're looking for,' said Jellison, parking on the right-hand side of the Firebird. As they came to a halt, Wilder walked out of the service station past the front of their station wagon. Jellison could see he'd very recently shaven; his face was well tanned except for the baby white skin where his beard had been. Their driver's window was open and both troopers shouted out, 'Stop!' at the same time. Wilder, who had been walking cautiously, made a dash for the Firebird's passenger door, grabbing desperately at the handle. It was locked. He turned, a frantic look on his face, and started to rush towards the back of the Firebird, locking eyes with Jellison.

The trooper shouted, 'Stop!' again as he leaped out of the police vehicle, adding, 'We're state police, we want to talk to you.'

Wilder stuttered several times, 'I . . . I . . . I . . .' and then bolted around to the driver's door, flung it open and bent down across the seat.

The manager of the service station saw a stocky-looking bear of a guy and his passenger shouting, 'Stop!' He later told FBI agents he heard them call out that they were state troopers, saw the guy from the Firebird try to get into the locked passenger door, then panic and run to the other side of the car, fling open the driver's door and launch himself across the seats, rummaging around on the passenger side.

VIC'S GETTY SERVICE STATION
MAIN STREET
COLEBROOK, NH

Jellison got to the driver's door of the Firebird a second after Wilder. The 188-centimetre, 115-kilogram trooper instinctively realised the fugitive was fumbling for a weapon. He didn't have time to draw his own gun from its holster, so he did the only thing that he could think of; he dived on Wilder's back and put the serial killer into a bear hug. Jellison squeezed Wilder's arms together as tightly as he could to prevent Wilder moving them. They were both large and powerful men grappling with each other in a very restricted space, and Wilder was wriggling his body while attempting to pull his arms free.

Fortier raced to the passenger door to try and help his partner, but the door was locked. He started to run around to the driver's door when he heard the gunshot.

Jellison felt a sharp intense pain in his chest, but he carried on gripping Wilder until he felt him go limp. As he pulled backwards, he saw a red dot in the centre of Wilder's back. He stood up, looked down at his own chest and saw an entry wound. The bullet had gone straight through.

'He just shot me,' Jellison told Fortier, astonished.

Fortier looked at the wound and then at the Firebird where Wilder lay facedown across the seats. Holding Jellison's arm, he led him to safety at the back of the Firebird, then, pulling out his service weapon, he shuffled towards the passenger door with his gun trained on the front seats.

Another gunshot pierced the silence. Fortier ducked down and peered in at the front of the vehicle and saw Wilder's torso rise up a few centimetres. The trooper hurried back around the vehicle, passing Jellison, who was walking slowly towards the police station wagon. Wilder was still facedown on the seat of the Firebird with his left hand free, but his right hand not in view. Fortier, his gun still drawn, reached down and moved him sideways until he saw Wilder's right hand curled towards his stomach. There was a revolver just above the hand, and the barrel was pointing at Wilder's own head. Fortier holstered his gun and lifted Wilder's head up by the back of his neck. His eyes were glassy, and the trooper saw a large amount of blood flowing from his chest.

In the background, through the ringing in his ears he could hear Jellison, who was now slumped in the station wagon, yelling his service number, 651, repeatedly into the radio.

'Go ahead, 651,' answered the Troop F radio dispatcher.

'651, code 1000, I've been shot . . . I'm at Vic's Getty station in Colebrook,' said Jellison, breathing heavily, blood seeping between the fingers of his left hand, which was pressed against his chest.

The Upper Connecticut Valley Hospital was only a three-minute drive from the scene, even less when it was an emergency call. Fortier sat talking with his partner until the ambulance arrived. Jellison, still bleeding, said he felt like vomiting, but he kept talking until the paramedics put him on a gurney. Fortier then went back over to the Firebird to check on the perp, but he couldn't find any pulse.

TROOP E STATE POLICE HEADQUARTERS
CANANDAIGUA, NY

Yates County chief deputy sheriff Ron Spike was in a strategy meeting at state police headquarters, discussing the Dawnette Wilt investigation and the search for Wilder, when the news came in that there had been a fatal shooting in Colebrook that could be the fugitive.

Phone lines lit up as calls went everywhere to try and establish for certain that the man's body sprawled across the front seat of a Pontiac Firebird in the town's main street, with his feet poking out the driver's door, was definitely the serial killer.

VIC'S GETTY SERVICE STATION
MAIN STREET
COLEBROOK, NH

Garage manager Wayne DeLong had ducked when the first gunshot occurred. His next action was to reach up to the counter for the telephone and dial the police. Fortier had not long secured the crime scene, after his partner was taken to hospital, when the phone calls started arriving at the garage from state police command, eager for a positive identification of the victim. The newly assigned trooper was ordered to remove the deceased's right boot and check his ankle. He left the line open while he walked outside and pulled off the size nine-and-a-half Wagner boot. He walked back, picked up the receiver and described a 12-centimetre scar just above the ankle. Linda Grober had detailed a similar scar on the right ankle of her abductor. Ten minutes later, Fortier got another call and was sent to examine the deceased's left hand for fingerprints. He took notes this time, and when he got back to the phone, he described his findings as, 'Left thumb, index finger, middle finger and little finger all had a loop. A whorl was on the ring finger.'

It was Wilder.

TREATMENT ROOM 126
UPPER CONNECTICUT VALLEY HOSPITAL
COLEBROOK, NH

Trooper Chuck Jellison was a hero, and a very lucky one. The bullet had passed through Wilder's chest, exited his back and then entered the lawman's chest and come to a stop near his liver. Thankfully, it hadn't done any irreparable damage, and less than one hour after the incident he was able to sit up in bed and be interviewed for his first statement.

VIC'S GETTY SERVICE STATION
MAIN STREET
COLEBROOK, NH

State police sergeant Robert Loven removed a brown wallet from the deceased's left rear pocket. It contained a Florida driver's licence issued to Christopher Bernard Wilder. Inside the Firebird, police recovered colour photographs of naked women, receipts, an address book, a large knife and forty-nine $100 bills. There was also a marked-up copy of *The Collector*.

It was 4 p.m. when the crime scene photographs had been taken and the undertaker arrived to take Wilder's body to the morgue.

TROOP E STATE POLICE HEADQUARTERS
CANANDAIGUA, NY

At the Troop E state police headquarters, where the search for Wilder was being coordinated around the clock, two phone calls came in a few minutes apart that changed everything. The first was from police in Colebrook to say a preliminary identification of Wilder as the dead driver had been made, subject to final fingerprint confirmation. While the state police captain was taking down the details, another phone started ringing. It was long-distance from the Torrance police department in Los Angeles with the news that Tina Risico had walked into the station ten minutes earlier.

FBI MIAMI FIELD OFFICE
MIAMI, FL

John Hanlon was on the telephone to the FBI's Buffalo office, discussing the new search parameters for Wilder, when a young agent monitoring the teletype machines ripped off a piece of paper and raced across the operations room. Hanlon was on his feet, staring at the touring map next to his desk and using his free hand to stab it with red push pins, when the agent thrust the printout under his nose. He read the first line and fell back heavily into his chair, unable to say anything. He could feel all eyes in the room on him, but he was speechless for a few moments. Christopher Wilder, the fugitive whose every movement and action had consumed his life for weeks, was believed dead following a shootout with state troopers in New Hampshire. It was only preliminary confirmation, the urgent message said, but everything pointed to the deceased gunman being the serial killer.

Hanlon had mixed emotions. He had known Wilder was going to feed his terrible appetite for torture and murder until he was caught or killed, but his death would leave so many unanswered questions for so many of his victims' families. As word spread of events in Colebrook, Hanlon fired off the necessary messages and quickly went through the formalities of closing down the fugitive hunt.

Then he did one of the hardest tasks of his career. He picked up the phone and called the parents of Rosario Gonzalez and Beth Kenyon to tell them the man who'd taken their daughters had gone to his grave, taking all knowledge of their whereabouts with him. Hanlon, standing and facing out the window, became quite emotional, and another agent walked over and put a supportive hand on his colleague's shoulder.

Hanlon's third call was to Wilder's brother Stephen to alert him to the news before he was contacted by reporters. When he was finished, it was almost dark outside, and downstairs, media crews were setting up for a press conference. Hanlon was asked if he wanted to take part, but he declined. He tidied his desk, walked quietly into the sticky and humid evening air, and started walking up the street until he found a liquor store.

'I bought a six-pack of Heineken, drove home and cried like a baby,' he remembered.

Back at the press conference, FBI special agent Joseph Corless summed up the general mood when he said, 'The one person who could answer all of our questions is dead.'

He told reporters the FBI's most extensive fugitive manhunt had come to an end with the apparent suicide of Christopher Wilder.

'At any given time, the FBI had several hundred agents working this particular case, especially in the last couple of days, and I would estimate that across this country . . . officers had to amount into the thousands.'

UPPER CONNECTICUT VALLEY HOSPITAL MORGUE
COLEBROOK, NH

Troopers went to the morgue and obtained prints from Wilder's palms and fingers. They were given to Boston FBI special agent Charles Walsh for comparison with a set from one of Wilder's previous arrests. At 9.10 p.m., he said he was certain that Christopher Wilder was dead.

SOLDIERS AND SAILORS MEMORIAL HOSPITAL
PENN YAN, NY

At around the same time, Dawnette Wilt was having an emotional reunion with her parents and being credited by Yates County sheriff Jan Scofield with bringing Wilder's murderous mayhem to an end.

'If we hadn't had the break with her in this case,' he said, 'I firmly believe that Mr Wilder would still be alive. It was unbelievable how a sixteen-year-old girl could go through what she had gone through. She was very, very concise, very thorough with all her descriptions. Her fortitude was unrelenting, she is worthy of our highest admiration and esteem.'

UPPER CONNECTICUT VALLEY HOSPITAL
COLEBROOK, NH

The autopsy on Wilder was conducted by forensic pathologist Robert Christie. He recorded the cause of death as 'cardiac obliteration' caused by a 'self-inflicted gunshot wound'.

'The results of the autopsy cannot establish whether or not death was accidental in an attempted homicide, or suicide,' he reported.

Dr William Gifford, who witnessed the autopsy and signed the death certificate, said both shots had torn through Wilder's heart, and the second had ripped it apart. 'We have no way of knowing if this man wanted to commit suicide; there's no way to tell.'

At the request of the FBI, blood and hair samples were taken from Wilder's body and the results forwarded to Australian police. Wilder's brain was also removed for scientific study at a Boston hospital. Professor Albert Galaburda from the Harvard Medical School sliced it into 0.015-millimetre-thick sections from end to end, but he didn't find anything structurally abnormal at the time. The human brain lab closed over twenty-five years ago, and the professor says today the findings could be different. 'If the brain was chemically different, or the circuitry of areas of the brain dealing with aggression was abnormal, we would not have been able to tell based on the methods available to us at that time.'

35

STATE OF MIND

SUNDAY 15 APRIL 1984

TORRANCE, CA

With Wilder dead, and grieving families across the country left without answers or the chance to bury their missing loved ones, the spotlight turned firmly to Tina Risico. She was only sixteen, like Dawnette Wilt, but instead of being a hero who had helped end Wilder's reign of terror, Tina was being treated like a suspect. There were many calls for her to be charged as an accessory over the kidnapping and attempted murder of Dawnette and the death of Beth Dodge. Her case wasn't helped, in the public's eyes at least, when a Redondo Beach lawyer, retained by her father, told Edna Buchanan and other news organisations Tina would be telling her story to the highest bidder.

'We'll be listening to offers and go from there,' said Laurie Belger. He added, 'This is a sixteen-year-old kid who's been through hell. It's hard to put a price on it. It's obviously a nationwide story. I could see where a lot of movie producers would be interested.'

Torrance police had wanted Tina to appear with them in a joint press conference on Saturday, after spending the night in hospital, but the lawyer refused. 'I put a quick end to that. I felt she's fragile. She's definitely going to be talking to somebody. It will help the kid pay for her college education.'

Edna's story in the *Miami Herald* also revealed the FBI were trying to identify four mystery young women, more possible victims, whose colour photographs were inside Wilder's briefcase along with his torture equipment and cash.

MONDAY 16 APRIL 1984
TORRANCE, CA

Tina was now in the eye of the storm and refusing to cooperate with the FBI or police. She was represented by a new lawyer, brought in by her mother, who said his client would not be interviewed again until they received official word she had been granted immunity. Steven Siegel said he was concerned that if Tina talked further with police she may be 'damaging herself' legally.

Her grandmother Genevieve told reporters that Tina 'still hasn't been cleared'. With tears in her eyes, she said, 'People in the east don't understand. They think that she had something to do with this.' Genevieve suggested Tina's upbringing had helped her to survive, saying she had 'led a very tough life, she learned to cope with very tough people'.

BUFFALO, NY

Over in Buffalo, New York, US attorney Salvatore Martoche described as 'premature' any decision on whether to grant Tina immunity. 'Based on the information we have,' said the federal prosecutor, 'we do not have any basis to consider her anything but a victim, but that can change. We don't want to get this kid all riled up. I don't want to sound harsh or hard on her, but we also have to be fair to the families of other victims involved.'

'She's just as guilty as Wilder,' said Theresa Ferguson's mother, Frances, when asked by reporters.

Buffalo FBI agent Mike Kogut said Tina had 'ignored' at least two opportunities to escape when she was driving alone in a car following Wilder, because she said she was in 'abject fear of her life'.

COLEBROOK, NH

In New Hampshire, authorities were piecing together Wilder's final moments and moving away from the theory that he'd committed suicide.

'We don't have any conclusions yet, but we think the evidence is mounting that he drew that gun to try to kill the trooper,' said New Hampshire assistant attorney-general Michael Pignato.

NSW POLICE HEADQUARTERS
SYDNEY, AUSTRALIA

Wilder's devastated parents, June and Coley, had spent the previous day, their fortieth wedding anniversary, heavily sedated as friends and family tried to comfort them. Meanwhile, news of Wilder's death was making big headlines in Sydney, and the focus of much of the coverage was whether police had allowed the Wanda Beach killer of Marianne Schmidt and Christine Sharrock to escape.

CIB chief superintendent Noel Morey publicly revealed for the first time that they had received information fifteen years earlier suggesting Wilder was responsible for the Wanda Beach killings. Morey admitted Wilder had become a suspect before he started his new life in the US, when his wife Christine had made a statement about his extremely violent sexual behaviour and that she believed he was responsible for the Wanda murders. Morey was not able to explain why Australian police didn't question him then. When Wilder was back in Sydney, behind bars, awaiting trial on rape charges, police apparently had made an extraordinary decision not to interview him about the brutal double homicide of Marianne and Christine until the rape case had finished. Again, Morey could not explain why.

Even when Wilder successfully applied for bail twice, first to live with his parents, and later to return to the US, detectives made no attempt to question him about the state's most notorious unsolved cold case. While the prosecutor opposed bail on both occasions, the magistrate was never informed of Wilder's links to the killings. There is a suspicion that the Manly police handling the rape case, although aware of Wilder's deviant sexual history and previous conviction for a sexual assault when he was a teenager, didn't discover he was a suspect for Wanda Beach until after he had returned to America. The information should have been available from the intelligence branch, but it is not clear if that simple check was ever made.

Superintendent Morey chose his words carefully when he addressed the media. 'It was our intention to question him about Wanda Beach, but, unfortunately, that was not to be,' he told them.

MIAMI, FL

Wilder's brother Stephen was smuggled, by Zeke Kimbrell, past pursuing reporters into a Miami TV studio, to record a satellite interview for Australian television. He told Channel Nine host Mike Willesee he was 'happy' that his brother had been stopped and no more young women would get hurt. Looking tired and drawn after two weeks in America, meeting the families of some of the missing girls, he said, 'This story you just wouldn't believe, we are talking about people's lives, that's what it is all about, innocent young girls.

'None of us is really normal, and you can't use that word with Chris. He had a strange – that's not the right word either – his personality was not what I would call normal. He was a loner and had a lot of trouble relating to people and establishing relationships with women. He thought the only way he could do it and get a relationship was to buy people. He was one of those guys who just had to make themselves look big.'

Stephen said his brother had been committed to returning to Australia for his rape trial until very recently. 'He was on bail and he had full intentions on going back. My opinion, and the opinion of all the people I have spoken to here, and the FBI, is that he went crazy.'

TUESDAY 17 APRIL 1984
MIAMI HERALD
MIAMI, FL
Edna's editorial in the *Miami Herald*, 'The Wilder Case', raised serious and uncomfortable questions about Wilder and how he had been allowed to operate and remain a danger to women for so long:

Christopher B Wilder was the most notorious outlaw in the nation for seven weeks and when he died some answers about the crimes attributed to him forever were snuffed out.

[. . .] One uncomfortable question that the Wilder episode raises is whether his wealth influenced the consideration he got from the courts, which repeatedly released him on bail. In a more-perfect world, all men would be judged as equal before the law. In the less-than-perfect real world, money too often is a principal factor.

NEWMAN FUNERAL HOME
COLEBROOK, NH

Police kept a close watch on the Newman Funeral Home, where Wilder's body was being embalmed and dressed, after desperate newspaper and magazine journalists offered locals cash if they could get a photo.

Finally, after four days, owner Bob Moore drove the serial killer on his final journey, packed in a white shipping container, and wearing underwear and smock pyjamas. It took almost three hours to drive him to the Portland Jetport in Maine, where he was flown to Boston, and then transferred to a Delta Air Lines flight to Palm Beach airport in Florida. A horde of reporters and camera crews was on hand when Delta L1011 touched down at 7.15 p.m., and sheriff's officers struggled to hold back the melee as baggage handlers transferred the 2-metre-long cargo into a white hearse parked on the airport apron. Five sheriff's cruisers, a van, two unmarked cars and two police-trained German shepherds then provided an escort, blue lights flashing, to the Palm Beach medical examiner's office.

John Hanlon had requested a plaster cast of Wilder's jaw be taken to enable a possible match with bite marks on the breasts of several of his suspected victims, and photographs were also taken of his scars and scratches for the same reason.

Finally, just before midnight, Wilder arrived back in Boynton Beach, at a local funeral home.

WEDNESDAY 18 APRIL 1984
SCOBEE-COMBS FUNERAL HOME
BOYNTON BEACH, FL

Stephen Wilder left it to Kimbrell to organise his brother's funeral, which was held at the funeral home chapel.

'It was fucking weird and cool at the same time,' said Kimbrell. 'It was a crazy scene with the FBI and local cops trying to stop all the media getting in. I organised the guest list and kept it to thirteen guests, and the last few I chose randomly to make up that number. I deliberately made it creepy because the whole thing was a mad circus. Chris was born on the thirteenth, he died on the thirteenth, the FBI believed there might be thirteen victims and I took thirteen photographs of him in the coffin.'

The impersonal thirteen-minute late-afternoon service was presided over by a Catholic priest. No-one else spoke. 'It's hard to grieve for a friend that's done such terrible things,' said Kimbrell's wife, Sharon, saying she only attended to make sure that Wilder was dead. 'There's a part of your mind that has to make sure he is gone and part of the nightmare is over. How else are you going to know?'

Wilder was cremated, and his brother Stephen took his ashes with him when he returned to Australia.

———

It was a very different scene at Beth Dodge's funeral in New York, where her four-year-old daughter, Stephanie, asked her father, 'Where's Mummy?' as she stood beside the casket. The hugely emotional service was attended by all Beth's friends, work colleagues and many of her Sunday school pupils. Little Stephanie looked all over the church for her mum.

'She's here with us,' her heartbroken dad told her. 'Just somewhere beyond our reach.'

THURSDAY 19 APRIL 1984
SOLDIERS AND SAILORS MEMORIAL HOSPITAL
PENN YAN, NY

Dawnette returned home after spending a week in hospital recuperating. She had given several interviews to Chief Deputy Sheriff Spike, at the request of the FBI, which was continuing to investigate the missing girls, other potential Wilder victims and Tina Risico. Spike wrote a report for the bureau based on Dawnette's answers, which said, 'She feels now that Tina Marie Risico on a few occasions could have aided her, as Wilder seems to have placed some trust in Tina as they were left alone in the car a couple of times etc.'

Dawnette and her parents were in tears as they were escorted to Penn Yan airport by Spike and emergency nurse Sue Bricker, who had cared for the teenager during her treatment. A local company donated the use of a private jet to fly the family home to Indiana. Dawnette left behind a short, handwritten letter thanking the local community for its love and financial support.

'The only sad thing about returning home is the feeling of loss of close, close personal friends,' she said. 'The nurses weren't only women in white, they were my temporary mothers.'

WEST PALM BEACH, FL

Local police throughout Florida, with the help of the FBI, were trawling through files on unsolved kidnapping and murder cases to see if Wilder may have been responsible.

'What's happening is several local departments are going

through their files now, looking for unsolved crimes against missing girls that might have something to do with Wilder,' said FBI
spokesman Dennis Aiken in West Palm Beach.

Lee County sheriff's department in south-west Florida said
Wilder was the best suspect in the 1981 disappearances of two
teenagers from the Edison Mall parking lot in Fort Myers several
weeks apart. Mary Hare, eighteen, was found stabbed to death.
Mary Opitz, seventeen, has never been found.

FRIDAY 20 APRIL 1984
PALM BEACH COUNTY PROBATE COURT
PALM BEACH, FL

When Wilder's will was filed in Palm Beach County Probate
Court, it was revealed Wilder had left the bulk of his estate to
his former partner Victoria Darling, his parents and Kimbrell.
Darling was left his Boynton Beach home, eight and a half acres
in Loxahatchee, Palm Beach, and property in Fort Lauderdale,
while his stock in the Sawtel Construction and electrical con-
tract firms was left to Kimbrell and two other friends. When
some news reports estimated the estate could be worth as much as
$7 million, the families of ten of his suspected victims filed claims
totalling more than $50 million. Police captain Don Ferguson,
stepfather to Theresa, filed a $2 million claim against Wilder's
estate. His wife, Frances, said her husband had done it 'out of
anger and frustration'.

She explained, 'You have to strike back when you get hurt. You
want to belt back but we couldn't do anything to Wilder because he
was dead. If you get a cheque in your hand, it's like they are saying,
"Here's for the life of your child." But you couldn't put a price on
her life – she was priceless.'

Three weeks after the will was filed, the Internal Revenue Service filed a preliminary $345 000 claim against the estate also, claiming that Wilder failed to pay any income tax in 1980.

TUESDAY 24 APRIL 1984
FBI FIELD OFFICE
DYER, IN

Meanwhile, the FBI was still wrestling over whether to charge Tina Risico. John Hanlon and the bureau's Miami office were not pressing to prosecute her but also believed granting her immunity was unlikely in view of Dawnette Wilt's statements. The FBI's Indianapolis office was asked to interview Dawnette again, 'in order that the US attorney's office at Indianapolis might be in possession of total details in order to make an intelligent decision as to whether it should proceed against Risico'.

With each interview she did, Dawnette's view about Tina seemed to harden. Dawnette was questioned at home and the agents reported:

> Wilt volunteered that subject Wilder, while holding her captive, repeatedly told her that he had killed before. To these statements, Tina Marie Risico responded with statements such as, 'yes I know, yes I know he will, yes I've seen it'.
>
> Wilt advised that her impression of comments made by Risico lead her to believe that Risico may have either witnessed the subject abduct other women or may have been told by Wilder details of other abductions. Wilt went on to state that Wilder had developed a trust relationship with Risico as he frequently left Risico unattended with his revolver and knife in positions where Risico could have easily accessed them.

The families of all Wilder's suspected victims whose bodies had not been discovered made approaches through the police, the FBI and Tina's lawyer to speak to Tina privately about anything Wilder might have told her about other victims.

Ken Whittaker Jr, still working for the parents of Beth Kenyon, managed to arrange a telephone conversation with Tina in her lawyer's office. He asked the teenager if at any stage during her odyssey with Wilder, he had mentioned any victims from Miami, anything that would help them in their search for Beth's remains. In her FBI statement, Tina had described how she had stayed in the car when Wilder took Dawnette into the woods and did not see him carrying any weapon. She told agents who interviewed her she was too afraid to ask him what he had done when he returned after half an hour 'or so'. According to Whittaker, Tina admitted to more in their phone chat, and she described how she could hear the knife being plunged into Dawnette. She told him it was the first time she ever panicked with Wilder, who then told her, 'Turn around, otherwise you will end up like the girls from Miami.'

FRIDAY 15 JUNE 1984
PALM BEACH COUNTY SHERIFF'S DEPARTMENT
PALM BEACH, FL

Tom Neighbors worked out one of his worst cases had probably been committed by Wilder. Two young girls, aged twelve and ten, had been walking in the centre of Boynton Beach in broad daylight when a man driving a white van pulled up alongside and pointed a gun at them. He told them to get inside and drove to a remote rural spot on a dirt road, where he laid out a tarpaulin and sexually assaulted them so badly, for several hours, that they both sustained serious injuries. Afterwards, he drove them back to town and let them go. The girls told their parents, who went straight to police, and Tom Neighbors was assigned the case.

Although they had given a good description of the El Camino truck their abductor drove, and helped an artist produce a sketch of him, it was well before Neighbors knew Wilder's history, and he struggled to make headway with the investigation. It is certain Wilder would have derived a sick pleasure from spending so much time in the home of the detective, who was investigating the case for which he was responsible, chatting away with Tom's wife, Dana. Following Wilder's death, Neighbors pulled the case file and got detectives to show the girls a photo line-up of suspects. It was done separately, but both of them picked out Wilder without hesitation. Also at the time, Wilder had been driving a white El Camino truck with Sawtel Construction written on the side, and going back to their witness statements, the girls had spoken about writing that said 'something construction' on the side. They'd also noted that the truck had been full of builders tools. Wilder's guilt was confirmed when forensics matched his blood with semen found on the tarpaulin he had carelessly left at the scene. The case confirmed Wilder was a paedophile as well as a serial-turned-spree killer.

WEDNESDAY 15 AUGUST 1984
TORRANCE, CA

Tina Risico didn't end up being charged, and she didn't sell her story. She did eventually break her silence after four months, agreeing to do an interview for the *Los Angeles Times*. She met the reporter at a McDonald's restaurant and talked while she ate a hamburger, the food staple she mostly lived on during her time with Wilder. Despite the nine days of absolute terror she endured at his hands, when she was repeatedly raped and tortured, it was describing their goodbye kiss that brought tears to her eyes. 'It was heartbreaking, it was so sentimental,' she said. Having had so long to think about her 'escapade', as she called it, Tina was convinced Wilder spared her life because 'he fell in love' with her and 'knew he was close to being killed'.

He didn't want her to die with him.

Asked whether she thought about the other victims, Tina thought a moment and replied, 'I care, but I'm not going to worry about it. You can't . . . brood over it the rest of your life. They're them and I'm me. I'm not God.'

WEDNESDAY 11 JUNE 1986
PALM BEACH COUNTY PROBATE COURT
PALM BEACH, FL

Retired Massachusetts district judge Albert Silverman, the arbitrator appointed by the court to oversee splitting the balance of Wilder's estate among the families of his victims, announced his recommendation. He based his payout figures on the gross worth of the $7 million estate, even though after mortgage debts, legal fees and the Internal Revenue Service had claimed unpaid taxes, less than $200000 would remain. 'I was told not to pay any attention to that,' Silverman said. 'They will all get a percentage of what I awarded.'

He gave the largest share of the estate, $1.2 million, to the family of single mum Beth Dodge, because she had left behind a four-year-old daughter. At the end of the day, he said her family would probably receive about $32000 of this amount. He awarded $1 million each to the families of Dawnette Wilt, Terry Walden, Sheryl Bonaventura, Michelle Korfman and Terry Ferguson, although they were expected to receive only 12 per cent of the amount remaining after tax, around $24000 each. Leo Jellison, the trooper shot apprehending Wilder, was awarded $75000, but this was likely to be reduced to little more than $2000 in the after-tax breakdown.

36

RIPPLE EFFECT

Following Wilder's death, Linda Grober flew home from the safe haven in Norway she'd fled to and struggled to settle back into her old life. It was two years after her ordeal before she successfully managed to return to her studies, but she stuck at it and went on to complete her PhD at Florida State University. Today she is a mother and a renowned marine conservationist.

She says: 'I was lucky. I could have done exactly what I did and ended up like all the girls before and after me. I don't think anybody can say why I survived and not them. I got a second chance and it really stuck with me that I had been given a new lease on life.'

Linda researched the girls who didn't survive their encounter with Wilder and made contact with some of their mothers, including ringing Dolores Kenyon nearly every Mother's Day. 'The more I learned about them, how they were teachers and nurses and some were mums themselves, I realised that I needed to make sure I did something worthwhile with my life, because they were all amazing, productive, beautiful women who never got the chance.'

Linda has strong views about Wilder that will come as a surprise to many. 'I don't think he was a monster,' she said. 'I was sad that he died, and I know people struggle with that. I definitely had some form of Stockholm syndrome, but he was a person who needed help, who had been crying out for help for a very long time and should not have been in a position to have access to young women.'

Every year on the anniversary of her kidnapping, Linda spends time alone, usually hiking, to remember a vow she made to herself when she got her life back on track.

'I had a really bad day a long time ago, and Wilder took that day from me, but he wasn't going to take the rest of my life. I realised Wilder never had it on his best day as good as my worst day.'

———

For eight years, Haydee Gonzalez and her husband, Blas, kept their daughter Rosario's bedroom exactly as it was on the day she disappeared. Then their home was destroyed by Hurricane Andrew. When they rebuilt, they turned the front garden into a shrine, and every year they hold a candlelit vigil mass on the anniversary of her disappearance. Like Beth Kenyon's parents, Haydee and Blas also consulted psychics to try and find their daughter, and all four kept searching together for the two girls for years.

Rosario's sister, Lisette, a midwife and mother of four today, said life stopped in her family for a long time. 'We didn't have any parties, we didn't put up a Christmas tree, didn't celebrate birthdays – they just couldn't because she wasn't here. For many years there was no happiness in the house.'

It was only when she got married and her parents' first grandchild came along that the gloom started to lift, although Rosario is never far from anyone's thoughts. 'I had so many kids because I never wanted any of them to be left alone like I was when Rosario disappeared,' said Lisette. 'I wanted my daughter to have a sister, because I enjoyed having Rosario for the short time I did; it is such a special bond.'

Four weeks after Wilder died, on Mothering Sunday, Haydee and Blas were arrested for breaking into his Boynton Beach home. Haydee had begged Rosario's fiancé, Bill Londos, to help her get inside, and he went on the Saturday evening with Beth Kenyon's father and forced an opening. 'We opened up the sliding door for her,' said Bill, 'but we didn't go in. I couldn't because I knew Wilder had taken Chary there. It was too much.'

When Haydee and Blas arrived the next day and went inside, a neighbour called police.

When Bill heard they had been arrested, he rang the station. 'I got the chief on the phone and I said, "I'm not going to be a jerk, but every news organisation in the country calls me every day, and I will tell them that you have this woman locked up on Mother's Day. Please let her out; she doesn't need to be there."'

They let her go.

———

When Rosario Gonzalez's fiancé received the phone call that Christopher Wilder was dead, he went berserk, destroying an entire bathroom at his college, tearing every basin and stall off the wall, breaking both his hands.

Bill Londos was besotted with the girl he called 'Chary' and, more than three decades later, still hasn't come to terms with her disappearance. He has been married and divorced four times and admits all of them were doomed to fail, because there were three people in each of the relationships, Chary always in his thoughts. In June 1984, two months after Wilder's death, on what should have been his wedding day, he still went to the church. 'Every news camera in the world, it seemed, was at my house. I snuck out the back door, I jumped over the neighbour's fence and jumped over another fence, and my best friend met me two blocks away, and we drove down to the church. I stayed for a couple of hours and sat there by myself. I had nowhere else to go and nothing else to do.'

He put on his wedding suit that day for the next ten years and returned to the church. He still has the wedding ring he was going to put on Chary's finger and is now planning a memorial so that he has somewhere to go where he can grieve and talk to her. It will help him get closure, he says.

He continued looking for Chary for a long time. 'I tried several times to contact Tina Risico,' he said. 'I just wanted to ask a very simple question, but she would not take my phone call, she would hang up on me. I know she was sitting there with him, and they had to be watching the news together, all I wanted to know is where was her body . . . did he ever mention it?'

Bill's marriages gave him three children, and his daughter works for him in the business he founded, which is one of the fastest growing companies in Florida and has made him very wealthy. He would give every cent away to know where his first love is buried.

———

When John Hanlon rang to tell Beth Kenyon's parents that Christopher Wilder was dead, Dolores Kenyon threw herself to the ground, knowing the best hope of finding her eldest daughter had been lost.

The Kenyons spent hundreds of thousands of dollars searching for Beth's remains over the next few years, travelling all over North and South America chasing leads, employing private detectives and psychics. They had all their daughter's belongings shipped to their family home in Lockport, New York, and re-created her bedroom there, Dolores insisting the light remain constantly on to act as a beacon in hope that she might one day return.

The couple never forgave police for acting so slowly after they tipped detectives off about Wilder.

'They had him in their hands and let him go,' said a bitter Bill Kenyon. 'He was a wealthy guy and they were watching out for his rights.'

'He'd been getting away with it for years,' Dolores Kenyon said. 'It was like the devil himself was riding on Chris Wilder's shoulder, watching out for him.'

Beth's brother Tim says his mother never recovered from her grief and died at age fifty-six from a broken heart. 'I heard Dad say to her once, "How do we get beyond this?" Her answer was, "I'm not."'

Bill Kenyon died two years after his wife, a shattered man.

———

Almost thirty-five years later, Ken Whittaker Jr still runs the investigation agency he founded with his late father and has never forgotten a fact about the Christopher Wilder case. He continued working for the Kenyons for some time after Wilder's death, trying to discover the whereabouts of their daughter Beth.

He developed a theory about what happened to the 23-year-old schoolteacher, but it isn't clear if the FBI took it on board or had the necessary technology at the time to check it out. Says Whittaker: 'I think Wilder took Beth home, had an argument with her, and when she said, "Take me home," or, "Take me back," things got violent.

'When he got the cleaning crew in after the sliding door was smashed, he took an active role in cleaning up with them, which he'd never done before. He had a bathroom that was off the pool deck, where you could gain access to inside the house through two doors. When one of the cleaners went to wash his hands in there, Wilder said, "No, no no, I got some glass and dirty rags in there. Don't worry about that, I will clean it up myself."

'The cleaners thought it was odd that the bathroom was locked from both sides – Wilder had locked both doors, which is significant. We interviewed Wilder's maid, and she said there was a new shower curtain in that bathroom the next time she went in.

'I have strong reason to believe that he had four or five construction sites that were at the pre-pouring stage at the time. We know he bought a shovel on the previous day, Sunday morning, at the True Value hardware store. I believe he went to one of his construction sites, pulled back the wire meshing, dug a shallow grave and put Beth in there, wrapped in the shower curtain.

'His employees said they had an account to buy shovels, rakes or whatever they needed, so why would Wilder need to go out on a Sunday to buy a shovel? It was never found.'

———————

Theresa Ferguson's parents divorced following her abduction and murder, after nineteen years of marriage. Her mother, Frances, said later she experienced something at her daughter's funeral that 'changed my life'.

She was adamant she started to feel Theresa's presence and said that, afterwards, fans and lights would turn on by themselves, and she would catch a whiff of Terry's favourite perfume on a gentle breeze.

'Terry gave me absolute proof that there is life after death,' said Frances. 'I was forty-five, about to go through the change of life, and my only child had just been murdered . . . I thought I was losing my mind until my mother and others started telling me that the same thing was happening to them.'

Frances became isolated and lonely. 'I couldn't talk about this to my friends because they absolutely didn't want to hear about it,' she said.

She left Florida and moved to Atlanta, wrote a book about Theresa and her experiences, then started a self-help workshop for people struggling to cope with the loss of a loved one.

Theresa's stepfather, Don, the police captain in Indian Harbour, had lost his daughter and his wife in quick succession, and admitted to harbouring anger and resentment towards the man who had wrecked his life. 'Yes, I'm bitter he died, but Wilder got what he deserved,' he said.

Today, the celebrated Pulitzer Prize–winning former crime reporter Edna Buchanan lives with her dog Harry overlooking Miami Beach. Like a number of the reporters who covered the Christopher Wilder case, she went on to become a hugely successful crime author. Edna has kept all her notes and interview transcripts on the case, and she still remembers checking in regularly with John Hanlon at the FBI and noticing the toll the fugitive manhunt was having on the special agent. 'He would go home and cry knowing they had failed to find him again, and that another girl would be dead or dying that night,' says Edna. 'It was very personal for him, and I could see the effect it was having.'

Edna says she knew straight away that Wilder was responsible for the abductions of both Rosario Gonzalez and Beth Kenyon, and she has always believed strongly the girls are buried together. 'In the same way that I immediately felt they were related, I felt the bodies of Beth and Rosario were together somewhere. They went missing only a week apart, and who knows how long Rosario was alive, maybe they were together and both alive at the same time?

'Bodies have a habit of turning up eventually, but Rosario's and Beth's never have, and there is nowhere in the country that has had more construction sites than south Florida.

'The best way for Wilder to know that they wouldn't be found is if they are somewhere hidden in a property, cemented into a wall or floor, and he could have done that very easily because he owned a construction company.

'I always felt the FBI should have taken his house apart brick by brick, board by board, because they could be anywhere in there.'

———

Two years after the death of Christopher Wilder, the agent who led the fugitive hunt to capture him almost died a violent death himself. John Hanlon was shot and seriously wounded in a wild shootout on a Miami residential street, on what is known as 'the bloodiest day in FBI history'. Two agents and two bank robbers were killed and five more agents seriously wounded in the gunfire, which involved more than one hundred shots from automatic weapons, shotguns and pistols. Hanlon, forty-eight at the time, was shot twice.

He had run out of bullets and seen one of his colleagues die at his feet. He was desperately trying to reload his gun, despite a bullet wound to his right hand, when one of the robbers shot him in the groin. 'I couldn't get up, and I thought I was going to die,' he said. 'I was lying there, trying to keep from bleeding to death, and I rationalised that he was going to kill me, and I had a fifty-fifty chance that I wouldn't know it was coming. Believing I was going to die, I started to think about those poor girls and what they went through with Wilder, that they knew they were going to die.' Reinforcements arrived, the two bank robbers were killed and Hanlon survived.

Hanlon knew that Christopher Wilder's friendly, harmless demeanour and cunning ability to flee so far and so quickly made him a killer that authorities were helpless to stop, but it would be a very long time until he stopped beating himself up over it. 'As horrible, as horrific as he was, it could have been worse . . . or we never could have caught him,' Hanlon said. 'As long as you're not unlucky, you can kill people whenever you want.'

Wilder had stayed lucky for forty-seven days.

After his recovery, Hanlon left the FBI and followed through with his plan to become a court prosecutor.

———

Wilder's company Sawtel Construction struggled once the media reported he was the co-owner. Contracts were lost, some employees quit and his business partner changed the name to try and escape the link to Wilder.

'It was a dark cloud, a stigma, people didn't want to be doing business with Sawtel with this guy out doing what he was doing,' Zeke Kimbrell said.

Wilder had been ripping him off for years, Kimbrell claimed. 'When we went into business, it was meant to be fifty-fifty, but I'd go out and do a job, and I'd have no fucking money in my account. I'd go to the people and say, "Did you pay your bill?" and they'd say, "Yeah, we paid Chris." I'd say, "How did you pay Chris?" and they'd say, "We paid cash, he gave us a real deal." He did this without telling me. I had no money, I was working six days a week, twelve to fourteen hours a day, and not seeing anything. He didn't bring shit to the business.'

Even though Wilder left the business to his partner in his will, Zeke didn't really benefit. 'I had to buy everything back, $123K. I was broke, it took everything I had just to get back what I owned.'

The shadow of Wilder looms even in death and he will be difficult for the world to forget. He was included in the 1985 edition of *Collier's Encyclopedia*, and the significance wasn't lost on his one-time business partner. 'He's in history now,' says Kimbrell. 'That's what Chris wanted. He wanted to go down in history.'

———

Tina Risico moved in with her boyfriend Billy after leaving hospital, and the couple rented a number of apartments in quick succession. Money was tight, as a number of promised job offers to Tina fell through when she came under suspicion for helping Wilder, but four months after the serial killer put her on a plane home following their goodbye kiss, Billy proposed and gave her an engagement ring.

Tina said at the time that she wasn't motivated by much, any longer, except for him. 'I live, actually, for Billy,' she said.

She said Billy struggled every time Wilder's name would come up. 'He gets all weird and says, "Leave me alone," and goes away and slams the door and hides out for a while. Later, when he apologises, I tell him, "Don't worry about it. You can't help it. That's fine. It's my problem. I don't want to bother you with it." So I don't.'

Eight years after she escaped, in February 1992, Tina was living back with her grandmother when she did the only television interview she has ever given about her nine days in captivity with Wilder.

It was very short and was used in an episode of the TV show *FBI: The Untold Stories.* Tina revealed how she had relieved the tension of her abduction by fantasising about shooting Wilder 'point blank in the back of his head'. She described her 'feelings of hate and anger' towards him, like all the other parents and victims of his, and thought, 'just to blow him away would be great'.

At the age of twenty-four, she said, 'I've come a long way and I feel very good about myself, that I've made it. I thank God every day about that. I've become a pretty good independent girl.'

Five years later she got married in Nevada, but not to Billy.

Dawnette went home to Dyer, Indiana, and quickly returned to school. Eight years after Christopher Wilder stabbed and left her to die in a field, she walked down the aisle to be married. Today, she is a very successful management professional and a mother. She has never spoken publicly about her experiences with Christopher Wilder or Tina Risico. A follower of the ancient Chinese philosopher Lao Tzu, she has posted several of his teachings on her social media profile, including, 'Life is a series of natural and spontaneous changes. Don't resist them – that only creates sorrow. Let reality be reality. Let things flow naturally forward in whatever way they like.'

———————

Both Leo Jellison and Wayne Fortier received the Medal of Valor, the highest award granted by state police, for their 'extraordinary heroism' in bringing to an end Christopher Wilder's murderous reign. They also received awards from the American Police Hall of Fame and the American Law Enforcement Officers Association.

———————

Wilder's mother, June, was battling cancer at the time her beloved eldest son went on his killing rampage, and she would never recover. She died three years later, aged sixty-one, full of shame and living as a virtual recluse. In the immediate aftermath of her son's death, her daughter-in-law Valerie, Stephen's wife, told reporters, 'At least now, the nightmare is over. We still have to live with the people who wonder what sort of family could have produced someone like Christopher.' June's best friend and long-time next-door neighbour Cathy Edwards said of June, 'She was a broken woman who wouldn't leave the house, thinking everyone was watching her.'

A couple of years after June's death, Wilder's father, Coley, got married again, to the daughter of one of his wartime sailor buddies. When he died in 1992, aged seventy-two, his ashes were placed with June's at the cemetery in Sawtell, and his second wife returned to America. Cathy Edwards describes the Wilders as too soft on their four sons, and Christopher particularly.

'June absolutely adored Chris, and as far as she and Coley were concerned, he could do no wrong,' she said, 'and if he did, they regarded it as someone else's fault. They used to speak about him all the time – how clever he was, and how very proud of him they were, and the success he was in America.'

Just before the news broke that Wilder was on the run, raping and murdering a different girl every few days, June and Coley asked to meet Cathy to tell her what was about to happen, and they were still making excuses for him.

'June wasn't accepting that Chris had done wrong – she was saying that it was all a misunderstanding, and that it was the fault of the girls. Coley just sat quietly next to her, listening.'

Cathy met Christopher Wilder when she hosted a wedding anniversary dinner for his parents one year while he was visiting from America, and she has never forgotten it. 'It was a creepy experience – there was something eerie about him. He had a strange hooded look in his eyes, and I was glad to get away. My intuition told me straight away he wasn't quite right.'

———

Suzanne Logan's parents, Jack and Agnes, sued Wilder's estate for $1.3 million within weeks of his death.

'We don't care if we get $1 at all,' said Jack. 'The main idea is to avoid any of what he had being turned over to relatives. If his estate was distributed, some people would live quite comfortably; it just disturbs us to think of it.'

In the end, the most heartbreaking but fitting epitaph to the tragic story was a devastating letter Agnes wrote about her daughter's case, which was published in the *Miami News* in 1985.

It has been a year since my beautiful daughter was raped, beaten and stabbed to death by Christopher Wilder. A year of intense pain, desolation and despair. No-one knows the trauma of losing a child this way unless they have experienced it. Suzanne was intelligent, sweet and kind to everyone and a wonderful daughter with so much to live for. She had been married nine months and I looked forward so much to holding her baby one day. All our dreams were shattered on March 26, 1984 by a man who should never have been walking amongst normal people, had everyone concerned done their duty. What is wrong with the criminal justice system in this country?

In 1984, after Beth Kenyon disappeared, the Kenyon family hired a private detective . . . who gathered enough evidence against Wilder to at least apprehend him. Yet Miami police . . . knowing Wilder's background, didn't even question him after being given the evidence . . . Why?

Metro police were also told about Wilder, but never questioned him either, as they, like Miami police also had to build their own case. Why?

My daughter's body lay in a morgue in Kansas for 10 days as no-one could identify her . . . Geary County, Kansas, Sheriff's Department put her description on the NCIC system nationwide. Meanwhile . . . the Oklahoma City Missing Persons Bureau had Suzanne's description and no-one in that department bothered to check the NCIC and compare descriptions. Why?

They didn't even search for her car. Her husband and I found it in the Penn Street Mall parking lot – five km away. It had been there five days, yet no-one had bothered to ticket it. Why?

In frustration, we hired a private detective, Bill Wilson, and in seven hours he found where Suzanne's body was and tied the whole case together – something the police could not do in 10 days. Why?

I have heard people complain about law enforcement agencies' indifference and incompetence, but never realised it until I experienced it myself. Should we increase law enforcement agents' salaries and maybe instill a better attitude and attract applicants with a higher degree of intelligence? Does anyone care?

Agnes died in 1999.

———

Widow Elizabeth Schmidt went to her grave with her greatest wish unfulfilled, finding out who murdered her eldest daughter at Wanda Beach. Marianne was on the beach that day with her four youngest siblings, but it was her seven-year-old brother, Wolfgang, who police are convinced saw her killer. The burden of being the only eyewitness was a heavy one, and Wolfgang's adult life was tough. He died of complications from diabetes, never getting an opportunity to identify Christopher Wilder as the 'surfie' youth he saw leading his sister and her best friend Christine to their deaths in the Wanda Beach sandhills.

Trixie Schmidt was only a couple of hundred metres away from her sister when she was being murdered, playing in the dunes with her brothers. Nine years old at the time, after more than half a century, many of her scattered childhood memories of the big sister she shared a bedroom with have faded away, and it hurts that she can't remember.

'That mongrel took a lot away from me,' she said, crying. 'He took a big part of my life away, he took the one female in the family that I really depended on. He took my memory of her, and it's not fair.'

37

WANDA LIMBO

2007
NSW POLICE HEADQUARTERS
SYDNEY, AUSTRALIA

Twenty-three years after Christopher Wilder's death, the police commissioner in Sydney set up an elite team of detectives to review the state's major unsolved cold cases using the latest forensic science tools and DNA-testing technology.

The first case that Police Commissioner Andrew Scipione asked the Cold Case Justice Project (CCJP) unit to investigate was the 42-year-old mystery of the Wanda Beach murders from 1965.

Inspector Ian Waterson, a 39-year police veteran, was handpicked to head up the CCJP after a decorated international career. Waterson and his team spent months in the state archives, reading and analysing fifty-two volumes of Wanda Beach case files. The killings had taken place well before computerisation, and everything had been written up and logged manually. They also spoke to colleagues in the Unsolved Homicide Unit who had carriage of the still-open case, as well as a couple of long-retired detectives who had worked on the original investigation.

The thousands of dedicated hours that had gone in to the inquiry over the years, and what those officers had generated, were quite intimidating. Wanda Beach was the biggest murder hunt in the state's history, with thousands of witnesses interviewed, every piece of possible evidence recorded and tagged, and all of it written up and logged by hand. The bookwork and record-keeping by the Wanda detectives was meticulous, and key information and leads were all cross-referenced with hundreds and hundreds of index cards. The CCJP reviewed every major case decision taken and re-assessed the key judgements made over decades that had seen the list of possible killers steadily dwindle, as suspects were ruled out.

It was hoped the application of the very latest forensic science techniques would bring about a modern-day breakthrough, but when the team examined the mountain of physical material that had been amassed half a century ago, they made an inconceivable discovery. The most crucial piece of forensic evidence that could categorically prove the killer's identity was missing.

Before bludgeoning her to death, Marianne Schmidt's murderer had raped her in the Wanda Beach sand dunes next to her dead or dying best friend, Christine Sharrock. A specimen of her attacker's semen had been recovered from her body, placed on a small glass evidence slide, then delivered to the government laboratory in Glebe for analysis, along with the other physical evidence gathered from the crime scene. All those other items, including the clothing the two girls wore that day, were still stored and had been maintained in good condition. But the glass semen slide, labelled and logged on the list of evidence, was lost. There was no entry showing it had been signed out for examination and not returned. The CCJP and the Unsolved Homicide Unit carried out separate and exhaustive searches in addition to those by laboratory staff. The health department gave permission for every single filing cabinet containing evidence samples to be opened and checked. It took white-gloved detectives two weeks to complete the painstaking process, but they still couldn't find the holy grail slide. Even in death, it seems, Wilder continued to ride lady luck and cheat justice.

The Wanda Beach murders took place two decades before DNA testing was introduced in Australia. Today, that small rectangular glass slide, if it still exists somewhere, would give investigators a clear-as-daylight window into the past and, in the case of Christopher Wilder, could enable them to identify him as the killer. They would need a sample to test for compatibility, and this is readily available. Both the police in Florida and the FBI have samples of Wilder's blood, and he has two brothers still living in Australia whose DNA could be used. The FBI even requested the serial killer's hands be removed and preserved following his autopsy, and Wilder's brother Stephen agreed.

While Ian Waterson described the loss of the semen sample as a 'major blow' to the case, following the CCJP team's assiduous study of all the evidence accumulated over more than fifty years, he said the Wanda Beach killer was Christopher Wilder.

'There's a number of suspects nominated five, ten, fifteen years after the murders that have been re-investigated but have been eliminated,' he revealed. These include the convicted child killer Derek Percy, who died in a Melbourne hospital five years ago after more than forty years in jail, and Alan Bassett, who was arrested for the murder of a teenage girl five months after the Wanda Beach killings and served twenty-nine years in prison.

'We looked at them, and based on reviewing the previous detectives' evidence, they were ruled out,' confirmed Waterson.

That leaves Wilder. 'He stands out far above anyone else,' he said, 'as the red-hot, number-one suspect, mainly because of his propensity for violence, his sexual appetite and history of attacking girls and murdering them.

'He's never been ruled out, he was in Sydney at the time, he looks like one of the suspect sketches, he liked to hang around beaches and photograph young girls, that was his modus operandi. There is a lot of evidence that points towards him, and a lot of the entries from older detectives show they thought the same thing.'

Waterson said Wanda Beach was Wilder's 'evil debut' as a killer. 'He used our beaches as a training ground,' he said, 'for what he did in America later.' The Wanda detectives were swamped with information at the time, and this led to delays which allowed Wilder to flee. 'These days, you would just log into the computer and he would pop up. In those days, it was all manual entries, and while it might look now like he was one step ahead, it was luck more than anything, we just couldn't catch up with him in time.'

———————

One person did quiz Christopher Wilder about the Wanda Beach murders, and his links to the crime, and it is a remarkable twist in an unprecedented story. Tina Williamson's father was the master builder who took on Wilder as a carpenter's apprentice when he was seventeen years old. He became a father figure to the teenager, and the two men remained close even when Wilder moved to America. Tina, who was ten years old at the time of the Wanda murders, grew up with Wilder, who acted like a protective older brother towards her.

Tina remembered the little MG sports car Wilder drove at the time of the double murder, and how Wanda Beach was his favourite surfing spot, where he liked to hang out in the sandhills and watch girls sunbathing in their bikinis. They remained in touch after he left Australia, as her dad was good friends with Wilder's father, Coley, and they caught up whenever Wilder was visiting from America. In 1984, in the weeks leading up to Rosario Gonzalez's disappearance, Tina and a girlfriend spent two months as houseguests of Wilder at his Boynton Beach home.

Tina never felt uncomfortable or concerned around Wilder, although her travelling companion did and spent as much time as possible away from the house when he was there. That left Tina, who was minding Wilder's two English setters, April and Mindy, alone with him in the evenings, when they would chat for hours. She was then twenty-five years old and could still remember Wilder's odd behaviour: he would suddenly fall quiet and go trancelike, he would sweat profusely and seemed very uptight, and would drink bottle after bottle of Gatorade. The next morning, he'd leave large amounts of money for Tina on the dining table and would suddenly disappear for days on end with no word or explanation. If it hadn't been for her father's long relationship with Wilder from his apprenticeship days, she shudders to think now what might have happened. 'Strangely, I think he respected my father too much to harm me, and I think that probably saved my life,' she said.

She remembered one night, in particular, when they were up late talking about old memories, and Wilder was teasing her about the beaches and places he liked to go and what he got up to there. He kept mentioning Wanda Beach, and Tina found herself asking him jokingly whether he had anything to do with the murders. Wilder, who had been chatting away all night, looked at her for a long time in silence and didn't answer.

She didn't know if he was responsible, but she did believe his hatred and contempt for women that emerged later had its roots in his relationship with his mother. 'She was a bitch and he despised her,' said Tina. 'She was very buxom and loud, especially after a few drinks, and loved to flirt with all the men at the big parties she liked to throw. Coley let her get away with anything she wanted, and when he wasn't around, she let the boys do the same thing. The Wilder family was a strange one. They were good at hiding things and playing happy family.'

The detail of what happened at Wanda Beach to Marianne Schmidt and Christine Sharrock is clear from the evidence, said Ian Waterson. 'Based on everything we reviewed, the girls clearly met a boy, he's made sexual advances to them, I'd say they rejected those and he's then become violent.

'There's no sign that he tied them up or anything, so I'm not sure if he's raped them while they're alive or dead, but Christine was hit with a blunt instrument when she tried to run away, which definitely would have slowed her down. I can't imagine how he would have controlled both of them while he raped one; the blunt instrument has probably rendered her unconscious, and then he's used his knife to finish the job off in quite a vicious way.

'He stabbed them numerous times, both of them, and cut Marianne's throat. That's a violent act to commit on such a young girl. He's just trying to control the situation, and he's finished it off so he's in total control.

'It happened quite quickly. Once the girls realised they were in trouble, he acted and would have drawn the knife to threaten and intimidate them. I think they continued to fight and that's why they suffered the fate they did. At that stage, Wilder was in his teens, and he had a propensity for sexual deviation and for violence, but I think it was just starting to grow within him. I believe they were probably his first murder victims prior to moving to America and continuing his ways over there.'

Waterson's view was that the two girls knew their killer. 'I think he may have known them or met them previously; it might have been at the beach that day. I think his basic instinct originally was to have sex with one or both the girls, and it probably got out of hand, and he's ended up making sure that he wouldn't be recognised.'

Now, he said, it was a case of playing the waiting game for forensic science to take another leap forward so that the case could be solved. He had sent the zipper from one of the girls' costumes for a newly developed low-copy DNA test at a lab in New Zealand, and they did produce a profile, but it turned out to be female. A second low-copy DNA profile was found on another item of clothing, which turned out to belong to one of the Schmidt brothers; however, Waterson said it pointed to the strong possibility that in the near future, science would finally catch up to Christopher Bernard Wilder and nail him for the Wanda Beach killings.

AUTHOR'S NOTE

My interest in the extraordinary story of Christopher Bernard Wilder originated with a chance discovery: the psychopath and serial killer lived as a teen in the same Sydney suburb where I was raising my own young family. Thirty years earlier, and we would have been neighbours, frequenting the same tiny strip of local shops, taking the same bus and train trips, visiting the same parks. Every day that I walked my dogs, I would pass the entrance to a small, nondescript cul-de-sac, halfway up a steep hill that overlooked a popular playground. It was in this street, with its towering, gnarled old gum trees and kookaburras cackling away to each other, that a broody and deviant Wilder spent his formative years.

I became determined to find out how such an ordinary family neighbourhood, as Aussie as Anzac biscuits, could spawn such a cunning and ruthless monster. During my career as a journalist, I have studied and written about many psychopathic killers. I've also interviewed a fair few: from Jeremy Bamber, who shot his parents, adoptive sister and her six-year-old twin sons at the family farmhouse, to Gareth Bunce, a tall and gangly father with rotten teeth who used his enormous hands to slowly strangle his ex-wife's step-sister. There is no doubt that Wilder was the most terrifying of all, mostly because of his unnerving ability to manipulate and control everyone around him. I have no doubt at all that, although the cold case remains officially unsolved, his first murder victims were the Wanda Beach schoolgirls Marianne Schmidt and Christine Sharrock. Several times law enforcement officers in both countries had Wilder in their clutches, and several times they let him slip through their fingers. The full story of just how he managed to outsmart so many people, even the best of the FBI, has never been fully revealed before.

I travelled many of the same routes (on both sides of the Pacific) as Wilder, visiting some of the motels where he molested and killed, stopping off at restaurants and gas stations he used during his deadly rampage. The story is based on first-hand interviews, names have not been changed and events are portrayed as accurately as possible. The thoughts and actions of Wilder himself are interpreted using a variety of source material: official medical reports and interviews with doctors and therapists who treated him, the views of his friends, surviving family members and the law enforcement officers who investigated and interrogated him.

This book is only a reality thanks to a long list of talented people. To my agent, Haylee Nash, for believing in the book from the beginning and for her smart and always honest advice, to publisher Cate Blake, for her insight and constructive encouragement, and good mate Mark Llewellyn for his unstinting support and friendship. Special thanks to my amazing wife, Louisa, whose countless rounds of editing, and endless patience and humour made the book a reality; to my children, Rachael and Harry, you will always be my proudest achievements; to my mother and late father, Gene, whose memory is my abiding inspiration. This is for you, Dad.